CAMPAIGN CRAFT

CAMPAIGN CRAFT

The Strategies, Tactics, and Art of Political Campaign Management

DANIEL M. SHEA

Praeger Series in Political Communication

Westport, Connecticut
London

Library of Congress Cataloging-in-Publication Data

Shea, Daniel M.
    Campaign craft : the strategies, tactics, and art of political
campaign management / Daniel M. Shea.
        p.   cm.—(Praeger series in political communication, ISSN
    1062–5623)
    Includes bibliographical references and index.
    ISBN 0–275–95458–7 (alk. paper).—ISBN 0–275–95459–5 (pbk.)
    1. Campaign management—United States.   I. Title.   II. Series.
JK2281.S49   1996
324.7′0973—dc20   96–21324

British Library Cataloguing in Publication Data is available.

Library of Congress Catalog Card Number: 96–21324
ISBN: 0–275–95458–7
        0–275–95459–5 (pbk.)
ISSN: 1062–5623

First published in 1996

Praeger Publishers, 88 Post Road West, Westport, CT 06881
An imprint of Greenwood Publishing Group, Inc.

Printed in the United States of America

The paper used in this book complies with the
Permanent Paper Standard issued by the National
Information Standards Organization (Z39.48–1984).

10 9 8 7 6 5 4

To Frederica Bowers
In Honor of Her Wisdom, Kindness, and Strength.

Contents

Series Foreword

Those of us from the discipline of communication studies have long believed that communication is prior to all other fields of inquiry. In several other forums I have argued that the essence of politics is "talk" or human interaction.[1] Such interaction may be formal or informal, verbal or nonverbal, public or private, but it is always persuasive, forcing us consciously or subconsciously to interpret, to evaluate, and to act. Communication is the vehicle for human action.

From this perspective, it is not surprising that Aristotle recognized the natural kinship of politics and communication in his writings *Politics* and *Rhetoric*. In the former, he establishes that humans are "political beings [who] alone of the animals [are] furnished with the faculty of language."[2] And in the latter, he begins his systematic analysis of discourse by proclaiming that "rhetorical study, in its strict sense, is concerned with the modes of persuasion."[3] Thus, it was recognized over 2,300 years ago that politics and communication go hand in hand because they are essential parts of human nature.

Back in 1981, Dan Nimmo and Keith Sanders proclaimed that political communication was an emerging field.[4] Although its origin, as noted, dates back centuries, a "self-consciously cross-disciplinary" focus began in the late 1950s. Thousands of books and articles later, colleges and universities offer a variety of graduate and undergraduate course work in the area in such diverse departments as communication, mass communication, journalism, political science, and sociology.[5] In Nimmo and Sanders' early assessment, the "key areas of inquiry" included rhetorical analysis, propaganda analysis, attitude change studies, voting studies, government and the news media, functional and systems analyses, technological changes, media technologies, campaign techniques, and research techniques.[6] In a survey of the state of the field in 1983, the same authors and Lynda Kaid found additional, more specific areas of concern such as the presidency, political polls, public opinion, debates, and advertising to name a few.[7] Since the first study, they also noted a shift away from the rather strict behavioral approach.

A decade later, Dan Nimmo and David Swanson argued that "political communication has developed some identity as a more or less distinct domain of scholarly work."[8] The scope and concerns of the area have further expanded to include critical theories and cultural studies. While there is no precise definition, method, or disciplinary home of the area of inquiry, its primary domain is the role, processes, and effects of communication within the context of politics broadly defined.

In 1985, the editors of *Political Communication Yearbook: 1984* noted that "more things are happening in the study, teaching, and practice of political communication than can be captured within the space limitations of the relatively few publications available."[9] In addition, they argued that the backgrounds of "those involved in the field [are] so varied and pluralist in outlook and approach, ...it [is] a mistake to adhere slavishly to any set format in shaping the content."[10] And more recently, Nimmo and Swanson called for "ways of overcoming the unhappy consequences of fragmentation within a framework that respects, encourages, and benefits from diverse scholarly commitments, agendas, and approaches."[11]

In agreement with these assessments of the area and with gentle encouragement, Praeger established the Praeger Series in Political Communication. The series is open to all qualitative and quantitative methodologies as well as contemporary and historical studies. The key to characterizing the studies in the series is the focus on communication variables or activities within a political context or dimension. As of this writing, nearly forty volumes have been published, and there are numerous impressive works forthcoming. Scholars from the disciplines of communication, history, journalism, political science, and sociology have participated in the series.

I am, without shame or modesty, a fan of the series. The joy of serving as its editor is in participating in the dialogue of the field of political communication and in reading the contributors' works. I invite you to join me.

Robert E. Denton, Jr.

NOTES

1. See Robert E. Denton, Jr., *The Symbolic Dimensions of the American Presidency* (Prospect Heights, Ill.: Waveland Press, 1982); Robert E. Denton, Jr., and Gary Woodward, *Political Communication in America* (New York: Praeger, 1985; 2nd ed., 1990); Robert E. Denton, Jr., and Dan Han, *Presidential Communication* (New York: Praeger, 1986); and Robert E. Denton, Jr., *The Primetime Presidency of Ronald Reagan* (New York: Praeger, 1988).

2. Aristotle, *The Politics of Aristotle*, trans. Ernest Baker (New York: Oxford University Press, 1970), p. 5.

3. Aristotle, *Rhetoric*, trans. Rhys Roberts (New York: The Modern Library, 1954), p. 22.

4. Dan Nimmo and Keith Sanders, "Introduction: The Emergence of Political Communication as a Field," in *Handbook of Political Communication*, eds. Dan Nimmo and Keith Sanders (Beverly Hills, Calif.: Sage, 1981), pp. 11–36.

5. Ibid., p. 15.

6. Ibid., pp. 17–27.

7. Keith Sanders, Lynda Kaid, and Dan Nimmo, eds., *Political Communication Yearbook:*

1984 (Carbondale: Southern Illinois University Press, 1985), pp. 283–308.

8. Dan Nimmo and David Swanson, "The Field of Political Communication: Beyond the Voter Persuasion Paradigm," in *New Directions in Political Communication*, eds. David Swanson and Dan Nimmo (Beverly Hills, Calif.: Sage, 1990) p. 8.

9. Sanders, Kaid, Nimmo, *Political Communication Yearbook: 1984*, p. xiv.

10. Ibid.

11. Nimmo and Swanson, "The Field of Political Communication," p. 11.

Preface

It can be argued with considerable force that the way in which candidates present themselves to voters is a key element in the democratic process. It can also be stated with little dispute that this process has changed significantly over the last few decades—particularly in the United States. With this said, however, the lack of scholarly research and insight into modern campaign is as stunning as it is bewildering. A new profession (campaign management) has emerged nearly overnight. Yet, these folks are *not* being trained, for the most part, in colleges and universities, rather they are forced to learn the trade from the "school of hard knocks." Much of this is due to a persistent wedge between the ivory towers and everyday politics. The number of college offerings and programs in campaign management and applied politics is growing, but so far it is too inconsequential for its import.

This book is designed to help fill that gap. It is an effort to provide students of modern campaign management with up-to-date information on how this process works. My aim has been to merge theoretical material, such as the history and rationale behind various activities, with practical information, such as how it is done and what pitfalls await. The book also contains hundreds of illustrations to help highlight significant points.

During the course of writing this book, several graduate assistants provided help. Greg Taylor was a tireless research assistant, as was Mia Mounts. Dominique Broyles was a superb copyeditor and Cresha Auck did a great deal with layout. Matt Nasman helped with research and Melanie Haskell with final preparations.

I am grateful to the Department of Political Science at the University of Akron, and the Ray C. Bliss Institute of Applied Politics at the University of Akron, for their support. John Green, director of the Institute, has been a steady sounding board throughout my career and many of the pages that follow owe their beginning to our chats over coffee. Jim Murphy of the New York State Democratic Assembly Campaign Committee provided keen insight and sound editing. At Praeger Books, Jim Dunton, Liz Leiba, and Lynn Wheeler did an outstanding job moving the book forward and cleaning up the final manuscript.

The reader will note that two of the chapters were provided by other authors. Mark Weaver, formally of Wilson Communications and currently assistant attorney general for the State of Ohio, was kind enough to spend some of his scarce time to compose a roundup of paid media. Jesse Marquette, director of the Survey Research Center at the University of Akron, answered my plea and wrote an excellent piece on survey research. Their astute understanding of these areas are clearly reflected in the chapters.

Finally, this book would not have been possible without the unwavering support of my family. It was written when my wife and I were expecting our first child. Not only was Christine instrumental in editing and drawing out ideas, she provided steady, kind encouragement to lift my spirits when things got a bit tough. Each day she helps remind me, without ever saying a word, that books and careers are important, but they are, after all, only fractions of a good life.

I would also like to thank our child (yet to be born) for being kind to his/her mother during *most* of their stay together.

CAMPAIGN CRAFT

Chapter One

Introduction: The Contemporary Campaign Craft

The rate of technological change in the latter part of the twentieth century has been nothing short of stunning. Only thirty years ago black-and-white television was the rage; today every home in America has at least one color set, usually boasting hundreds of channels. Want to watch a live cricket game in Scotland?—no problem! Sitting on this author's desk is a machine thousands of times more powerful than the first computer developed only a few decades ago, weighing thirty tons. Cordless telephones, once faddish, have been replaced by cellular phones—now standard ware for the upwardly mobile. By utilizing satellite triangulation, hikers can find their way out of the woods with a hand held global positioning system (GPS). Of course, the use of fiber optics is changing everything: four billion bits of information can be sent over the information superhighway at once—that means three copies of the *Encyclopedia Britannica* per second. And these changes represent just the tip of the iceberg.

As we might expect, the technology revolution is changing American social fabric as well: how we teach our children, converse with one another, and entertain ourselves; and what we do for a living and what are our expectations about the future. Less obvious, but no less profound, are adjustments to our system of government. This notion may seem odd to some, since the basic structure of our system has remained about the same over the last two centuries. Yet the Framers would not recognize a core element of the process: the way we now elect public officials.

Regardless of one's precise view of democracy, few dispute that elections are not at the center of the process. How candidates are offered to voters and the way in which citizens structure and process this information speaks volumes about the democratic character of a popular system. "Elections can produce high drama or infinite tedium, but they are the key institutions of representative democracy" (Butler and Ranney 1992, 1).

In this light, it can be argued that the contemporary election process represents one of the most significant transformations in our nation's history. In the recent past, campaigns were conducted by volunteers, usually local party activists and the candidate's network of friends and family. Time-honored methods were used, mostly face-to-face canvasing and a modest range of printed material (e.g, pamphlets, posters, and newspaper advertisements). By the mid-1960s, many of the skills and tactics used by product marketing specialists began to appear in presidential and congressional elections. Carefully conducted random sample surveys, for example, proved to be a better and more cost-effective means of identifying and responding to the wishes of voters than simply keeping a finger to the wind.

Today, pure grassroots campaigning seems archaic for all but the most local races. Even town and city council races are utilizing expensive, high-tech methods and the tricks of the last decade are quickly becoming passé. Instead of conducting large- scale polls, focus groups are frequently utilized; rather than sending out printed direct mail, video tapes are distributed; satellite teleconferences have replaced smoke-filled rooms; and radio beepers and television satellite feeds may be more important than written press releases. Simply put, no other area of American politics has so drastically changed over the last few decades than the way in which candidates pursue votes.

Changes in campaign technologies have had, and will continue to have, a serious impact on governance. For one, the importance of money in the election process has been well documented. Candidates with enough resources can bypass traditional screening mechanisms, such as party support and other ways of "paying dues." Those without sufficient funds rarely stand a chance, particularly if they are challenging an incumbent. Political parties, the center of campaign activity for over 150 years, have taken a back seat to campaign consultants and political action committees (PACs), and they are struggling to regain relevance. Without viable parties, many suggest, there is serious doubt as to whether the structure of our system can endure.

The type of campaign information provided to voters has also changed. We are now inundated with thirty-second spots and ten-second bytes. Perhaps this is behind the increased level of cynicism and distrust among voters, and a corresponding decrease in turnout at elections, but at the very least the type of campaign information citizens receive these days is much different than it was in the past. Image has replaced substance. Moreover, the volume and tone of negative campaign advertising appear to be at a fever pitch. The media seem more interested in who is ahead in the polls and in how each campaign is being run, than in the policy stands of the candidates. There is even some evidence to suggest that the type of person willing to undergo the rigors of modern campaigning has changed—leading to a much different crop of public officials and a new approach to governance (Ehrenhalt 1991).

Modern campaign technologies have also begun to spread to Central and South America, as well as to the emerging democracies throughout Eastern Europe. For citizens in many of these countries, high-tech campaigning will be the only electoral process they have known. How this will impact the development of these systems is only speculation at this point. Surely the process and the result will be different from the American experience.

THE STUDY OF CONTEMPORARY ELECTIONS

It was not until voters had moved away from partisan cues as the basis of voting that electioneering seemed to matter. Several of the earliest election studies, conducted in the 1950s and 1960s (Berelson, Lazarfeld, and McPhee 1954, for example), found little evidence of campaign effects. Voters, it was believed, stuck closely to their partisan badges, and it was not until a dramatic, crosscutting issue divided the electorate that voters would be swayed by candidate appeals. This rigidity was believed to be especially strong at the local level. Scholars found little utility in studying campaign activities, as opposed to voter behavior, because they simply had little bearing.

Much has changed to suggest that campaign activities deserve close attention. Fewer people are guided only by partisanship when voting, implying volatile elections and uncertain outcomes. Elections do matter in this environment, especially for the growing number of low-involvement voters (Nimmo 1970). Second, the amount of money being spent by candidates at all levels has skyrocketed, and it takes scant investigation to discern a tight fit between campaign war chests and electoral success. Third, although urban party *machines* have withered, party organizations seem to be providing candidates greater assistance than in the past. This paradox has underscored the need to understand what parties can offer if not activists. Finally, by the early 1970s, students of congressional elections detected a sharp decline in the number of close incumbent reelections—and conversely a sharp decline in incumbent defeats. Concerned about the very stability of the competitive election process, the race was on to discern incumbent advantages. Each of these elements underscored the need for shifting the analysis from the voter to the campaign process itself.

Yet, the recent focus on elections has caught only part of the picture. Over the last decade, for example, scores of studies have been published on voter alienation, distrust, declining levels of efficacy, and diminishing turnout, but only a handful have focused on the tactics and techniques of campaigns. To complete the picture one would hope to know more about *how* candidates attempt to persuade voters, as well as the role of the various players in this process. Scholars also seem fixed on the losers in the campaign technology battle. Countless texts mourn the passing of party-centered elections and caution the emergence of candidate-centered politics and PAC overload. We know a good deal about why parties may have failed, but little about what has taken their place. Candidates run without the aid of party machines, but are campaigns really candidate centered? Conceivably there are other players in the game as well.

In brief, election studies of late have examined primarily the motivations and choices of those involved in campaigns: determinants of vote choice; why people run for office; the role of the media gatekeepers; why contributors give; the roles of consultants, party activists, and special interests actors; the role of negative campaigning on individual attitudes; and the contours of the incumbent advantage debate. With the exception of a modest literature on campaign strategies, there has been scant discussion of campaign technologies. That is, how candidates and other players in election process attempt to win office remains a mystery in the political science literature. We know that favorable media coverage gives candidates a big boost, but how, precisely, does one go about getting it? Money is the mother's milk of elections, but what are the options in raising it? We have gotten a better look at the forest, but not the trees.

CAMPAIGN MANAGEMENT LITERATURE

This is not to suggest campaign that technologies have been altogether neglected. Several books did emerge in the 1970s, as professional campaigning moved beyond the presidential level, most notably those by Agranoff (1972), Napolitan (1972), and Brown and Seib (1976). Of note in the 1980s, Blumenthal (1980) and Sabato (1981) drew attention to the emerging campaign profession. Hershey (1984), Beaudry and Schaeffer (1986), and Salmore and Salmore (1989) shed much needed light on the interworkings of electioneering. One of the most frequently used texts in this area has been Sabato (1989), which is a collection of reprinted articles from *Campaigns and Elections* (a trade journal for campaign consultants). More recently, Diamond and Bates (1992) have provided an in-depth examination of media advertising; Jamieson (1992) has explored the rise and implications of "dirty politics"; and Selnow (1994) has taken a good look at the role of computer technology in elections. Thurber and Nelson's edited work (1995) provides an up-to-date mix of the theoretical and the applied material.

Beyond a general shortage, campaign management texts to date have generally been of two types. The first is what might be termed "manuals"—where the emphasis is on directing the reader through the steps of each campaign activity. Although informative, this approach is considered rather dry and distant from real-life settings. Readers are left with the impression that campaigning is a mechanical process, rather than a tumultuous, unpredictable mix of craft and art. The second type tends to rely upon case-study material, where a small number of elections are reviewed, often skimming over the details to get to the big bang. This material is more lively, but it provides little instruction on how these activities are undertaken and the strategies behind them.

This book is designed to merge these approaches and help fill a gap in the campaign management literature. It is intended for the student of modern electioneering. It combines theoretical and practical information about the nature and function of various election activities. Each chapter reviews the background of the topic, the logic behind its use and importance, the most up-to-date tactics and technologies, and illustrations of their use and misuse. More than anything else, the goal of the book is to help debunk this complex new aspect of American governance.

THE RISE OF NEW-STYLE CAMPAIGNING

The phrase "new-style campaigning" is used frequently in the pages to follow. Originally advanced by Robert Agranoff (1972), it continues, with some modifications (noted below), to symbolize the state of modern electioneering. The established view of the shift from "old-style" to "new-style" campaigning can be summarized in four dimensions: (1) new players, (2) new incentives, (3) new tactics, and (4) new resources.

New Players

The exact role of candidates in elections, as discussed in greater detail below, has clearly changed in the past few decades. Yet in a sense it has remained constant—there is still only one person from each party running for an office. The supporting cast in elections, notwithstanding, has greatly changed.

From the 1830s until the 1970s, candidates were *run* for office by party organizations. Their fortunes were linked to the success or failure of the party. Candidates were expected to contribute to their election effort—often a donation to party coffers was a precondition of their nomination—but the task of voter contact was left to party activists. If there were "professionals" in the campaign business, they were the most seasoned party workers. Their training was "the school of hard knocks." To be sure, the idea that campaigning could be learned in schools or from books was antithetical to the party organization credo of trial by fire and working your way up the ladder. This notion is well captured in the words of George Washington Plunkitt, a powerful party leader in the Tammany Hall Democratic organizations, located in New York City around the turn of the century:

Tammany district leaders ain't bookworms and college professors. If we were Tammany might win an election once in four thousand years. Most leaders are plain American citizens, of the people and near the people, and they have all the education they need to whip the dudes who part their name in the middle and to run City Government. We got bookworms in the organization too. We keep them for ornaments on parade days.(Riordon 1948, 60–61)

The decline of party organizations, and leaders such as Plunkitt, is well documented and needs only be summarized here. Party atrophy had begun in earnest by the turn of the century, as members of the Progressive movement set their sights on reforming the corrupt city machines. They pushed forward with civil service, the Australian ballot, direct primary elections, and in some states nonpartisan municipal elections. By the midpoint in the century, sociological changes, such as decreased immigration, urban flight, higher education levels, and changing family patterns, further reduced the position of party organizations. By the 1970s, presidential nomination reform stripped the role party leaders once had in selecting their party's candidate, and campaign finance reform led to the creation of PACs, further diminishing the relative weight of party assistance to candidates. By this point, most students of the American system were led to conclude that "the party's over" (Broder 1971).

It was assumed that candidate image would replace party-based appeals. Beginning first at the presidential level, observers of elections noticed a growing number of candidates willing to head into the trenches unaided by political parties. This was quickly dubbed the era of "candidate-centered" politics. With a flood of special-interest money at bay, and able to reach voters with target electronic media, candidates at all levels soon found inadequate utility in linking their fortunes to the party organization—especially if the party provided little assistance during the campaign. As either cause or effect, the electorate's movement away from party labels as voting cues—termed dealignment—made candidate-centered choices seem all the more logical and inevitable. Voters and candidates alike gave up allegiance to the party. Finally, the new campaign medium of choice, television, was perfectly suited for image and character-based appeals; there was simply no need for the party.

New-style election consultants quickly emerged as well, responding to the new demands of candidates—and in some ways fueling that demand (Sabato 1981). Carrying bags of tricks garnered from the public relations and product marketing professions, these folks seemed to fit the bill precisely. At the top of their list of skills, consultants were able to measure voter preferences and direct messages to specific groups. The profession further specialized, and some thirty branches of campaign professionals could be listed in 1972 (Agranoff 1972, 17).

New Incentives

Incentives for helping candidates prior to the 1970s were diverse. Party organizations did so in order to control the reins of government—to regulate patronage disbursement and manage government contracts. Family and friends would lend a hand out of personal loyalty; and some individuals would even assist a candidate because they believed that the candidate, and other members of that party, would do the right thing once in office. It was also common to find campaign workers lending a hand expecting that, after the election they would get a job—perhaps as part of the elected official's staff.

More recently, "volunteers" have continued to lend a hand for a variety of reasons. But volunteers are only supplements to the overall effort, and professionals form the center of the campaign team. Their incentive for involvement is simple—cold, hard cash. The campaign consulting profession can be very lucrative; top pros garner over $250 per hour for their time. As noted in many of the pages to follow, consulting firms can pull millions of dollars each election cycle. It is further common to find top pros working for both Democrats and Republicans—suggesting a disregard for purposive concerns. It could be argued that ideology takes a back seat to fees when it comes to who a consultant will work to elect. A former leader of the Republican party, Ed Rollins, recently jumped ship to aid Ross Perot's efforts to oust George Bush. Perhaps the $1 million he received from Perot played a role in his decision.

New Tactics

Possibly the best way to summarize old-style campaign tactics is with a "shotgun" analogy. The candidate's message would be spread out over the electorate in a broad, imprecise way. The goal was to reach as many people as possible (not necessarily voters) and to stress either partisan-based appeals or the concerns of most voters. The means to get the message out were newspapers, rallies, and district wide door-to-door canvasing. Each of these tactics was effective in contacting people, but not necessarily the best *voters*, and it surely did little to link the right message with the right person.

Again drawing their expertise from product marketing, new-style consultants chose to use a "rifle-approach." This means carefully discerning voter preferences through scientific survey research, stratifying voters based upon these preferences, and then providing a tailored communication to each group. The credo for new-style consultants is to find and push the right message for each voter. As noted at several points below, no word better captures the tactics of modern campaigning than "targeting."

Beyond the general movement away from a shotgun- to a rifle-based approach, scores of high-tech tactics now lie at the doorstep of the campaign professional. Television and radio have allowed candidates to enter more living rooms in thirty seconds than a party organization might reach by foot in a month. By using cable or paying careful heed to format, target groups of voters can be tapped. They can also use these media to highlight image and personality—especially strong voting cues among nonpartisan voters. Computers have aided campaigns immensely, particularly in direct mail, survey research, list development, fund-raising, targeting, and just about everything else a campaign might seek to accomplish. About the only thing computers do not do in campaigns is directly ask for votes—but this may be changing as well. New technologies allow a candidate simultaneously to meet with several groups of voters with satellite hookups, and "actualities" can be fed to radio news stations over digital couplers. Even the most basic voter contact tactics, such as the door-to-door canvas, are being given a high-tech upgrade. Some tactics, as will be seen below, have remained constant over the years, yet for the most part new-style campaigns only shadow those of just twenty or thirty years ago.

New Resources

Finally, the resources of campaigns have changed. In the past, the partisan preferences of the district was a prime resource. If most voters hitched themselves to a party and the candidate was a member of that party, the fix was in. If the distribution of preference was roughly even, party activists and other volunteers provided the fuel for the campaign engine. Campaigns have never been altogether cheap, but certainly "people" were considered the most precious resource in the campaigns of yesteryear.

New-style campaigns run on money. Nearly all of the tactics and tricks of this emerging profession hinge on financial resources. There are examples of recent candidates overcoming large financial deficits, but they are rare. In fact, there is a startling close fit between money and success on election day, as will be seen in Chapter 10 on campaign finance. Volunteers and activists still matter, but money is simply more fungible; it cannot convert all resources, but a deficiency in most areas can be more easily overcome with money than with any other resource. Scant new-style consultants would swap volunteers for money.

The massive weight of money in new-style elections has created a number of new issues—including where it should come from, what contributors expect, how it might be raised, and how much is enough? The rising cost of elections and the growth of special- interest money at all levels have startled observers of the democratic process. Agranoff, for example, seemed surprised in 1972 when he noted that state legislative campaigns might then cost between $10,000 and $20,000 (1972, 27). By the mid-1990s, ten times this amount is customary in some states, and even in midsize states, such as Ohio, state legislative races can reach the $5 hundred thousand mark. There have been renewed calls for reform, but currently neither the federal government nor many states regulate the amount of money in elections. The prime resource of new-style campaigning is money—and trunks of it!

NEW-STYLE CAMPAIGNING IN THE 1990s

As noted, Agranoff's view of new-style campaigning goes a long way in describing the state of affairs in the 1990s, but it is not a perfect fit. Two adjustments must be made to the traditional view: the resurgence of party organizations and a movement from candidate-centered campaigns to what might be termed "consultant-centered" elections. Each is briefly outlined below.

The Resurgence of Party Organizations

It was taken for granted by the mid-1970s that political parties no longer mattered in electoral politics. Partisanship among voters was down, presidential candidates ran with their own blessing—outside the official party apparatus—and members of legislatures were inclined to stray from the wishes of the caucus leaders whenever it seemed to better their reelection chances. At the same time, however, the national party organizations and the thousands of state and local party units throughout the nation seemed to be hanging on. They did not completely disappear, as many expected.

A decade later, a few scholars thought it best to set aside party-in-the-electorate and party-in-government, and accurately gauge the stability of state and local party *organizations*. The Party Transformation Study (PTS), undertaken by Neil Cotter and his colleagues in 1984 and published under the title *Party Organizations in American Politics*, systematically surveyed thousands of party leaders across the nation. Their principle finding was that, contrary to popular wisdom, most party organizations remained vibrant and in fact were often stronger than they had been since the turn of the century. On close inspection, although the relative weight of party activity had declined in light of PACs, they were by far the largest single source of assistance to candidates. Office seekers relied upon parties to carry petitions, organize volunteers, give some money, make telephone calls, and canvas door to door. The PTS was followed up by a number of other studies, all of which found basically the same thing—"the party goes on" (Kayden and Mahe 1985).

At first the contradiction seemed puzzling. How could it be that fewer voters tied themselves to a partisan label and legislators saw fit to abandon the party at will when, at the same time, party organizations were expanding? Joseph Schlesinger (1991) provides one answer. It is precisely because partisanship does not matter among the voters, he argues, that elections have become more competitive and less predictable. In this new environment, party organizations have been forced to adapt—and this adaptation has been to provide more campaign service to candidates. Moreover, because candidates face uncertain elections, they look to merge with others in the same boat as a form of collective protection. This merging of "candidate-centered nuclei" has occurred in party organizations.

Today, fully funded, aggressive local party organizations can be found in most counties across the nation. Many have moved full steam into the high-technology age and boast computer targeting systems, direct mail operations, survey apparatus, and telemarketing centers, while others provide significant grassroots help. Several finance reform measures, established in the 1970s, also seem to be aiding state and local parties. In an effort to get around contribution limits (discussed in Chapter 10), PACs and individuals can give generously to state and local party organizations. This process, called "soft money," has helped parties remain key players.

Most important, the national and state party organizations have developed new structures specifically geared to legislative elections. At the national level they are termed the "Hill committees." First brought to our attention by Herrnson (1988), these organizations gear all their activities toward winning more seats in the House and Senate. Each party boasts two units—one for elections in each house. The Democrats, for example, have the Democratic Congressional Campaign Committee (termed the "D-Triple C") and the Democratic Senatorial Campaign Committee (DSCC). Republicans have a similar set up. These organizations are well financed, professionally organized, and staffed by state-of-the-art campaign consultants. Combined, the four units spent over $150 million on House and Senate candidates in 1992 (Herrnson 1995, 79). Their goal is to win elections—period!

Similar organizations have appeared at the state level. Now found in forty-two states, legislative campaign committees (LCCs) provide a host of campaign services (Shea 1995). In some states, such as New York, Ohio, California, Michigan, and Wisconsin, they have become the dominant player in state legislative elections—far surpassing the efforts of PACs and special-interest groups. In New York, for example, the Democratic Assembly Campaign Committee (just one of four), spends nearly $5 million each election (Shea 1995). Legislative campaign committees are quickly becoming the "800 pound gorillas" of legislative elections.

The services and resources provided to the candidates by these organizations are vast. They give money, but more important they provide expertise and assistance. A candidate can expect to be invited to Washington, D.C., or the state capital to attend a training session. They can use the media studios to make radio and television spots, and they receive assistance on their direct mail. In some states, LCC operatives join races in the field, essentially running the show. Perhaps the foremost help provided by these units is what Herrnson has termed a "brokerage role." That is, they link candidates with potential contributors and discount service vendors. If a candidate is interested in a survey, for example, they can be put in contact with a top-notch pollster—and receive this service at a bargain price. (The pollster is able to do so because of the volume of work provided.) They also bring PAC decision makers and candidates together as part of a fund-raising match making service.

While the Hill committees at the federal level and the LCCs at the state level have transformed the role of parties in legislative elections, there is a catch. Unlike traditional party structures, which are inclined to spread the resource pie to all members of the ticket, these organizations target their efforts on competitive races. In other words, if a candidate's race is deemed good, he or she can expect significant help, but if it is believed to be a long shot or a forgone conclusion to win, he or she will get nothing. This can be one of the most frustrating aspects of modern campaigning—how does one become competitive without first getting assistance? In short, party assistance through Hill committees and LCCs can be a tremendous help to candidates—at the state level candidacies often live or die based upon party funds and expertise. Yet not all candidates can count on it.

Overall, it is appropriate to reconceptualize the role of parties in elections outlined by Agranoff and others at the dawn of new-style campaigning. Party machines are relics of the past, but new organizations, staffed with cutting edge professionals, have taken their place. Plunkitt's thoughts on the role of college- educated party workers would surely seem out of place in the 1990s. Party organizations are very much an element of new-style campaigning.

The Rise of Consultant-Centered Campaigns

With that said, however, the process has clearly *not* returned to party-centered elections. Although parties provide the largest single source of funds to candidates, this amount is just a fraction of the overall expenditures. Moreover, few candidates overtly link themselves to a party ticket to appeal to the voters. It is indeed rare to find a candidate even mentioning his or her party in campaign advertisements. Image and character are deemed more portentous. This movement away from party in elections was, as noted above, described in the political science literature during the 1970s and 1980s as candidate centered. "The candidate, rather than the party," writes Agranoff, "tends to be the chief focus of today's campaign communication" (1972, 4). This notion falls short in the 1990s. When it was first coined, candidate-centered campaigns reflected what was going on in presidential elections. During the 1950s, for example, Dwight Eisenhower demonstrated that voters could be pulled from their partisan leaning by drawing attention to character and by conveying this message through the electronic media. Jimmy Carter ran as an "honest person," rather than a Democrat, and Ronald Reagan epitomized strength and character—not necessarily Republican ideals. Lower-level candidates, realizing the advantages of this approach, began highlighting their images to win elections.

But candidates were not able to accomplish the transition from party to image without help. Rather, the shift was brought about precisely because the "image makers" began providing their services. Simply put, image-based campaigns emerged at the presidential level because survey and marketing experts were there to push presidential candidates in that direction. It was only after persistent appeals from his new-style advisors that Richard Nixon, for instance, made the transition from party to image—leading to his success in the 1968 presidential election (McGinniss 1969). As new-style consultants began providing congressional and state-level candidates with their services, partisan appeals were dropped.

Today few serious candidates, beyond the most local races, head out into the trenches without the aid of campaign consultants. These folks measure public opinion, shape candidate appeals, raise funds, and implement the most efficient voter contact methods available. Campaigns are not party centered, nor are they candidate centered. Today elections are consultant centered. As noted by Dan Nimmo (1985), "Campaigns may no longer be battles between candidates but between titans of the campaign industry, working on behalf of those personalities" (as cited by Baer 1995, 50).

As will be seen throughout the pages to follow, new-style campaigning is professional. Everything from fund-raising activities, to direct mail, to television advertising, to grassroots activities is now coordinated by well-paid campaign consulting firms. It has become big business. One media consulting firm alone collected over $11 million in 1992, *just for their service in congressional races* (Morris and Gamache 1994). Only about 10 percent of competitive congressional races in 1992 were conducted without the aid of professional staff (Herrnson 1994b, 64–68), and even as far back as the mid-1980s not a single challenger for the U.S. Senate or for state governor was successful without the help of consultants (Luntz 1988, 45).

The number of people employed in the campaign consulting profession has skyrocketed. Significantly more people now make their living with campaign consulting firms than by working for political parties. Over the last decade the American Association of Political Consultants (AAPC), for example, has gone from a membership of less than 50 to over 3,500. On top of this, most party organizations are no longer staffed without the aid of campaign consultants—at least on a part-time basis. The operatives of the Hill committees and LCCs are more likely the product of graduate schools, such as the Bliss Institute of Applied Politics at the University of Akron or the Campaign Management Institute at American University, than they are of party units.

Moreover, when it comes to media coverage, the precise makeup of each candidate's consulting team has become just as important as the policy stands of the candidate. Candidates able to secure top consultants have a better chance than those unable to do so, without ever asking a single voter their thoughts. No serious candidate would not have a team of political consultants at bay. For one, they carry with them the tools required to compete in politics today; second, if they do not have the party organizations, PACs, potential contributors, and the press, they will not be taken seriously. This is deemed especially important for challengers.

In brief, the role of candidates in their own campaigns has been forever altered—very few do not recognize the skills and tricks afforded from these new "wizards of American politics" (Luntz 1988). It makes sense that we rethink the nature of new-style campaigns. Perhaps they are best described as consultant centered.

HOW THE BOOK IS ORGANIZED

As noted above, each of the chapters to follow is designed to cover several areas: the history of the topic, the logic behind its importance, cutting-edge technologies, and its place in the overall campaign plan. The goal is to merge a general understanding of the topic of the chapter with new-style tactics.

Also, unlike many works on new-style campaigning, the focus in each chapter is on subpresidential elections. Few consultants will have the opportunity, particularly straight out of school, to plan media buys, organize direct mail, or raise funds for a presidential candidate. Several illustrations are drawn from this level, mostly to accent a topic with an identifiable figure; but for the most part, the book addresses the strategies, tactics, and technologies most appropriate for mid level elections, such as congressional, state legislative, county executive, and city council.

Chapter 2 provides a brief look at the importance of campaign plans. It will be argued that plans not only guide the course of the campaign, provide deadlines, and assign specific responsibilities, but also suggest how plans can be used to begin the process of leading critical external players, such as the media and potential contributors, to see the candidate's chances as reasonable.

The next set of chapters examines the "campaign context"—the list of givens in any campaign that should become key elements in the overall campaign strategy. Chapter 3 looks at a mix of factors, such as the level of office and the status of the candidate. This is followed with an extended look at demographic research (Chapter 4) and then an overview of prior electoral targeting (Chapter 5). It is argued that prior electoral information is one of the most important, yet often overlooked, aspects of new-style campaigning. Part One is concluded in Chapter 6, which examines the opposition research—why it works, how it is collected, and how it might best be used.

Part Two looks at the elements of strategic thinking. It begins with a discussion of survey research (Chapter 7), moves to the development of a campaign theme (Chapter 8), and ends with some general thoughts on strategy (Chapter 9). Much of the "art form" element of new-style campaigning comes from the interplay of what the voters want, the candidate's theme, and the campaign strategy.

Part Three looks at voter contact techniques, beginning with fund-raising (Chapter 10). Although it is possible to reach voters without money, races with enough cash have a tremendous advantage. The history of money in elections is provided, followed by a lengthy discussion of how to go about getting it. The numerous avenues of paid media form the topic of Chapter 11. If there is anything that distinguishes new-style campaigning it is the use of electronic communications to reach voters. Chapter 12 tackles earned media. It will be suggested that, although press coverage is exceedingly difficult to get—especially for lower-level races—it can be accomplished with tenacity and ingenuity. Finally, Chapter 13 takes a look at the importance of grassroots voter contact techniques.

Like mushrooms after a summer rain, a critical transformation of American governance is all around us. Modern campaigning has taken hold from the presidential level on down to town council contests. We have taken steps toward understanding much of this process, but the details have eluded us. Gerald Pomper noted some two decades ago, that although Americans choose over half a million public officials through the ballot, "elections are a mystery" (1974, 1). This book is intended to make them a bit less baffling, underscore the artistic element of electioneering, and help begin the process of training a new generation of political activists.

Chapter Two

The Importance of a Campaign Plan

This book speaks about the transformation of campaigns. In many ways new-style campaigns only shadow those of yesteryear. There are a few elements, however, that have remained basically the same over the years. One is the utmost importance of a campaign plan.

The presidential election of 1896 was one of the most intensely fought in the history of the United States. The nation was in the midst of an economic recession; there was high unemployment, labor strife, and farmer discontent (especially in the Midwest). Partisan loyalties were being dislodged, as divisions over the proper role of government widened. The Democrats, under the helm of Grover Cleveland, had seen their strength in Congress and in state legislatures dwindle during the preceding years. The Populist party, appealing to agrarian interests, and the Republicans; primarily the business interests of the Northeast, had made great strides in the 1894 midterm election, suggesting trouble for the Democrats. Things appeared so turbulent in 1896 that Cleveland decided to pass up the chance to secure a third term.

The Republicans quickly settled on William McKinley, a longtime member of Congress and former governor of Ohio, as their candidate. The Democrats, although at first divided, settled on William Jennings Bryan. Bryan who was just thirty-six years old, and came from an electorally irrelevant state (Nebraska). On top of this, his race was seriously underfinanced, and the media seemed unwilling to lend a hand. He was, however, a gifted orator. Bryan proceeded to break a long-standing tradition that presidential candidates "stand" for office, and he delivered his message directly to the people. He traveled to twenty-six states, talking to an estimated 5 million folks. By distancing himself from the failures of the Cleveland administration and by taking on the cause of the "common man," Bryan had turned what was believed to be an easy Republican win into a horse race (Dinkin 1989, 114).

McKinley, sensing trouble, harnessed the talents and ingenuity of his longtime friend and political godfather, Mark Hanna, as his campaign leader. Hanna was arguably the first true campaign consultant. He fashioned the McKinley race along "business principles," putting together an elaborate organization with an extensive staff to handle each phase of the race (Troy 1991, 105). He instituted different bureaus to appeal to different constituencies—Germans, blacks, wheelmen, merchants, and even women. Hundreds of speakers were deployed and roughly $250 million in pamphlets were distributed. In order to target the appeal, many of the pamphlets were printed in foreign languages and handed out in relevant neighborhoods. To finance the race, Hanna systematically approached the captains of industry, raising more money than had ever been raised for a presidential race and an amount unmatched until the election of 1920.

As for the candidate's efforts, McKinley was unable to travel during the race. For one, the custom held that only candidates in "trouble" actively campaigned; second, his wife was an invalid; and most important, he feared he would be upstaged by Bryan at every stop. Unfortunately, the race was too close to keep the candidate completely out of it. Instead, Hanna crafted an extensive plan to bring the campaign to McKinley.

He orchestrated one of the most finely tuned "pilgrimages" *to* a candidate in the history of American politics. Among other things, he enlisted the aid of leading GOP railroad moguls to offer excursion passes to those journeying to McKinley's front porch in Canton, Ohio (Jamieson 1984, 18). Of course, once these delegations reached the candidate, every step was carefully choreographed, and the media were always given a prime seat. Even the introduction speeches supporters gave McKinley were carefully scrutinized by Hanna's team for the appropriate content and message. In the end, McKinley's front porch campaign captured the attention of the nation: "The desire to come to Canton has reached the point of mania," reported Francis Loomis (Troy 1991, 105). From midsummer until the election, McKinley gave over 300 speeches and had nearly 1 million visitors. Many of these visitors saw fit to snatch twigs, grass, stones, and even pieces of the famous porch as souvenirs of their experience; others left gifts for the candidate.

Election day saw one of the largest voter turnouts in history. McKinley won with just 51 percent of the vote, thanks in large measure to the careful planning and skill of his top aid, Mark Hanna.

This chapter briefly examines the importance of planning in new-style campaign management. It begins with a look at the rationale for written plans and proceeds from there to the various elements. There is no record of Hanna's written plan from the 1896 election, but his adherence to business practices and professional management strongly suggests that a written, finely tuned document guided much of what he did for McKinley. Because the race was extremely close, this organizational tool might surely have made the difference. In today's turbulent, competitive political environment, the victor is usually the most organized; that means close adherence to a well-devised plan.

WHY HAVE A CAMPAIGN PLAN?

The greatest function of a campaign plan is that it creates order out of an otherwise chaotic process. Far too many candidates and novice consultants head out into the trenches expecting to "take things as they come." Hard work, they presume, will overcome any obstacle. They are wrong. As noted by a top Democratic consultant, "A campaign without a map is like a journey without a map. Although Saint Brendan did find North America without a map, Neil Armstrong could never have reached the moon simply by pointing the rocket" (Sweeney 1995, 15).

Campaigns are filled with scores of details, deadlines, and changing circumstances. Without written plans, campaigns flounder, and in competitive races they fail. Plans provide a step-by-step blueprint of how to win the election.

Written plans serve as a reference tool and a timetable during the heat of battle. They define what is to be done, when it should occur, who should be doing it, and what resources are needed. All too often races pause because of uncertainty over the next step. With plans, there is little question; no one wonders what to do next. Specific timetables help push staff and volunteers to get the job done. Open-ended assignments are generally failed assignments.

Plans keep the staff calmly focused on the task at hand. Campaigns can become volatile, and often emotions are stronger than logic. A plan also helps keep the *candidate* fixed on the predetermined strategy. A candidate may find it nearly impossible, for example, to resist fighting back when he or she is assailed by an opponent, or a candidate may want to come on strong at the wrong time. But consultants realize the importance of timing. Plans go a long way toward appeasing an infuriated or overly anxious candidate. Many times nothing works!

Thoughtful plans also minimize second-guessing during races. This can come from the staff or from the candidate. Competitive races take many turns. Although plans should be somewhat flexible, they do speak to the long term. The only critical day in a campaign is election day. Plans keep every player focused on that goal and are less concerned with coming out on top in any given day, week, or month preceding it.

Plans delegate responsibilities and command accountability. Time and resources are precious commodities in campaigns. A lucid definition of responsibilities eliminates waste. In some instances, duplication can be damaging rather than simply wasteful. For example, as is mentioned in Chapter 12, only one person should be responsible for working with the press. Contradictory statements from various members of the campaign team can lead to no coverage and possibly to negative coverage.

Written plans provide a record of ideas received by informal brainstorming or conversation. They signify hard work, discipline, and a commitment to the product that is impossible without formal documentation. "If it's not in writing, it doesn't exist" (Sweeney 1995, 16).

Less obvious but equally important, plans inspire confidence in potential supporters and the media. It is suggested throughout this book that one of the most difficult obstacles many candidates must overcome is the public's perception that they stand a chance. "Sure losers" are given scant attention by the press and even less help from money sources. One way to get the ball rolling in a positive direction is to tout a finely tuned plan. It leads "the influential" to believe that one's race will be conducted in an organized, efficient manner and will not waste resources.

ELEMENTS OF A PLAN

The precise contours of a new-style campaign plan vary from consultant to consultant. There is no step-by-step guide to building one. Nevertheless, certain core elements must be addressed. A plan carefully lays out contextual information, audience considerations, strategy and tactics, and staffing and resource requirements. These topics are addressed in depth throughout the pages to follow; nevertheless, a brief listing here illustrates that they should be incorporated into a written plan.

Contextual Information

District Profile. This section of the plan provides information on district geography, industry, housing patterns, community organizations, transportation infrastructure, and other fixed variables. This profile is a condensed version of a larger research project, discussed in Chapter 3, but during the heat of the campaign it may prove to be a handy reference tool.

Demographic Profile. As highlighted in Chapter 4, students and practitioners of elections long ago discerned a close fit between the characteristics of a voting population and election outcomes. For example, districts with a large number of union members tend to vote Democratic. This section sketches demographic characteristics of the voters. A narrative is suggested along with maps and summary tables.

Prior Electoral Targeting. One of the best ways to predict future voter behavior is to look at past voter behavior. This section provides summary information from prior electoral targeting, discussed in Chapter 5.

Candidate Qualifications and Background. It will not be possible to note all candidate information in this section, but a summary is convenient during the race. It might include personal and professional highlights and spend a bit more time on the candidate's elected office background, such as past experience, committee posts, bill sponsorship, appointments, and so on.

Opposition Profile. As voters have moved away from partisan voting cues, new-style campaigns have become increasingly "comparative." It is critical to have all legally available information on the opponent. This section should note the high points of this investigation.

Audience Considerations

Issue Papers Abstract. This section should include one-page summaries of the candidate's stand on all possible issues of the race. These stands are derived from the concerns of voters, the candidate's background, the opponent's background and expected stance, and the candidate's core values. A set of more detailed position papers should be developed and stored elsewhere. The idea here is to provide a synopsis.

Polling Plan and Schedule. This section provides an overview of the polling that will be done in the race. It lists the dates, survey technique, estimated costs, and the goals of each phase.

Voters Concerns (Polling Highlights). This section should contain an overview of voter concerns, as well as an overlay with targeting subdivisions—in other words, a summary of the topics of interest to voters throughout the district.

Strategy and Tactics

Campaign Theme. Developing a campaign theme is the subject of Chapter 8. It is argued that this is derived from what the voters want, what the candidate has to offer, and what the opponent has to offer. This section should note the theme and a one-page justification.

Overall Time Frame. Noted at several points below, voters pass through three phases during a campaign: cognition, where they discern who is running; affect, where they begin to make a choice; and evaluation, where they reach a decision. Strategy and tactics will vary according to the stage. This section provides an estimation as to when each phase will be reached.

Paid Media Voter Contact Schedule. This piece, closely linked to the overall time frame, provides a detailed framework for the various voter contact tactics. This should be broken into subsections for each medium. For example, there might be a direct mail plan, a radio schedule, a television plan, and a literature drop scheme. This is one of the most important pieces of the plan so great care should be taken here. Unlike in several of the aforementioned sections, details should be stressed. The subject of paid media is covered in detail in Chapter 11.

Earned Media Activities. Acquiring favorable press coverage can be one of the most difficult chores of new-style campaigning. Careful planning will help. This section, also quite detailed, lays out the topics and schedule for earned media efforts.

Candidate Activities. It is wise to include in any plan a fairly exact description of the candidate's obligations and duties throughout the race. Among other things, this helps optimize the candidate's time and compels him or her to do things he or she might not otherwise wish to undertake.

Resources and Staffing

Necessary Resources (Budget). Obviously, it takes resources to communicate with voters. This section is derived from the time frame, the paid and earned media plan, the polling schedule, and the staffing and operations requirements. Simply put, it specifies what types of resources the campaign needs and, even more important, when they are needed.

Fund-Raising Plan and Schedule. On the heels of the campaign budget is the fund-raising strategy. This section carefully discusses when and how the campaign war chest will be built.

Staffing. Here the duties, responsibilities, and chain of command for the campaign staff are noted. For all but the smallest staffs, it is profitable to divide this section into several areas, or teams—such as the fund-raising team, the press team, the grassroots activity team, and so on.

Organizational Requirements. This section outlines the organizational needs of the campaign, such as headquarters, telephones, cars, computers, fax machines, and so on.

SOME THOUGHTS ON IMPLEMENTATION

Obviously, the integration of numerous elements into a blueprint is no simple task. The timing of each step often depends on preceding ones. Little in a campaign can occur, for instance, prior to fund-raising, and certainly no voter contact activity should take place without survey data. Conceivably more important than timing considerations, there must be careful harmony in voter contact activities. That is, messages are most effective when they are mutually reinforcing. Paid and earned media advertisements should complement each other—address the same theme. If the plan calls for an all-out attack in the second week of August, nearly all communications during this period should strike the same chord. This idea is discussed throughout the book.

Republican consultant Mark Weaver suggests a flowchart be devised after the plan has been established. Across the top would be the campaign teams or departments, and along the side are dates—preferably weekly rows for most of the race, but daily ones by October. Recorded at the intersections are specific duties. This allows the campaign to distinguish clearly the projects and the goal.

Campaign plans are win oriented. In other words, it should be assumed that, if everything is completed in the plan, the candidate will receive at least 50 percent plus one share of the votes casts.

The candidate should always play an integral role in the development of the plan. For one, he or she must be comfortable with every step. If a candidate finds aggressive attacks against the opponent unpalatable, for instance, the plan would have to be modified accordingly. Second, the candidate must be the center of many of the campaign events, and problems will surely arise if scheduled activities do not conform to set plans. The amount of time a candidate will be able to take off from work to campaign, for example, will be an important consideration. Moreover, candidates must feel as though they have a personal stake in the planning of the race. This will, as noted above, reduce the level of Monday-morning quarterbacking and keep everyone on the same track.

It is also important to recognize that campaign plans should *not* be considered ephemeral to the strategy team. They are based upon honed research and the best available information. It is imperative to have faith in the analysis and stick to the strategy. This is often hard to do when things get tight and election day draws near.

With that said, neither are they set in stone. In many ways, they are based upon prior assumptions, and these guesses can prove to be wrong. There are also unforeseen developments in every race (carefully developed campaign plans eliminate many of these surprises). The best approach is to establish benchmarks and milestones throughout the race to review the progress of the race (Beaudry and Schaeffer 1986, 54).

Part One

THE LAY OF THE LAND: UNDERSTANDING THE CAMPAIGN CONTEXT

Chapter Three

The Campaign Context

If one were to ask an average voter, a member of the media, or even someone politically active what the most important piece of a campaign might be, he or she would probably respond with notions about strategy, finances, or tactics. The responder might even develop a sophisticated answer to your query; nevertheless, he or she would be incorrect. The most significant element in a modern campaign is the context. Consultants will use different terms, such as "the landscape," "the environment," or "the political terrain," and others may pull together the same idea with several related concepts, but they have in mind the same thing: the list of givens in any campaign.

By a "list of givens," it is meant those pieces of the campaign that cannot be altered by your candidate, the opponent, or by anyone else (Salmore and Salmore 1989, 11–12). A partial list includes the office you are seeking, your candidate's status (incumbent, challenger, or open seat), your candidate's qualifications, the opponent's qualifications, the election year, the media market, national trends, who else is on the ballot, demographics, the predisposition of the electorate, and so on. No one element will dictate the tone, direction, or strategy of a campaign, but in any race astute care must be given to the list of givens—as all strategy, tactics, message resources, and decisions must originate from this foundation. One might even go so far as to suggest that everything that occurs in a campaign is driven by its unique context.

Because this topic is so consequential, it is divided into several chapters. The chapter at hand lists many of the more basic, yet often discounted, contextual pieces. The goal is to describe why each matters and how a better understanding of their importance can lead to a strategic advantage. Illustrations of their uses and misuses are provided. In 1992 Bill Clinton's campaign team found it useful to remind themselves of their core message by posting a sign on the wall which read; "It's the Economy Stupid!" We might go one step further by reminding ourselves: It's the Context Stupid!

THE OFFICE SOUGHT

Strange as it may seem, the certainty that the office sought guides the course of any campaign often gets lost in the hustle and bustle of activities. Consultants jetting from one client to another, or party activists working for a full slate of candidates, will sometimes fail to recognize the impact of the office sought. One might group these differences into three categories: what the voters expect, what the media expect, and the overall interest in the race.

What the Voters Expect

Simply put, voters often expect candidates for certain offices to highlight a particular set of issues, to hold different qualifications, and to stress a somewhat different campaign style. It would be overly optimistic, for instance, to conduct one survey for three or four candidates running for different offices among the same electorate and expect one theme to emerge for each. Understanding the subtle nuances of varying expectations is as much an art as a science, and much of the research in this area is underdeveloped. But these distinctions are real and campaign strategists must consider their weight.

Regarding issues, as will be seen in several chapters to follow, the candidate message is a complex matter—discerned through survey research, what the candidate has to offer, what the opponent brings to the table, and much else. The office sought also plays a role in this calculation. It may be a miscalculation, for example, to stress foreign policy concerns in a race for the U.S. House even though it jumps out on early surveys and your candidate has impressive qualifications in this area. A candidate running for the state house would certainly want to downplay national policy matters and highlight state policy concerns. What is more, candidates for judicial posts are expected to stress legal matters and nonpartisan issues and, if anything, stick to personal qualifications instead of controversial issues.

The 1992 congressional election produced one of the true surprises of the decade and provides a telling illustration for our discussion at hand. Stephen Solarz, a Democrat from Brooklyn, New York, was first elected to Congress in 1974. In most of his reelections he ran either unopposed or received over 75 percent of the vote. By all counts he had served his constituents skillfully and had quickly risen to the higher ranks of the Democratic Caucus, including chair of the prestigious Foreign Affairs Subcommittee. He was doing so well that there was even speculation about his ascendance to the speakership.

After the redistricting of congressional boundaries in 1990, Solarz's district (the 12th) was changed, forcing him to develop a relationship with a new set of voters. He proceeded to run his campaign on what he, and his advisors, deduced to be his strengths—a solid foreign policy prowess and his prestigious post in Congress. Apparently, this carried much weight with his colleagues in Washington and among the national media, but it was of secondary concern to the voters because he was defeated in the primary election. Solarz's rising congressional career had ended, leaving the Washington establishment stunned.

It would be simplistic to suggest that Solarz was defeated solely because of his overreliance on his foreign policy experience, or that congressional election voters never care about these issues. In some districts, such as those with a large immigrant population, foreign policy matters may be of great interest. But it is perhaps not a coincidence that "between 1970 and 1984, three consecutive Senate Foreign Relations chairs were defeated in reelection bids by opponents who charged that they had cared more about world politics than local concerns" (Nelson 1995, 21). Conceivably, Solarz's team misread the polls, or simply could not offer what the voters wanted. To be sure, the new district contained a large number of Hispanics, many of whom voted along ethnic lines. And no doubt his 743 overdrafts from the House Bank caught the eye of many voters. But it is also likely that Solarz did not anticipate what voters demand from U.S. House candidates.

Voters also have a basic notion of which issues are "national" and which issues should be dealt with at the state and local levels. Conceivably this is why U.S. Senate and House candidates have had difficulty in making hay out of topics surrounding education, even though it shows up on every survey. Simply put, it is perceived to be an important, but local concern—something best dealt with at the community level. Conversely, crime—traditionally a state and local issue—has recently been nationalized, and federal office candidates today neglect it at their peril.

Constituent service is certainly an issue legislative candidates must stress. There is a growing body of research to suggest case work—taking care of the folks back home—has single-handedly led to exceedingly high reelection rates among members of Congress and state legislatures.[1] The ability to deliver goods and particularized benefits often makes or breaks reelection campaigns. On the other hand, this sort of thing rarely figures in gubernatorial, mayoral, or other executive post elections. Voters seem more concerned with policy and programmatic success from these candidates.

How does one discern what types of issues are best addressed in House, Senate, or mayoral campaigns? There are no clear guidelines here. One possibility is to look at the political history of the district, paying close attention to the themes of prior successful and unsuccessful candidates. Another possibility is to incorporate into survey questions not only what issues are important, but also what office is best able to handle these concerns. Carefully conducted focus groups, discussed in Chapter 7, will also help in this regard. At the very least, a wise campaign strategist understands the office sought will, in part, guide the choice of issues and themes.

A similar element of voter expectations relates to candidate qualifications. There appears to be a good bit of variance in the qualifications voters prize in candidates for certain offices. Research in this area is a bit underdeveloped, but a rough breakdown is that candidates for executive posts are expected to have leadership skills and the ability to implement programs. Stephen Wayne, a distinguished scholar of the presidency, conducted a survey of what voters most admire in presidents. Topping the list were "strong," "ability to get things done," and "decisive" (Wayne 1982, 192–195) One would expect to find similar attributes admired in gubernatorial and mayoral candidates. Candidates for legislative posts, on the other hand, might stress bargaining and conciliation skills, as well as a close connection with the average voter. Asked whether members of Congress should look after the needs of "their own district" or the "interest of the nation," a Harris survey found respondents overwhelmingly favor the former: 57 to 34 percent (Nelson 1995, 17).

It is likely that voters are less interested in programmatic leadership skills from legislative candidates because, after all, a legislator is just one out of a large group. That is to say, it is more difficult to affix blame or give credit to one member of a legislative body, than it is to a mayor or governor. Certainly legislators are more anxious to highlight their successes—which are often narrow, district-specific programs—than their broad-based policies. Another possibility is that voters see legislators as their chance at the national/state pie, and legislators are therefore assessed on how well they deliver. In 1990 incumbent Romano Mazzoli barely held on to his Kentucky congressional seat when both primary and general election challengers charged he was ineffective at bringing federal projects back to the district (Craney 1990, 3311). Representative Harley Staggers (D-W.V.) was not so lucky in 1992. He was defeated in his primary bid by Allan Mollerhan, who repeatedly charged that Staggers had failed to deliver. According to one television ad: "You [Staggers] didn't get one single dollar for your district in the recent highway bill. You even missed a key vote funding the FBI Center in West Virginia" (Parsinos 1994, 23). Executives, such as mayors and county executives, represent all the voters and are expected to lead. Here, an emphasis on leadership skills may be more fitting—indeed anticipated. Bringing home the pork may be less expected.

It has long been held that U.S. Senators should rise above mere constituent service and stress programmatic themes. In fact, if a legislative candidate were to underscore foreign policy, it might be one running for the Senate. Congressional scholar Eric Uslaner (1981) suggested some time ago that senators downplay constituency service in favor of seeking national forums. "Most senators would prefer to appear on *Meet the Press* or *Face the Nation* than to address a garden club or listen to a constituent's personal problems" (170). And the voters, he suggests, may be accustomed to this. But even this may be changing. Senator Al D'Amato (R-N.Y.) was elected, and continues to be reelected, on his unabashed willingness to secure federal projects for New York—so much so that he has been dubbed "Senator Pothole" in reference to his ability to garner funds to fix the streets and bridges of his own state. More and more Senate candidates appear to be heading down this path.

A final element of what voters anticipate relates to the style and tone of the campaign. Again, this is a speculative area of research, but some generalizations can be made. In some states or districts, voters expect executive and judicial candidates to run serious, issue-based campaigns, while legislative candidates are more free to "mix it up." In some districts, a loose, relaxed style may be appropriate for all candidates, while in others it might be unacceptable for all posts.

Traditional wisdom holds that U.S. Senate candidates should remain somewhat stately during the course of the campaign. Once again, this may be changing. During his 1992 bid for the Senate, Russ Finegold made mileage out of using a television spot featuring Elvis, who had finally come out of hiding to lend his endorsement. The spot, highlighting the King in full regalia, was very humorous—something infrequent in U.S. Senate races, especially in Wisconsin. Finegold, nevertheless, won the election.

Only a short while ago, it was also believed that candidates for all offices should appear in public wearing business-like clothing. Even if they were to attend a plain-folks event, such as a barbecue or ice-cream social, they should take off their jackets and loosen their ties, but always don professional attire. In some areas this still holds water and in many others just the opposite may be occurring. In 1994 Ohio U.S. Senate candidate Mike DeWine ran a series of television ads featuring himself wearing a plaid flannel shirt. This sort of down-home look would not have been appropriate in Ohio several years ago, especially for Republican candidates; and it may still be out of place for gubernatorial candidates. Yet, Dewine now represents his state in the Senate.

A campaign guided by "traditional wisdom" and "the way we've always done things" may prove successful, particularly when a candidate is ahead in the polls and faces a similar thinking opponent. In today's volatile election arena, however, campaigns willing to test and rethink old adages often rise to the top, as did Dewine and Finegold. It would be a mistake to adhere only to what has been done in the past. This does not mean, however, that local traditions and norms are irrelevant. The key is to understand what voters expect, how deeply they adhere to these beliefs and customs, and what might be done within these parameters to accent your own candidate.

Media Relations

Just as the office sought may impact voter expectations, it may also greatly influence what members of the media expect. As will be discussed in detail in Chapter 12, successfully obtaining media coverage can be one of the most important voter communication techniques. In order to acquire coverage, the campaign team must understand what the local and national media expect from candidates for different offices.

For starters, candidates are expected to have a basic, if not good, understanding of the issues confronting the level of office to which they aspire. Federal candidates should be up on national issues, state candidates should know about state issues, and local aspirants should understand community concerns. To many voters, the line between local, state, and national problems is a bit hazy, but to reporters it is clear.

Second, generally speaking, the higher the aspired office, the greater the expectation that the candidate has intimate knowledge of issues. To be sure, U.S. Senate candidates are often surprised by the rigorous grilling they are put through by the media. Candidates perceived by the media as unprepared are tagged as "incompetent" or "green," an impression difficult to shake. In 1990 challenger Bill Schuette was unsuccessful in his bid to oust incumbent Carl Levin (D-Mich.) because, among other things, he was tagged by the media as unprepared. According to Holly Idelson of *the Congressional Quarterly*, "Schuette has had to battle perceptions that he was more gloss than substance, and he did not help himself on this score by refusing to debate his Republican primary opponent" (Idelson, October 13, 1990, 3318). In 1992 Spence Abraham defeated Ronna Romney for the GOP Senate nomination in Michigan by suggesting that she was unqualified for the job and did not have a solid grasp of the issues. By the end of the campaign, the media agreed; the *Free Press* called Romney "unbelievably shallow" after a poor showing in a debate (Beiler 1994a, 32). This is not to suggest that state and local office candidates can run unprepared, or pay little attention to the issues, only that these posts may be viewed as a training ground for budding politicians, and some leeway may be available. One should, however, never bet on it!

Another issue to keep in mind is that shortcomings, either professional or personal, are *less* likely to be overlooked the higher the level of office to which one aspires. Whereas a reporter may uncover dirt on a state legislative candidate and never report it, that same information might be reported on a congressional candidate. And in the media feeding-frenzy atmosphere, U.S. Senate candidates should be squeaky clean. This may be due to greater media scrutiny for higher level offices, or it could simply be that media gatekeepers—those who decide what is news and what is not—have double standards. In any event, this is a an important contextual nuance to understand. Again, candidates for lower level offices are not free from media scrutiny, only that higher level aspirants should be especially wary.

It is also a certainty of modern campaigning that the ability to level charges against an opponent, often robust ones, increase for lower level offices. Whereas most assaults waged against Senate or House candidates will be inspected by the media for accuracy, and be reported if found to be untrue, this is not the case in lower level campaigns. Reporters and news people are overworked and underpaid, and there are only so many hours in the day. Rather than track down every charge candidates make against one another during an election, they choose to concentrate on higher level races. Reporters also suggest, when challenged on this, that it is their job to report the news, not play referee in a fight (Dunn 1995, 117). Since 1992 "ad watch" journalism has come into its own, where there is an emphasis on disclosing inaccuracies (Ansolabehere and Iyengar 1995). Because of time and resource constraints, this effort is primarily focused on presidential, U.S. Senate and House races and, in off years, on mayoral races.

Of course, this is not to suggest that campaigns for any level of office should play fast and loose with the truth. It is not only unethical, but very risky. A campaign found to have relied on false or misleading material will nearly always, in the end, be uncovered. Yet, as discussed in several chapters below, what is factual during campaigns is often a matter of interpretation and spin. A candidate may have a 97 percent attendance record, but still have missed "385 important votes." Candidates for lower level offices simply have an advantage when it comes to a broad interpretation of the facts.

A final issue to consider with regard to the media, and much related to each of the aforementioned, is the amount of coverage a campaign can expect. All things being equal, U.S. Senate and mayoral races receive a good deal of coverage, and House campaigns get a modest amount. City council, county legislative, state legislative, and judicial races are generally starved for attention. A state legislative candidate who puts a great deal of stock in earned media might well rethink his strategy. There are opportunities for coverage in these lower level races, yet the office sought will often dictate the extent of media coverage.

Overall Interest in the Campaign

Not only are political novices shocked to find that their campaign rarely makes the front page, but they are even more surprised to find it is of little interest to most voters. Candidates, party activists, volunteers, and even some consultants get deeply enmeshed in the races and begin to expect everyone is equally interested. What they forget is that most voters think about their jobs, children, bills, vacations, cars, spouses, and a vast pool of other matters long before they think of politics. Elections are, at best, a secondary concern to most voters.

With that noted, not all offices are ignored equally. There is, you might say, a hierarchy of interest, starting with presidential races and quickly dropping to Senate and House races—the rest fall a distance behind. Perhaps at the bottom of the list are campaigns for judicial posts. The logical question would be what difference does the level of interest make in a campaign's strategy and tactics?

For one, there is "drop-off." Simply stated, the number of voters to cast ballots in any given election will vary from office to office. Lower level offices can often anticipate as much as a 15 to 20, or even a 40 percent drop-off from the top of the ballot (presidential, gubernatorial, or mayoral, depending on the election year) to the bottom. Precisely estimating the number of likely voters in your race will greatly impact when, how, and to whom you communicate your message. A 37 percent turnout is markedly different than an 41 percent turnout. Much more will be said about drop-off and turnout in Chapter 5.

The interest in your campaign will also affect fund-raising. Individuals and organizations give money to candidates because they are aware of the race and expect the outcome to matter. If few are interested or even familiar with your race, an outpouring of money should not be expected. This, of course, is a self-fulfilled prophecy—more money makes for greater awareness, which brings in even more money. Conversely, high- profile races can expect seed money and, in the end, larger war chests.

Finally, the level of awareness, tied closely to the office sought, will impact how your message will be communicated. The campaign cannot proceed with messages as to why they would better serve the district before voters even know that person is running for office. As noted in Chapter 9, voter attitudes go through three distinct phases during any election: cognition, affect, and evaluation (Salmore and Salmore 1989, 13–14). Much more will be said about the overlay of these phases and strategic decisions in the chapters ahead. It may be enough to note at this point that how you proceed during an election—the tactics and strategy used to communicate with voters, as well as the message chosen—will depend on the store of information voters have about your candidate. And this level of awareness is very much linked to the office sought.

CANDIDATE STATUS

No other contextual element has a greater bearing on the outcome of the election than candidate status. There are three possibilities here: incumbent, challenger, or open-seat candidate. By "incumbent" it is meant the candidate who already holds the post and is running for reelection. A "challenger" is a candidate who is running against an incumbent. An "open-seat candidate" is running for an open seat—there is no incumbent in the campaign because the office holder is not running for reelection or has otherwise vacated the seat. As Figure 3.1 notes, there can never be one open-seat candidate in an election.

Figure 3.1
The Three Types of Candidate Status

When Candidate A Is:	Candidate B Must Be:
Incumbent ————————————>	Challenger
Challenger ————————————>	Incumbent
Open-Seat Candidate ——————— >	Open-Seat Candidate

Incumbency far outweighs any other resource a candidate might possess. They generally have higher early name recognition, better and more frequent relations with the media, more experienced staff, better finances, more volunteers, and superior connections with parties and interest groups in the district. Often they will have "worked" and "cultivated" their relationship with the electorate through massive franking (publicly financed mailings), town hall meetings, and scores of receptions. Furthermore, by definition, they have voter appeal—they were at least once selected to hold that post.

It is not surprising that nine out of ten incumbents win reelection to Congress and state legislatures. Even in the Republican sweep of 1994, 90 percent of the incumbents were returned to office. (It just so happens that all who were defeated were Democrats.) This percentage is a bit lower for executive posts, but it remains above the two-thirds mark.

If your candidate is a challenger, and absent a big mistake on the part of the incumbent, it is only honest to admit the chances of celebration on election night are slim. Whereas your opponent will begin the race, for example, with a 50 percent hard name identification, you may work hard through the spring and summer only to get to 15 percent by Labor Day. Political action committees and other regular contributors to campaigns will be hesitant to give heavy backing to your races for fear of alienating themselves with the incumbent—the person most likely to be making public policy after election. They will give to competitive races, but how does your candidate become competitive without money? From 1984 to 1992, the average challenger for the House of Representatives spent only one-third of what the average incumbent spent. Even in 1994, a year considered to be a "breakthrough" by a leading scholar of campaign finance (Malbin 1995), the ratio of incumbent to challenger spending was

2:1—$599,490 to $225,503, on an average. Added on top of this is that incumbents will often have even the most insipid news release printed by the local paper, while a challenger cannot get a reporter to cover his or her announcement speech. Incumbents nearly always attract more attention and a bigger crowd. It is an unfortunate reality in contemporary American politics that most elections are simply biased in this way.

Fortunately, there is some light at the end of the tunnel. With skill, good judgment, and a bit of luck, many of the advantages of incumbency can be turned around. There is a strong "throw the bum out" movement in politics these days, and outsiders and fresh faces seem increasingly appealing. As much as they may try, it is exceedingly difficult for an incumbent to run on a platform of "change." Incumbents also have records, much of which they will attempt to highlight, but there are also blemishes on every elected official's public scorecard. "The choice for voters often comes down to a referenda on the incumbent's performance in office" (Bradshaw 1995, 38). Challengers can benefit from not having such liabilities.

In the spring of 1994, the voters of the 28th state senate district of Georgia shocked the rest of the state by rejecting their powerful, long-term senator, Danny Corbett, in favor of State Representative George Clay. Corbett first elected in 1982, was considered unbeatable. Three issues seem to have come together to upset this prestigious incumbent. First, early polls indicated that Corbett had high negatives. Just as years of service can build a foundation of support, it also can amass a pool of hostile voters. According to pollster Jim Kitchens, whose firm conducted the survey in the 28th, "[Incumbents] usually survive because challengers aren't very credible and can not match their resources" (Koelemay 1994). Second, those same polls found overwhelming discontent with the performance of the legislature itself; 72 percent disapproved of the job it was doing. Corbett may or may not have been part of the problem, but he was certainly caught up in it.

Third, and perhaps most important, he had developed a legislative record hostile to a resourceful, powerful interest group—the Business Council of Alabama (BCA). As chair of the Senate Economic Affairs Committee, Corbett had repeatedly blocked probusiness tax, tort, and workers compensation reforms. As a result, the BCA contributed $200,000 of Clay's $255,000 war chest (Koelemay 1994, 48). Finally, Clay was a well-regarded challenger, who compiled a skillful, well-coordinated campaign team. Among much else, his campaign pursued an aggressive telephone and paid advertising program, as well as a carefully targeted mail effort. "We had all the right elements to pursue a very aggressive effort—a vulnerable incumbent and a credible challenger," noted lead Clay consultant George Burger (Koelemay 1994, 49).

Many incumbents have a habit of running the same campaign each election. This is one of the warning signs, according to polling consultant Neil Newhouse, of "incumbentitus." Incumbents often look upon a past successful campaign as the model for all future campaigns (Shea and Brooks 1995, 24). Closely examining past elections can offer a strategic edge. If the challenger is a political novice, the incumbent will have nothing similar to review. As noted by columnist John Persinos, "The most difficult opponent is somebody who's never run for anything" (Persinos 1994, 22).

Challengers may find it easier—more palatable in that district—to attack; in some areas, it is perceived as undignified for an elected official to go on the offensive (yet, this too may be changing). All incumbents, on the other hand, should expect to be attacked by both the opponent and the media. There is an old adage, and there continues to be some truth to it, that challengers do not win elections, incumbents lose them.

Once picked up by the media, challengers can benefit from underdog and bandwagon phenomena. In most elections it is assumed that the incumbent will win, and when a challenger begins to move it catches attention—it becomes news and more people jump on board. There will always be more stories and talk about an underdogs catching up, than about the perceived victors plodding along.

As for the qualifications, incumbents have records of achievement to run on. They must do their best to highlight their successes. This should come easy because much of what they do can be described in a positive light. They also have constituencies cultivated through committee assignments or official activities which can be counted on. They have lists of donors to resort to, and a record of volunteers from previous elections. They also have an edge on "experience," "knowledge," and "leadership" qualities. Just as incumbents can never be outsiders, challengers rarely can be more experienced.

Although open-seat candidates run on an even footing, there are several other issues to keep in mind. In the recent past, many open seats were considered noncompetitive; the partisan predisposition of the voters was overwhelmingly one-sided, giving the candidate of that party an immense edge. Today, with the decline of party identification as a meaningful tool for selecting candidates, many open seats are toss-ups. A fitting illustration occurred in Pennsylvania's 13th congressional district (suburban Philadelphia) during the 1992 election. Marjorie Margolies-Mezvinsky broke a seventy-six-year Republican reign by defeating Jon Fox in an open-seat contest. No Democrat had received more than 44 percent since 1968, and there continues to be a two-to-one Republican registration advantage (*Congressional Quarterly*, January 16, 1993). Unfortunately for Margolies-Mezvinsky, the seat returned to its Republican leanings in 1994. Because open seats are generally up for grabs, the media, as well as interested PACs and individuals, pay close attention.

As neither open-seat candidate may have an extensive public record, attacks may focus on other professional or personal affairs. Another possibility is that, although there is no incumbent in the race, that does not mean that one candidate cannot be tagged as such. The candidate of the same party as the national or state administration, for example, may be labeled as "part of the problem" and serve as a referendum target. Perhaps one of the candidates had worked, at one time or another, for the departing office holder. Sometimes older candidates can be portrayed as members of the party of the status quo.

In the spring of 1994 there was an election to fill a vacated congressional seat in Oklahoma. The Republican candidate was Frank Lucas, a rancher from the rural part of the district. The Democratic candidate was twenty-seven-year old Dan Weber, a congressional press secretary, who had spent his entire adult life in Washington, D.C. (Beiler 1994d, 47). Although Weber was aggressively backed by former governor and three-term U.S. Senator David Boren, he clearly suffered by being linked to Washington. Lucas ran a series of television spots highlighting Weber's home in Washington, juxtaposed to his own home in rural Oklahoma. The comparison was frequently made, followed by the kicker: "Get the picture?" (Beiler 1994). The race was an open seat, yet Lucas effectively turned his opponent into the incumbent.

Open-seat campaigns may also turn to partisan or ideological differences. In 1994 Democratic open-seat candidates for all levels of office struggled to declare themselves "different from Clinton," while the Republicans sought to stamp them as "part of the problem." One Democratic candidate for the New York State Assembly went so far as to denounce his association with then Governor Mario Cuomo, also a Democrat.

THE ELECTION YEAR

As noted above, the number of voters expected to cast ballots in a race will be a critical component, and certainly the office sought has a direct bearing. Another key piece of this calculation is the type of election year.

When discussing types of election years, there are three possibilities: on, off, and odd. "On" elections are simply those years when there is a presidential election, which occurs every four years: 1984, 1988, 1992, 1996, 2000, and so on. "Off " years are also even numbered, but there is no presidential election. "Off " years also occur every four years: 1990, 1994, 1998, and so on. Finally, "odd" year elections are simply those that occur in odd-numbered years.

The number of people heading to the polls is always highest during on years. This is due to the attention given to presidential campaigns; however, all of the House, one-third of the Senate, and most state legislatures (both houses) hold elections during these years as well. The percent of citizens legally registered to vote on election day who actually go to the polls (turnout) will vary from state to state, and from district to district, but within that state or district it always reaches its zenith during on years. Lower level offices holding elections during on years will therefore have a turnout higher than those held during other times.

Generally speaking, off years will have the next highest turnout. This is because all of the House of Representatives, one-third of the Senate, most state legislative posts, and a majority of gubernatorial, as well as many other statewide, elections occur then. Together, these races kick up interest and bring people to the polls.

The lowest turnout will nearly always occur during odd years. This is when most municipal and judicial offices are filled; only one state (New Jersey) holds statewide posts during odd years. There is simply less campaigning and media attention during these years, and fewer people go to the polls.

Table 3.1 presents a tabulation of prior turnout in a hypothetical town—Smithville. As it suggests, it is not uncommon to see turnout levels dramatically shift from year to year. In Precinct 2, the turnout dropped 21 percent between 1988 (an on year) and 1990 (an off year). And the difference between 1988 and 1989 (an odd year) is 35 percent. The reader should note several additional items from the table. For one, precincts are rather consistent over the years; that is, a precinct with a relatively high turnout in 1988 will have a relatively high turnout in other years.   For example, Precinct 2 had the highest turnout every election, not just in 1988. The converse is also true; areas with low turnout in one election will generally always have a low turnout.   Second, the examination of turnout is not an exact science.   Precinct 5 experienced a higher turnout in 1991 (an odd year) than in 1994, an off year. Sometimes a hotly contested local race during an odd year will push turnout up more than during congressional races.   Moreover, districts/precincts are not *always* consistent year after year—there are patterns, not perfect pictures.

Table 3.1
Hypothetical Prior Turnout: "Smithville"
(In percent, by precinct*)

Election Year	1988	1989	1990	1991	1992	1994
Precinct 1	77	50	66	47	79	67
Precinct 2	89	54	68	57	83	71
Precinct 3	71	47	61	49	71	62
Precinct 4	63	42	52	40	62	55
Precinct 5	55	27	33	36	51	35

* A precinct, often termed an election district, is the smallest geographic electoral subdivision.

Another item to keep in mind is that, during some years, a campaign may be competing for the voters' attention much more than in some others. During on years especially, the airways, billboards, and mail will be filled with campaign messages. If you are running a state legislative race during these times, you must either accept that your message may get lost in the torrent of campaign communications, or do something different. One strategy may be simply to outdo all the others, but this requires massive resources. During off and odd years, there is a bit less competition for voter consideration, yet there may also be less overall interest in elections.

Occasionally, "special elections" are held at an odd time during the year (other than in November) in order to fill a particular post. This occurs when the office becomes vacant for some reason, such as resignation or death. Jill Long (D-Ind.), for example, was first elected to Congress in February 1989, in a special election to fill a seat previously held by Dan Coats, who was appointed to fill a vacancy in the U.S. Senate. Ron Lewis (R-Ky.) won a hotly contested race for the House in May 1994, filling the seat vacated by the death of William Natcher. These elections do not have to compete for voters attention—they are the only shows in town. Unfortunately, there is less interest in politics during these times, and turnout is generally low.

Just as voter attention waxes and wanes depending on the election year, so does media interest. During on years, the media are geared up for politics and spend much time covering it. This is somewhat less true during off and odd years. It may require more effort to secure coverage in one election year than in another.

Finally, the import of the "surge and decline" phenomenon should be understood. It is an peculiar occurrence in American politics that, in nearly every midterm congressional election since the turn of the century, the party of the president loses seats in Congress. The election of 1990 provides a clear illustration. It took place just two years after George Bush's impressive victory. In the months leading up to the election, public opinion surveys indicated voters were fed up with business as usual in Washington. The savings and loan scandal, the budget deficit crisis, and allegations of misconduct by scores of elected officials suggested that voters were prime for a change. Because the Democrats controlled both houses of Congress, one might have expected the Republicans to take over or, at the very least, to pick up a few seats. In actuality, the Democrats *gained* seventeen seats in the House and one seat in the Senate. While idiosyncratic factors clearly contributed to the election outcome, 1990 was consistent with a long-standing trend. Today, most pundits accept that there will be a loss for the president's party during midterm elections, and they speculate only how big it might be.

What causes the surge and decline phenomenon? Social scientists have wrestled with this question for some time, and a clear answer has yet to emerge. One possibility is that the electorate is different during the two elections. That is, a large group of citizens go to the polls during presidential elections but do not cast ballots during off year elections. These people, generally less partisan and less ideological, are responsible for a president's success, as well as an influx of congressional office holders of the president's party. During off year elections, the pool of voters shrinks and returns to its "normal" position. In other words, off years are the norm and presidential elections are the exception—without this influx of voters, congressional candidates of the president's party would not have been elected to as great a degree.

Unfortunately, this view is a bit unsatisfactory; it does little to explain the consistency with which the phenomenon occurs. Another possibility is that, as a president takes over, voters are naturally excited by the possibilities of his administration. As the term progresses, however, they become disillusioned and cast their congressional votes to the other party. A third premise is that the type of candidate changes between the two elections. Perhaps aggressive candidates of the opposing party emerge in response to actions taken by the new president; they become angry at what they see happening and decide to do something about it. As a result, they run hard, determined campaigns and win the election. Along very similar lines, conceivably, political action committees and special-interest groups upset with the new administration respond by contributing heavily to the opposing party, in order to minimize the damage.

None of these explanations may accurately describe what happens in midterm elections, and a complete understanding may be elusive. Being on the wrong side of this strange affair in no way means a sure defeat. For campaign strategists, a basic understanding that subtle forces during midterm elections may work for or against your candidate helps set the context, and thus the development, of an appropriate strategy and message.

CANDIDATE BACKGROUND QUALIFICATIONS

Another contextual element that will surely help guide the strategy and theme of any race is the qualifications of the two candidates. In fact, one prominent student of elections goes so far as to note:

[For many voters] the choice rarely, if ever, comes down to an evaluation of a candidate's position on any one issue or combination of issues. Rather, the selection is made more on the traits and characteristics of the candidates, and issues serve as a backdrop. (Bradshaw 1995, 37–38)

Very often candidates and campaign professionals put their fingers to the wind and attempt to shape their candidate accordingly. The traits and characteristics stressed are simply pulled from the polling data. If, for example, their surveys suggest the voters are looking for someone tough on crime, they will do their best to offer that candidate. They may also find the electorate is looking for an aggressive, outspoken leader and again try to mold their candidate accordingly. The hard truth is that this strategy too often fails because the qualifications and capabilities of *both* candidates are not given enough heed.

An illustration of this pitfall pertains to "experience." The experience issue can be a two-way street. On the one hand, voters are often anxious to elect someone who knows the ropes—someone who can get things done from the first day in office. On the other hand, voters today are increasingly anxious to see new faces in government, as noted above. Inexperience can be an equally strong prerequisite for office. The term-limit movement has caught steam across the nation precisely because voters seem to value fresh insight at least as much as experience.

So what are candidates to do—how are they to be pitched? The answer is not just what the polls say most voters want, but what the candidate has to offer. If your candidate is running for reelection and has held that post for twelve years, it would seem out of place and indeed even insulting to suggest he or she is a political novice. Nevertheless, it is surprising how often candidates do no less, occasionally with success. In the 1992 Washington state U.S. Senate race, Patty Murray (D) ran as the ultimate outsider; her campaign slogan was that she was "a mom in tennis shoes." Murray, however, had served in the state senate since 1988 and had risen to the ranks of Democratic whip, leading the *Seattle Times* to exclaim that she was "neatly packaged as unpackaged" (*Congressional Quarterly*, January 16, 1993). Although she narrowly won the election, it is doubtful she will be able to rely upon the same unpolished, outsider image in her reelection campaign.

Perhaps a better solution to overcoming the "change" bandwagon if your candidate is the incumbent (or tagged as such) is to agree to the need for change—but not in this particular instance. After reading the polls that suggested voters wanted a change—any type of change—George Bush had no choice but to discredit Clinton on a personal level. The message was although change was necessary, Clinton could not be trusted. Bush lost the race, but this may have been the only available strategy given the context.

Much the same can be said about the drive to be more experienced. Often candidates with little experience will stress their modest accomplishments in an attempt to stand on an even footing with their opponent. Or they may stress a qualification they simply do not have. One example here would be the voters' desire to elect average citizens. Many budding pols see this trend but are simply not average folks; they are professional, wealthy, the products of private schools, and owners of luxury cars. Occasionally, candidates can paint their backgrounds as something that they are not, but generally this fails.

One of the earliest candidates to declare his aspiration for the Republican nomination for the presidency in 1996 was Lamar Alexander, former governor of Tennessee and secretary of education in the Bush administration. Wishing desperately to appear not only as an average citizen, but also as a Washington outsider, he donned a flannel shirt during his announcement speech. It backfired, as scores of journalists and politicians noted the hypocrisy. Instead of a discussion of his ideas and qualifications, radio, television, and newsprint commentators focused on his flannel shirt. Alexander, a multimillionaire, is far from average. One journalist noted, "Although he's currently posturing as a political 'outsider,' Alexander has been on a well-greased inside to political power since he was a pup"(Ireland 1995, 517). Even presidential advisors can neglect the most basic contextual elements.

If the candidate has been on the wrong side of the issues, it would certainly be a mistake to backtrack. Flip-flopping is viewed as a cardinal sin. A better strategy would be to downplay the issue or to rephrase it into a statement with which no one could disagree. Another possibility is to acknowledge the position and move on to other topics. If it is something that will inevitably come out, why not address it early thereby making it "secondhand" news as the election approaches. If the election hinges on the issue, however, the candidate could be in big trouble. It may be the case where one candidate "owns" a particular issue domain. For example, agricultural concerns may emerge as the most pressing issue during a campaign. Your candidate, having little farm experience, may nevertheless wish to develop positions and tackle the problem. The opponent, however, *is* a farmer and has served six terms as the director of the Agricultural Cooperative Agency. No matter how your candidate might try, he or she may never be able to outdo the opponent on issues related to farming. Statements and positions must be developed in order to minimize damage, but the campaign should look for another area of concern to highlight. If the election were run on farming alone, your candidate would probably lose, but few elections are won or lost on a single issue. Perhaps the candidate has his or her own issue domain—a topic *also* on the mind of voters. The point here is that surveys are not the only criteria for selecting issues.

A campaign must consider the idiosyncratic qualities of the candidate and the opponent. A candidate may have poor interpersonal skills and not be well suited for direct voter contact or personal solicitation of contributions. Age might be an issue, where pictures should be either highlighted or avoided. In 1992, twenty-nine-year-old Cleo Fields was able to capture Louisiana's 4th district by heavily drawing from the students in the district, many of whom attended Southern University. Some candidates are better looking than others, and some are simply brighter. A candidate may be intelligent and well versed but freeze up under pressure. Candidates' spouses can often make a big difference, either positively or negatively. Any scandal, no matter how distant, could come into play, as could associations, memberships, and prior job posts. It is hard to run on a family values platform, for example, if your candidate is divorced and has missed child support payments. Ethnicity and racial background can obviously matter and affect strategy and tactics. Finally, among many other things, the candidate's gender can be a decisive contextual element.

More will be said about gender in the coming chapters. A few points are worth highlighting here in our discussion of candidate qualifications. Despite the growing number of female office holders, many voters still perceive male and female candidates differently. For example, it is believed that the public pays more attention to a female candidate's family status than a male candidate's. Voters expect married women to have the support of their husbands, and those who have children face scrutiny about what will happen once their mother is elected to office (Shapiro 1992, 53) Some female candidates are perceived as wishy-washy regardless of their commitment to policy goals, overly reliant on others (husbands, advisors), single-issue candidates (only interested in women's issues), or unstable and immature (they have not been tested and are not ready for office) (Allen 1995, 28).

The public also feels the need for female candidates to prove that they possess strong character traits. Women who are running for Congress must show that they are tough on crime, for example, and that they are even knowledgeable in the areas of foreign affairs and defense—topics male candidates can often avoid. Females running for an executive office must prove that they are especially strong willed and able to lead (Shapiro 1992, 52).

MINOR PARTY CANDIDATES

A vast majority of general election campaigns in the United States pit two candidates against one another. But this may be changing. In recent elections third-party candidates have had played a large role in outcomes. In 1990, for example, Democrat Doug Bosco lost his congressional seat to Frank Riggs by one percentage point. "In that election, Peace and Freedom candidate Darlene Commingore took 15 percent of the vote directly from Bosco's base of support" (Fairbank and Goodwin 1993, 51). In the 1992 Georgia U.S. Senate race, Wyche Fowler, the Democratic incumbent, was denied a second term because of a third-party candidate. Fowler got slightly more votes than his Republican challenger, Paul Coverdale, in the general election. But Georgia law mandates a candidate receive 50 percent in a statewide race to avoid a runoff, and Libertarian Jim Hudson's 3 percent kept Fowler from that goal. Coverdale won the runoff election by about 15,000 votes. In fact, significant minor party candidacies are popping up all over the United States. In nine of California's 1992 congressional elections, for instance, third- party candidates received more votes than the spread between the Republican and Democrat. Much the same was true in Montana, Alaska, Missouri, Maine, and Ohio (Hood 1993, 40). As for state legislative races, minor party candidates were elected in eight states and made a difference in who was victorious in scores of campaigns across the nation.

One reason for the success of recent third party candidates might surely be the strong showing of Ross Perot in 1992. Notwithstanding, the public does seem open to the idea—perhaps more so than at any other point in American history. A *Time/CNN,* poll conducted in February 1995, found that 56 percent of the public favor the formation of a third party (March 1, 1995). Campaign strategists should take note of this prospect and not only watch for third-party spoilers, but also perhaps begin to look to these races for clients.

Although they rarely win themselves, their party candidates can capture vital pieces of a major party candidate's base of support, undercut a theme, attract volunteers, and draw media and public attention away from your message. The best way to prepare for a three- party race is to take a close look at the history of minor party candidates in the district. If there is a viable organization already in place and they run candidates in most elections, it is a good bet they will run one in yours. A wise strategist will take a close look at where they have done well in the past and begin to sort out the rationale for their support. It may even be possible to meet with the activists and discuss how your candidate might address their concerns. In other instances, the candidate created the "party" just for their own candidacy, making any sort of endorsement impossible.

Survey research information should also indicate existing support for their party candidates, potential support, and the extent to which this candidate will cut into your candidate's base. These polls can also suggest the best ways to minimize the message of the third-party candidate, and aid in the development of a strategy that can respond to attacks from them. It is also a good idea to oversample independent voters in these districts, as they are more likely than strong partisans to vote for third-party candidates (Fairbank and Goodwin 1993, 51–52).

One should understand that third-party candidates do not affect incumbents and challengers equally. According to congressional election scholar Paul Herrnson, in 1992 House members who faced both major and minor party candidates won almost 10 percent fewer votes than those who did not (1995, 209). One reason for this disparity is that minor party candidates usually get into these races because they are dissatisfied and frustrated with the incumbent. That is, they are doing it to oust the incumbent, and they frame their campaign around this one goal.

Finally, in some states, such as New York and Connecticut, election law allows candidates to combine their vote totals for two or more ballot positions (parties). This is termed "cross over party endorsement." Again, third- party candidates rarely win outright, but if a major party candidate also secures this line, and the vote totals are combined, they can have a strong bearing on the outcome. Many state house and senate candidates in New York aggressively seek the endorsement of one of the three standing minor parties (Right to Life, Liberal, Conservative). Another twist is to gather enough signatures to create a new party, which will last only for that election. Gubernatorial candidates do the same. In the 1994 gubernatorial race, George Pataki defeated Mario Cuomo by less than the margin he received from this Conservative party line.

NATIONAL TRENDS

Former Speaker of the House of Representatives Tip O'Neill commented that "all politics is local." It was a reminder that while national and international concerns may envelop an elected official's time, they still need to be elected—and elections are, after all, local affairs.

As wise and useful as this notion may be, in today's political world there is no escaping national trends, moods, and obsessions. Each year the media highlight some concerns and discount others. It is unclear whether they do so because the issue is on the minds of voters, or it becomes a concern of voters because they draw persistent attention to it. In other words, which is the chicken and which is the egg? For our concerns, it is imperative to understand that national tides can have a profound impact on local elections. A campaign should never discard local concerns in a relentless pursuit of being on the correct side of a national movement, but it is necessary to understand them and incorporate these concerns into one's message when appropriate.

One example of a national trend is the crime issue. For social scientists, the media's fixation on crime is a bit of a paradox. Statistics suggest that criminal activity is on the decline. For example, according to the Justice Department's National Crime Victimization Survey, larceny and burglary declined nearly 20 percent between 1982 and 1992. Even violent crimes, such as rape and assault, appear to be on the decline. Nevertheless, the three major networks ran 1,700 news stories about crime in 1993. This massive coverage, an average of five stories per night, was double the number of stories in 1992. As a consequence, the number of people who feel that crime is the nation's worst problem jumped from 5 percent to 31 percent in less than a year (Edmondson 1994, 2).

The lesson for candidates is to pay close attention to this issue regardless of what the crime statistics suggest. It would be a serious mistake to tell voters that their obsession on crime is ill founded, or that the facts do not bear out their concerns. It makes little difference if crime rates drastically decline; voters may still be attentive to crime because the national media have chosen to accentuate it. Misreading this trend, or trying to convince the voters otherwise, would be a grave miscalculation.

We have certainly seen our share of "tough on crime candidates" in recent elections. In 1994 Republican George Pataki was able to upset New York's three-term governor, Mario Cuomo, by stressing his tough-on-crime platform. Cuomo, while emphasizing planks such as life without parole for murderers, suffered from having repeatedly vetoed the death penalty. Also in 1994, Pete Wilson (R) was reelected to the governor's mansion in California by, among other things, stressing his "three strikes and you're out" law, which mandates a life sentence for anyone convicted of three felony crimes. This trend was not limited to gubernatorial races. In 1993 Congress passed the Omnibus Crime Act, which stiffened the penalties for federal crimes, tightened gun control, and provided funding for more police officers. To be sure, scores of Senate and House candidates stress this and other actions against the "crime epidemic" in their 1994 reelection bids.

Another recent trend is the desire to shake up the old-boys' network in politics. One implication may be the public's desire to elect more women to office (1992 was dubbed "The Year of the Woman"), and another would be the term-limit movement.

Scholars of elections have long discerned a tight fit between national economic trends and vote choice. Much related, presidential popularity also seems to impact lower level elections. In the early 1970s, for example, congressional election scholar Edward Tufte found that 98 percent of the variability of congressional elections can be explained by the economy and the popularity of the president (Tufte 1975). Although found to be a bit overstated, and scholars have continued to refine the import of these variables, the point is well taken: voters may reward or punish the president's handling of the economy by using their vote for lower level offices. And if the economy is doing well, we might expect the party in power to be rewarded down the ticket. Another possibility, as will be discussed below, is that these measures are used by potential candidates as cues, thereby leading to certain outcomes. Beyond the overall state of the economy, a wise strategist will keep a keen eye to consumer confidence, the unemployment rate, business trends, and new home construction, particularly in the district at hand.

National moods and trends are not merely a passing media fixation, and the public is not simply being pulled around by its nose, likely to change course with every bit of new information. National trends matter because voters are deeply distressed about an issue; precisely how these anxieties develop we might leave to the social scientists to discern. For our interests, it is vital to understand that national trends can impact local-level elections.

CANDIDATES FOR OTHER OFFICES

Another "given" in any race are the candidates for other offices during the same election. Other office candidates, by simply being on the same or opposing ticket, can help or hinder a candidate's efforts.

The notion of "coattails" is deeply ingrained in American electoral politics. This notion suggests that candidates can benefit from the popularity of another candidate of the same party running in the same election year. The popularity of one candidate will translate into support for others of the same party. In 1980, for example, a large class of Republicans were swept into office, some would argue, because of Ronald Reagan's mass appeal. On the state level, many would argue the capture of the Ohio state legislature by the Republicans in 1994 was due, in part, to the popularity of their gubernatorial candidate, George Voinovich. Conversely, if a candidate is very unpopular, office seekers of the same party might suffer because of it. Some Republicans claim to have been hindered by George Bush's lackluster popularity in 1992.

As logical and straightforward as coattails may appear, it is hard to support the idea empirically. Leading congressional election scholar Gary Jacobson has looked at this closely and suggests that the "congressional vote is determined by evaluations of candidates as individuals, often with little reference to national policies or personalities" (Jacobson 1987, 155).

What then explains the apparent success of party tickets that have one or two very popular candidates at the top? One possible answer has been dubbed the "strategic politician" phenomenon (Jacobson 1987). This theory asserts that all aspiring politicians wish to win elections, and that any defeat is perceived as a blow to career aspirations. As such, strategic politicians pay close attention to early polling data, particularly as the information relates to other members of their party. When these surveys indicate that no member of their party is popular, they decide to sit the race out, not wanting to lose. They leave the party nomination open for lesser candidates (essentially anyone who wants it). Of course, because these candidates have poor qualifications, scant finances, and minimal name recognition, they lose the election. On the other hand, when one or two members of the strategic politician's party appear popular, they enter the race—believing wholeheartedly in the coattail effect. Because they are well qualified and adequately financed, they win. In brief, there need not be any connection in the minds of voters between candidates of a party ticket to see an *apparent* coattail effect.

Very much related, often an unpopular candidate at the head of the ticket will propel good candidates of the other party to enter the fray. Quality Republican candidates for all offices are gearing up for the 1996 election because they perceive Bill Clinton to be vulnerable, and they expect to be the beneficiaries of voter disdain. Again, the outcome of these races may appear to mirror Clinton's unpopularity, but it will have more to do with the decisions of potential candidates.

There are several implications for campaign strategists. In actuality, the quality of the candidate and the conduct of the campaign may have more to do with the outcome than any cognitive link between candidates. One should not become lulled into believing that because the head of the ticket is extremely popular, that this will spill over into support for one's own candidate. There is simply no *direct* connection. If you are on the other side—the popular candidate is of the opposing party—take heart because the race is far from over. A well-run campaign can overcome this apparent advantage.

This is not to say that coattails are inconsequential. In fact, they are often a pivotal contextual element. The *perception* that coattails exist will not only bring certain pols into the race and leave others out, but will also impact finances, volunteers, media coverage, and much else. If others believe that a candidate will get a significant boost from a member of the ticket, they will be more likely to give money, lend a hand, cover campaign activities, and simply be part of the process. Everyone wishes to be on the winning side, especially contributors. In the end, it becomes a self-fulfilled prophecy—because people believe a candidate will win, they jump on board; and the more they jump on board, the greater the likelihood of success.

The real fight, then, is over perceptions. If a candidate is on the same ticket as a popular candidate, the struggle is to convince everyone that coattails are real and that they will help propel the candidate to victory. It is a good idea, for example, to bring the polling results showing the extent of the popular candidate's support to the media, interest groups and associations, and potential contributors. Moreover, the popular candidate should be brought to the district as often as possible, again, not so much for the voters, but for the media and potential contributors and volunteers.

Unfortunately, if, on the other side, the battle is to convince everyone that coattails do not exist—often an uphill struggle. One way to do this is to stress your candidate's strengths, particularly juxtaposed to the opponent's. Although not on the ballot, you might bring to the district prominent politicians from your party to offset visits by the popular candidate. You may also attempt to convince contributors and the media of your momentum by showing polling data or other positive signs, despite the coattail issue: "with all that stacked against her, look how well she is doing." In the end, you may simply have to work harder and be more resourceful and skillful to get the same attention.

Beyond the coattail issue, others on the ballot can compete for resources, divide or unify the ticket, and decrease or heighten turnout. There may be, for example, a particularly "hot" race in your district, which siphons off financial supporters and fills up the news media. Your race may be low on the totem pole. On the other hand, a set of low-profile races on the ticket indicates a very different set of strategic concerns.

Finally, one should take careful note of ballot initiatives. In most instances, referenda draw only modest public and media attention and will do little to alter a campaign plan. In other cases, they can have a profound impact. In 1994 California's Proposition 187, designed to limit state-funded services available to illegal aliens, overshadowed even the U.S. Senate and gubernatorial races. This highly emotional issue brought people to the polls who would not otherwise vote, activated a diverse set of volunteers for and against the measure, and drew a massive amount of voters and media. Moreover, careful attention was given to each candidate's position on the matter. Failing to understand the weight of highly charged initiatives, such as Proposition 187, nearly always spells disaster. There are strong indications that referenda will appear on more ballots and in more states in the future.

GEOGRAPHY AND MEDIA MARKET

The geography of the district is important for several reasons. For one, the range of campaign activities may be limited or controlled by the shape of the district. Districts in urban areas, for example, tend to be geographically small, making face-to-face voter contact techniques easier. It is certainly possible to organize a series of door-to-door projects in the state senate seats encompassing San Fanscico's east side, for example. In particularly compact inner-city areas, it may be difficult to conduct a door-to-door canvas because high-rise apartments and condominiums generally have security systems and do not allow nonresidents. On the other hand, some districts are geographically larger, making personal contact difficult.

Second, geography may be critical in assessing the candidate's base of support. Very often, a candidate's base may extend beyond his or her political jurisdiction. By frequently being in the news, a mayor, for example, may also be well known throughout the neighboring towns and counties. If the district is relatively contained within the proximity of the candidate's base, this can be quite helpful. On the other hand, the population centers of a district may be separated by a good distance and be fractionalized between two or three media markets. While the candidate may be well known in the eastern part of the district, he or she may be an unknown in the western area, 200 miles away. Some congressional districts cover a vast geographic area, often linking cities hundreds of miles apart. A candidate may be well known in Keene and unheard of in Berlin, even though they are the two largest population centers in New Hampshire's 2nd Congressional District.

The spread of the district may dictate a candidate's activities. It is possible in some districts to move the candidate from one side to the other with ease, but in others it may require hours of driving or even frequent plane trips. Along similar lines, it is much easier in small districts to place the headquarters; in larger ones, a carefully calculated decision must be made. Perhaps it would be necessary to open two or three headquarters to cover the district adequately. Moreover, the layout of the district may define travel patterns, which may indicate potentially viable campaign activities, such as working a subway stop used by a large group of commuters.

Of true concern, the geography of a district may signify distinctive neighborhoods and communities. The interests and concerns of two population centers, even in the same district, may be fundamentally different. This knowledge will help fine-tune the candidate's message in order to push the proper voter button.

The geography of a district says a good deal about a district's media market. Often, a state house, senate, or congressional district is but one of many with a city area. There are, for example, roughly sixty assembly, twenty-five state senate, and fifteen congressional districts in the greater New York City area. Accordingly, they are contained in the same media market, and it is nearly impossible for lower level office candidates to buy radio or television spots. (Cable television, a much more targeted possibility, will be discussed in Chapter 11.) The market is simply too big, ergo expensive; a vast majority of the viewers and listeners would not be able to cast a ballot for the candidate. By default, campaigns for most offices in large cities rely upon direct mail, door-to-door techniques, and other more targeted activities.

Another possibility is that the district contains no real media market. In the fifteen counties of Michigan's Upper Peninsula, for example, the closest significant television market is Detroit, some 350 miles to the south. It is simply not cost effective to consider television ads in these districts, no matter how well financed the campaign. On the bright side, most rural areas do contain a few radio outlets, where spots can be purchased at a modest expense.

The best scenario occurs when a district contains, or is near, a relatively small media market. Spots can be purchased without excessive waste. An illustration is the state house and senate seats and the congressional district in New York's Adirondack Region. There are two media market possibilities, Wattertown and Plattsburgh. Both host roughly five radio and two television stations, where spots can be purchased for a song. More important, they are the only local media outlet for voters in the region—Albany and Syracuse are some 100 miles to the south.

OTHER PIECES OF THE CONTEXTUAL PIE

Any attempt to describe in detail all the givens in a campaign would fill volumes. In the chapters to follow, three additional key elements are carefully examined:

demographics, candidate records, and prior electoral data. As a final part of this chapter, several pieces of the contextual pie are briefly touched upon.

The Industrial/Business Profile

With the exception of one's family and friends, few factors are more important in a voter's life than how and where they make a living. Many districts are dominated by one or two professions and employers, and wise consultants will understand their significance. Keeping an attentive eye to where people make a living will not only accent issues and styles, but highlight certain campaign activities and potential endorsements, volunteers, and contributors.

Community Organizations

In every district certain community organizations stand out. Some may be more politically active than others, providing endorsements, contributions, and so on. At the very least, a keen understanding of the types of powerful groups can provide vital information. In some areas, for example, volunteer fire departments are huge, both in size and status. While these organizations are generally nonpartisan, it would be a serious mistake to believe that elections are not a topic of discussion at their many functions. The same can be said about the scores of professional and social groups in any district. This information must be understood.

Profiles of Elected Officials

Simply put, a campaign should know everything within reason about the elected officials in the area. These people will certainly become involved, one way or another, in the race, and a candidate must be prepared to accentuate their assistance and minimize their harm. Often, elected officials wish to be paid homage. A quick telephone call or visit can set them on your side for the campaign. Political figures can help attract media attention, contributors, and volunteers and make introductions to other prominent members of the community. They can do endorsements, advertisements, and in most states transfer some of their campaign account into yours. Officials of the other party can, of course, do the same for the opponent.

Political Heroes of the Past and Present

In every town, city, county, and state in the nation, past and present political heroes linger in the minds of voters. These figures can be a powerful force in an election, as they can suggest to voters a preferable style and approach to politics, as well as provide a cue on policy matters. At the very least, endorsements can make a big difference. A wise consultant will ascertain the extent of their popularity, both overall and regionally, and attempt to understand why. This should be done for heroes on both sides of the partisan fence. The next step is to discern how this popularity can help or hinder your own chances.

The Villains of the Past and Present

Although the public's esteem of elected officials increases after they leave office, some depart on a particularly bad note. A campaign should be wary of the mistakes made by these ex-officials, and be sure to steer clear of endorsements, pictures, or any other means that might tag a close association. A candidate should not rely upon the ex-politicians themselves to reveal the scorn of voters; far too many campaigns have been lured in to believing that an endorsement will help, only later to find out the full extent of the public's wrath. Much the same can be said about current villains. Before linking your fate to another public official, understand their prominence, or lack thereof, in the community.

Social and Political Customs

Every community in the nation adheres to a set of political customs and norms, albeit loosely. In some districts it may be acceptable, for example, to saturate the area with yard signs and posters. In others this may be seen as "littering the lovely community." In certain places it might be acceptable to use profanities while stomping, and in others not. Some places or times might be off-limits to campaigning.

Parties, Bosses, and Interest Groups

More will be said about parties and interest groups in the pages to follow. With regard to the campaign context, it should be noted that in some areas aggressive, well-funded party organizations are eager to assist their candidates, while in others they are simply no help whatsoever. Expecting too much from most party organizations is a common mistake. One way to discern their potential assistance is to examine their past performance. This can be done by talking to party or elected officials, or simply by looking at past campaign contribution disclosure information. The same can be said about interest groups and political action committees.

Where party organizations are strong, it is common to find a powerful leader at the helm. In a sense, the two are inextricably linked. In Akron, Ohio, for instance, Alex Arshinkoff heads one of the strongest Republican organizations in the nation. In such instances, it is often necessary to bring party leaders into the decision-making structure of the campaign early and pay the necessary homage.

The History of the Area

Understanding what the community has gone through, either recently or in the distant past, can yield valuable insight. Natural disasters, social or political turmoil, or even something as simple as having won the state girls' basketball title can be momentous. Again, elections are a secondary concern to most voters. By linking vote choice, even in the most subtle of ways, to more immediate interests can pull voters to your side.

Tourism and Recreation

Knowing what voters do in their spare time not only helps channel activities to more productive places, such as bowling leagues and at ball games, but allows candidates quickly to develop a connection. It is a nice icebreaker if the candidate can talk about the hobbies and interests of the voter. A candidate in northwestern Pennsylvania, who knows nothing about waterfowl hunting, for example, might want to take a crash course. And an aspirant for office in Houston, who has never heard of line dancing, should get out more before heading off to meet the voters. Also, tourist areas, such as ski resorts and stadiums, are often the leading employer in the area.

CONCLUSION

This chapter was designed to introduce the importance of contextual information in modern campaigning. By understanding the list of givens, it was argued, strategy, theme, message, and expectations regarding resources can be developed from a solid foundation. Far too few campaigns proceed without an understanding of the landscape, only to find themselves unprepared and at a disadvantage. Today's elections are won and lost on the fringes, and advantages must be seized. Solid contextual information provides just such an edge.

NOTE

1. For an excellent review of the literature on the causes of high reelection rates among members of Congress, see Linda Fowler (1993), Chapter 4.

Chapter Four

Demographic Research:
The Theory of Aggregate Inference

Even though the way in which we market and choose elected officials has fundamentally changed the nature and function of American governance and the new campaign profession is fast paced and exciting, these topics are rarely found in books, television, or at the movies. One exception was the modestly enlightened, and in some ways insightful, 1986 film, *Power*. In one scene, the character played by Gene Hackman, an old-style campaign consultant, confronts his fast-paced, new-style protégé, played by Richard Gere. Hackman is looking for assistance to impress a new client. Does he seek money, strategy, or media tips? Rather, he exclaims, "The demographics, God damn it, I need the demographics." The viewer never really understands why demographics are so important, as opposed to fund-raising lists or strategic advice, but we surely know it must be important.

The term "demographics" is often tossed around campaign circles. New ways of dealing with it are hot topics in professional trade journals. Suggestions of improved systems are labeled "magic" (Robbin 1989), "revolutionary" (Sutherlin 1992), or even a step toward "precision politics" (Beiler 1990). With such platitudes, one would expect this type of research to be highly complex—beyond the reach of beginning campaign consultants. The truth is, however, this form of contextual data stems from what we already know about politics and human nature, and much of how to use it requires only a basic understanding. Make no mistake, demographic information is a key ingredient in modern campaigning, but there is no mystery to using it.

During the early stages of any race, a wise consultant will seek a complete understanding of the voters. Before moving to strategy, finances, themes, and a host of other complex issues, astute care must be taken to pinpoint what makes the voters of that particular district tick. An efficient, inexpensive technique to help in this regard is to create and study the demographic profile. This chapter is designed to acquaint the reader with the logic of demographic inference, how this information contributes to the overall campaign plan, and techniques available to access it quickly and accurately. Gene Hackman may have been right to ask for the "damn demographics." The aim of this chapter is to understand why.

THE LOGIC OF DEMOGRAPHIC RESEARCH

The goal of modern campaigning is to tailor the appropriate message to each voter— to find the right button to push. If the electorate is small—when the consultant or candidate has first-hand knowledge of the interests of each voter or we have the opportunity to survey every voter—then coming up with the right buttons is a straightforward task. Another possibility is that the campaign is in an area with a larger network of activists, perhaps party workers, who know the ins and outs of every voter in their neighborhood. In the days of party bosses and precinct captains, there existed a clear voter-feedback mechanism. Unfortunately, neither of these scenarios is usually possible today, and other means of targeting must be devised. Demographic research heads us in that direction.

Simply stated, the word demography means the study of the characteristics of a given population: size, growth, education, gender, race, ethnicity, and other untold possibilities. The logic of demographic research, as it relates to modern campaigning, holds a number of basic assumptions which are outlined below.

First, there are telling differences among voters in any population. That is to say, no matter how homogeneous a district may appear, the voters who constitute it are distinctive. For example, we may be running a race in a neighborhood where all the houses seem to be the same and all the voters are white and middle class. We might assume similar interests, concerns, hobbies, outlooks, and so forth. On closer inspection, we would find that few voters are actually alike.

Second, voters in any district can be theoretically merged, based upon personal characteristics, into a set of groups, or what are sometimes termed "cohorts," "communities," "strata," or "clusters." What distinguishes one group from another can be a rudimentary bit of information, such as those separated by a single characteristic. For example, if we were to choose gender as our variable, there would be two clusters: males and females. Often using just one characteristic will lead to numerous clusters. With ethnicity, for example, there might from ten to fifteen possibilities in any district: Irish, Polish, Italian, Hispanic, Asian, French, and so on. Still other times we may wish to define the cohort based on a set of criteria, such as several characteristics combined. A possibility here might be race, religion, gender, and age. One group, then, might include white Catholic males over the age of sixty-five. We can assume there will be X number of voters in each group, depending on the distribution of the selected characteristics in the district, and the ranges used to divide each characteristic. Do we break down age into twenty different groupings or simply two? Because there are an infinite number of characteristics that define a population, there are an infinite number of theoretical groupings.

Third, members of a theoretical cluster will often have similar interests. This notion, of course, is dependent upon the criteria we choose to define the group. If we use eye color, there is little reason to expect blue-eyed people will have the same interests as brown-eyed people. On the other hand, characteristics like age, gender, occupation, educational background, ethnicity, race, and many other possibilities may help define a set of voters who have at least some overlapping concerns. We might reasonably expect blue-collar workers, generally speaking, to have a somewhat different outlook than white-collar workers. When shared concerns relate to politics, these groups are termed *politically relevant strata*. It would certainly not be far fetched to assume that women share a number of common interests, or that doctors have some like-minded concerns. By no means does this suggest that every member of the politically relevant strata have identical interests, or that they all agree upon any one item. There are women who do not believe in abortion rights and many doctors who are against Medicare reform. The idea is that politically relevant strata have at least some concerns that link a significant number of the members.

Fourth, by discerning the interests of politically relevant strata (as a group), we can reasonably predict the interests of any member of that group. This idea is much related to the above, but it is worth a bit more elaboration. It assumes that we need not know anything about an individual other than some demographic information to have an idea about his or her political leanings. If we have a general understanding of the attitudes and perceptions of most people in a group, and we find that an individual belongs to that demographic cluster, we can infer that this individual also shares the beliefs. If we discern most citizens over sixty years of age are interested in protecting Medicare, we can infer that an individual, say sixty-eight years old, will also hold this view. Again, often it is not a perfect fit. Knowing a voter's gender alone may tell us something about his or her partisan leanings. For example, social scientists and pollsters have found that women are somewhat more likely to vote Democratic than men. Even so, a vast number of women do not consider themselves Democrats, nor do they ever vote for Democratic candidates. In fact, a majority of women in any given district might vote Republican. The point is that, if we were to know *only* a voter's gender, we could improve the prediction of her vote beyond guessing. The same can be said about issues. We know, for example, as a group, Roman Catholics believe that abortion should be outlawed. This does not imply that every Catholic holds this view, only that if this was all we knew about the voter, our guess as to his or her view on abortion would be improved.

Finally, our deduction regarding the interests and concerns of any voter increases as we know more and more about their politically relevant demographic characteristics. That is, it may be helpful to know a voter's gender, but it is still better if we know his or her gender *and* age, and even better yet if we know that person's gender, age, *and* occupation. Simply stated, the more demographic information we have, the better we can predict someone's interests.

In a nutshell, demographic research seeks to find the electorally relevant groups that define a population, understand their concerns and interests, and make appeals to the individuals in these groups based upon this information. It is a process of *aggregation* and *inference*—pulling together information on groups and connecting the data to individuals (Robbin 1989). Instead of accumulating complete information on every voter, it is necessary only to understand the interests of the groups that constitute a district. Once this information is known, we can discern which group(s) an individual belongs to and push the right button(s).

The idea behind demographic research is therefore quite simple. It is something we intuitively know. If we want to please a little girl, we would be more likely to give her a candy bar than a salad. This is not to say that every child likes chocolate more than vegetables. This knowledge helps us improve our predictive power, making it more likely that we will please the child. When it comes to campaigning, the same logic applies. It makes sense that college-age voters would be more interested in programs affecting student aid, than would a senior citizen. It again makes sense to tell college students about student aid programs, rather than the highlights of your six-point senior citizen medical prescription drug plan.

Moving from this basic understanding to a more sophisticated use of demographic information will require a bit more inquiry. Nevertheless, one should be pleasantly surprised at how much they already know about aggregation and inference.

DEMOGRAPHIC RESEARCH AND MODERN CAMPAIGNING

By now a few points should be apparent from the logic of demographic research. It is critical to understand the political relevant strata that define a district. Next, close attention must be paid to the concerns of these groups, and finally voters must be labeled accordingly. Demographic research helps with this three-step process. Yet, as will be seen below, the way in which this information has been accessed and manipulated has dramatically changed over the years.

The Traditional Approach

In the early days of targeting, the first step was to amass as much information on the attitudes, perceptions, and political leanings of voters in the district as possible. Because it is difficult to collect information from every voter, inferential tools were used. One way was to spend a great deal of time "listening to the multitudes"—that is, talking to people, listening to the concerns of group leaders, reading the papers, going to community events, and generally keeping a finger on the pulse of the people. While this type of research was routine, exclusive reliance on it was scorned as haphazard. At the very least, what a voter tells a politician or campaign worker may be very different then what is actually on his or her mind. Also, it is human nature to surround oneself with supporters, yielding a much more optimistic picture.

A more accurate means of learning the concerns of voters was found to be random sample survey techniques. As will be discussed in Chapter 7, accurate assessments can be made about the overall population from a relatively small number of respondents. Once the concerns of the voters were found, early targeting would stop at this point. That is, the campaign team would look at the polls, find the issues of greatest concern, and point their candidate accordingly.

As logical as this might sound, it was possible to run a campaign on a set of issues favored by a majority of the voters and still lose. One possibility is that other contextual elements come into play. Another explanation is that the best-issue approach fails to discern the intensity of voter attitudes. As consultant Wayne Johnson notes,

From the first surveys we learned things like: 62 percent of the voters favor taxing the wealthy. So we would send mailings to all voters telling them that the wealthy need to pay more taxes. The problem was that the positive data (the majority position) was as likely to be a lukewarm opinion as a strongly held opinion. In this case, the wealthy mail recipient was far more likely to react than the middle income person receiving the same mailing. We soon found it was possible to mail on a 70 percent plus issue and still lose by a landslide. (Johnson 1992, 51)

The obvious solution was to mail only to middle- and low-income voters.

To target messages more accurately and avoid backlash, such as this, it was imperative to combine voter opinion data with divisions among the electorate. Aggregated findings were simply too risky. But what divisions should be used? One possibility was geography. The voters in the north end of the district must surely have some different concerns than those in the south. In some instances this idea may be effective, but in others it is of modest help. Using our example from above, are there not both wealthy and middle-class voters in the north end of the district? Also, many times there exists little variance in the geography of the district; it may be very small.

It became obvious that population-based characteristics (i.e., "demographics") was a more refined approach. Instead of merely looking for the issue of greatest concern to the greatest number of people, survey results could be overlaid, or "crosstabbed," with demographic information. The question was no longer what the voters wanted, but what males, females, the wealthy, the Irish, the well- educated, and so forth wanted. By relying on the logic of demographic inference, campaigns could hit the bull's-eye with their message. If a poll found low-income respondents favor an increase in the minimum wage, it was assumed most poor people would feel the same. Taken one step further, any appeals to voters in low-income areas should stress, if consistent with other contextual issues, an increase in the minimum wage.

To a large extent, the simple mix of survey research with demographic data continues to form the backdrop of campaign activities. Mario Cuomo ran his first campaign for governor of New York in 1982. Early surveys found Cuomo especially popular among voters of Italian descent. As election day drew near, operatives throughout the state were instructed to kick up turnout in Italian-American communities. On election day they were instructed to call Democrats to get them to the polls; and when this list was exhausted, they would call all voters with Italian surnames.

Along similar lines, consultant Mike Dawidziak encourages close attention to an "ethnic targeting program." Pointing to his success in local elections, Dawidziak notes such a program "is where you identify what ethnic group an individual or family belongs to primarily by looking at and analyzing the last name" (1991, 52). A table of surnames is created and, by using the last name, a notation of each voter's ethnicity is recorded. He writes, "A last name beginning with O' would be Irish [and a] last name ending with 'ski' would more than likely be Polish"(52). The final step is to create ethnic-based mailings for each of the groupings, based upon their presumed interests. Obviously, putting together an ethnic targeting program for a large group of voters is a time-consuming chore. Dawidziak believes it is worth it.

In 1992 Cleo Fields successfully targeted young voters in his bid to fill Louisiana's 4th Congressional District seat. While serving in the state senate, Fields, only twenty-nine himself, won the enactment of bills to get high school students to register to vote at seventeen, before they graduated, and to register college students when they signed up for classes. These accomplishments, combined with the fact that Southern University was located in his district, suggested a youth-based targeting strategy would work. The polls too suggested this group would respond to Fields' message, and the campaign proceeded to reach out to as many students as possible. The strategy was a stunning success, as Fields captured 74 percent of the runoff vote (*Congressional Quarterly*, January 16, 1993).

There also has been a growing interest in the electoral relevance of Hispanics. The number of Hispanic voters in the United States is growing five times as fast as the overall U.S. population; by 2010, this group will make up 15 percent of the American population (Power 1992, 63). Because it is believed that Hispanics will share a degree of like-mindedness, the rush is on to understand these interests and to fashion credible appeals. In a recent article, consultant John Power outlines the tactics for reaching these voters. Among other things, he suggests candidates "learn to habla Espanol" (Power 1992, 63).

In sum, today there are few campaigns that do not rely upon the logic of demographic inference to fine-tune their survey results. Demographic information is used because it works. It is generally not possible to chat with every voter about his or her political concerns and then fashion a message accordingly. This does not mean that campaigns must head into the woods without a flashlight. Inferential survey techniques, combined with demographic groupings, help cast a strong beam.

WHERE TO GET DEMOGRAPHIC INFORMATION

We now know that modern survey techniques overlay issue responses with demographic characteristics. A poll might tell us that college-educated, white females under the age of thirty-five are very concerned about reproduction rights. We would then go find these people and push the pro-choice button (other contextual issues aside). A logical query, however, is where we might find these people—where do we get demographic data on individuals? Do we have to rely upon surnames to discern an individual's ethnic background? Must we go to college campuses to find college-age voters? How do we find the white-collar voters in a district, or ones with less than a high school education?

The earliest use of demographic data came from an intimate knowledge of the district. The politician would simply know where the Italians lived and where the wealthy could be found. Efforts in this regard were aided by relatively homogeneous neighborhoods. By the 1950s, urban flight and the decline of tightly knit communities made neighborhood-based assessments onerous. More important, new-style campaign practitioners would be unsatisfied with the accuracy of this method. We might know, for example, that Baton Rouge is a "college town," but it is difficult to know which voters in the city are under twenty-five.

The U.S. Census Data Prior to the 1990s

United States Census data provided an answer. Every ten years the federal government undertakes a massive project to record the statistics of the nation's population. Unlike assessment techniques that rely upon sampling, the Census Bureau fulfills its constitutional mandate and attempts to enumerate *every person living in the United States*. For their part, each resident is legally obliged to fill out and return a questionnaire. An abbreviated list of recorded information includes age, gender, race, income, marital status, ancestry, household composition, value of the home, education, language spoken at home, veteran status, work experience, religion, transportation, and much else. There is even a broader list of questions (called the "long form") given to a random sample of residents—roughly one in six.

Census data are provided in two basic formats: summary data and "microdata." In the summary data files, the basic unit is a specific geographic entity, for which counts of persons, families, and households or housing units in particular categories are provided. We can find, for instance, the number of home renters in Weston City, or the ancestry of those living in Smithville. Microdata, on the other hand, use the individual housing unit as the basic unit of analysis. These files contain records for a *sample* of all housing units, with information on the characteristics of each unit and people in it. We might wish to know how many bedrooms there are in a typical house, the property value, or the age of each person per home in a given area. There are over seventy microdata characteristics available, but unfortunately these samples are put together by the Census Bureau only for those areas with at least 100,000 people. All told, every decade the Census Bureau compiles a massive amount of demographic information.

Thankfully, census data is published—as well as periodic adjustments based upon trends and updated forecasts. Campaign consultants have had at their disposal all of this information. Most libraries contain census material, particularly for the state in which they are located. Aiding their efforts further, census data are published not only as lists of variables, but several characteristics are crosstabulated in advance.

Census data are immensely helpful. Unfortunately for campaign professionals, this material, while extensive, is not available at the individual level. In other words, census information is collected anonymously. Even within the microdata files, all identifying information is removed to ensure confidentiality. It is not possible, for instance, to look up how much money your neighbor makes, or the ethnic background of your mail carrier. To use U.S. Census Bureau data, a geographic unit must be defined by the researcher, and the characteristics of the residents within that area can then be examined. We can know, for instance, that, according to the 1990 Census, Escambia County, Florida, has a 20 percent black population, but we cannot know who in the county is black and who is white. We know that of the 45,857 residents of Flagstaff, Arizona, 7,231 are of Hispanic descent (15 percent). But to determine precisely which residents are Hispanic, we must look elsewhere.

How, then, is this an improvement over neighborhood-based inference? First, abundant characteristics are available to the researcher. While local politicos might be able to say which area is predominately Polish or Italian, or which neighborhood is upper class and which is lower income, census information can not only do the same, but also say a good deal about how many people in the area own their homes, how many are headed by a single parent, how may are blue collar verses white collar, how many are farmers or clerks, how many are over the age of sixty-five, and so on. Second, Census data allows for a range of geographic options when breaking down the information. Summary statistics can range from the entire nation all the way down to the block. It might seem logical always to use the smallest unit of analysis, but in some cases this is impractical. In a statewide race, for example, county- or town-level data may prove valuable, particularly when a quick decision is needed. When using census data, the researcher has this option.

Combined, the ability to select from a vast set of variables and to choose among several geographic units has made census data a quantum leap over neighborhood-based estimates. Campaign professionals can select a block or county and scrutinize an immense set of population characteristics. Moreover, by overlaying these variables, an even more refined picture can be developed. Again, census data does not allow for individual-level assessments. Yet, as noted by political communication professor Gary Selnow, "[census-based research] can result in inaccurate information for some individuals, but statistical averages often are accurate enough for campaign activities, and they may be a lot better than no information at all"(Senlow 1994, 95).

The Rise and Fall of Geodemographic Clusters

One of the shortcomings of traditional census-based research has been the reliance on a small set of characteristics to construct target groups. Similar to the examples noted above, campaigns would look to survey results to find a small set of variables believed to isolate groups of voters. For instance, ethnicity and age might be combined to create twelve groups of voters. This was seen as an improvement over neighborhood-based targeting, but many scorned the approach as "unrealistic" and "imprecise." They argued that humans are vastly more complex. Recall that one of the basic tenets of demographic inference is "the more characteristics the better."

A related criticism was that survey results could not be accurately overlaid with more than a small set of demographic variables. Even if the researcher was anxious to expand the number of descriptive variables in order to tackle the complexity of human life, they were constrained by sample size. The end result was to retreat to two or three "key" variables (Robbin 1989, 109).

The solution was heralded as an innovative methodology, based upon a simple idea. In some ways it was a new twist on an old approach. In the early 1970s, the Claritas Corporation, headed by Jonathon Robbin, advanced the geodemographic cluster concept. It was based on the notion that humans gather into areas where the resources—physical, economic, and social—are compatible with their needs (Robbin 1989, 109). They create or choose neighborhoods based upon their lifestyle and stage of their life cycle. These neighborhoods make up distinct social groups that share a *broad* set of demographic characteristics.

By systematically examining a whopping 535 variables for the entire U.S. population, Robbin claimed to have found forty uncorrelated factors, explaining 87 percent of American diversity. In other words, humans are certainly complex, but by using computer technology to add, subtract, and sort 535 variables into millions of possible combinations, forty distinctive groups were found. Put a bit differently, 87 percent of the complexity of people in the United States can be explained with forty clusters.

The next step was to label each cluster with a nickname that provided a fairly good idea of the type of demographic group at hand. For example, one group was tagged "Share Croppers." These people were defined as, among other things, low income, rural, poorly educated, Southern, white, and so forth. It was argued that people falling into this profile create a distinctive cluster. A few other nicknames were "God's Country," "Blue Blood Estates," "Archie Bunker's Neighbors," and "Bohemian Mix." Each of these clusters was thought to be unique and bound by like-minded folks. If campaign professionals desired to know which clusters were found to be in their state or district, they needed only to send away to the Claritas Corporation for the information or to access America Online on the Internet.

Theoretically, the final step was to conduct a random survey of the entire constituency, with appropriate subsamples from each of the clusters in the district. It was assumed that only a portion of the forty clusters would be found in a single state or district. Once the views of voters in each of the relevant groups was assessed, the logic of demographic inference was applied and all voters in the cluster were furnished with the appropriate message. "Obviously, any procedure that can accurately generate numbers detailing the opinions of small groups of people in relatively minute geographic areas by simply using a statewide survey has enormous potential" (Atlas 1989, 128).

In a sense, then, geodemographic cluster sampling represents a computerized spin on an old idea. By moving beyond mere "neighborhoods" and compiling scores of voter characteristics, this technique took basic demographic research a step further. As consultant David Beiler noted, "Seasoned political operatives generally conceded that the geodemographic has some merit" (1990, 34).

Shortly after the arrival of this cluster-based targeting, notwithstanding, pundits began to sound warning bells. Was the new system magic or merely smoke and mirrors? Was it an improvement over the census approach or simply a marketing ploy to bolster the profits of the Claritas Corporation? In a rather harshly worded assault, consultant Mark Atlas argues that geodemographics cannot live up to its billing. For starters, there does not appear to be any statistical evidence to support the claims of improved targeting. In fact, the before-and-after evidence provided by the company, when reexamined, shows the system does little to change the outcome of the election. There is an entire set of questions related to methodological issues, such as the process of determining each clusters. Atlas writes, "Clusters derived from the entire nation's Census data may be very different from clusters that would be generated if each state's data had been clustered individually (1989, 134). Finally, there is again the problem of sample size. He suggests a rule of thumb is to have at least fifty respondents per sample, and because many districts or states will have most of the forty clusters, overall sample sizes of over 2,000 are necessary—as is a large budget to pay the bill. In sum, Atlas argues that "the allocation of campaign resources is too critical a task to be undertaken when there is substantial uncertainty about the targeting procedure's validity [as there is with Claritas Clusters]" (135).

Most consultants now agree that reliance on clusters derived from a national data set are imprecise and unnecessarily expensive. Claritas received a good bit of mileage among consultants and even within the media because the names for the clusters were intuitively handy and "catchy." We all know what type of person belongs to "God's Country." In fact, even Richard Gere, in the movie *Power*, makes reference to these labels. Yet it is altogether another thing to assume that these groupings accurately define voters in a given district. The profession has *not* again retreated to two- or three-dimensional targeting. Rather, as seen below, the ability to manipulate census data and combine scores of additional lists allows each campaign team to define their own clusters, based upon the unique context of the district.

ACCESSING CENSUS DATA IN THE 1990s

The information available from the U.S. Census Bureau has generally remained uniform over the years. There has been a refinement of collection techniques, a few new questions, and an improvement of forecasting techniques, but on the whole the type of data available has remained fairly constant. The way researchers can access this data, however, has drastically changed.

The mainstay of census data has been the hard-copy volume. To be sure, it is overwhelming to stand before a stack of U.S. Census Bureau publications. Smaller libraries will have selected pieces, but in larger ones, such as at colleges and universities, census publications take up several shelves—often an entire wing. Accessing this information is a formidable task, requiring a good amount of pulling from the shelves and cross- referencing, and more than one experienced researcher has gone back to the campaign headquarters frustrated.

It was a revolutionary decision by the Census Bureau in the late 1980s that broke the lock on the treasure chest of information (Selnow 1994, 92). This computer-oriented transformation of census data has taken several tracts. Beginning with the 1990 census, all information would be made available on computer tape reels, computer tape cartridges, and microcomputer compact disks (CD-ROM). For new-style consultants, the availability of CDs has created a whole new ball game. Each of these light plastic disks can hold a remarkable one-quarter million pages of data—about five hundred hefty volumes! Not only was the data made infinitely more manageable, but vastly more available. Once the computer disks are purchased, trips to the library are no longer necessary. Today, campaign strategists can carry in their briefcase more information than a consultant only a few years ago could cart in a pickup truck.

As for selecting the proper disks, two criteria must be considered: the geographic area and the variables to be examined. Regarding the former, all statewide, congressional, and local races will be covered on one disk. For example, all of New

Jersey and Pennsylvania are covered on one CD in the Summary Tape File(STF). As for content, there are numerous files to choose from, depending upon the campaign's needs. Some of these files cover a broad range of population characteristics, such as the STF, and others that are much narrower, including the Economic Census, the Truck Inventory Use Survey, and the County-to-County Migration Special File. The Census Bureau provides a listing of the information contained on each file, making selection uncomplicated. In all, roughly three disks should cover most races. The CDs are relatively inexpensive, ranging from about $50 to $250 apiece.[1]

In the fall of 1991, the voters of Louisville, Kentucky, were confronted with a ballot initiative regarding the imposition of a "library tax." The sponsors of the measure believed there was a desperate need to improve Louisville's library system and the best way to secure the money was to ask the voters to pay a bit more. Knowing it would be an uphill battle, they hired a prestigious campaign consulting firm, Wilson Communications, who moved ahead with surveys and focus groups. Data indicated that the idea was popular with homeowners, well-educated people, professionals, and people with children. To best locate these voters, they hired a demographer, who secured the appropriate CDs from the Census Bureau and proceeded to analyze the city. In the end, the campaign had at their disposal precise, clearly defined clusters of voters who fit the target group profile. The organizers moved ahead in a rifled, rather than shotgun, manner. Although the campaign to raise the tax was ultimately unsuccessful, they had improved the level of support for the measure from below 20 percent in spring, to 47 percent on election day.[2]

Second, the Census Bureau is not simply providing information on a computerized format as a service, but they view it as a money- making venture. What this means for consumers is extensive support services and an ever-refined set of retrieval software, called Go92, Extract, and DocView. With most CDs they provide QUICKTAB software to run frequency distributions and cross-tabulations. Their aim is to provide this information to large and small businesses, campaigns, and individuals. Accordingly, they are dedicated to making the technology user friendly.

One of the true shortcomings of census data has been the gap between Census Bureau–defined boundaries and actual political boundaries. What the Census Bureau defined as a block or set of blocks, for example, had little correlation to precinct boundaries. A third development has taken a giant step toward solving this problem. As of 1991, census maps have been incorporated into what is conceivably the most "revolutionary tool yet unveiled in political tacticians eyes: a detailed computerized mapping system known as TIGER (Topologically Integrated Geographic Encoding and Referencing)" (Sutherlin 1992, 43). With the aid of Census Bureau–provided Landview I software, these files transform statistics into digital maps, where voting precincts can be established as the lowest common denominator. Included on the files are, among other things, street names, address ranges, and zip codes. What this means for campaign professionals is that any number of precincts can be combined for extensive demographic analysis. Scores of population characteristics can be overlaid with an infinite set of geographic divisions. "At a glance, the user can assimilate patterns and pockets of statistics that otherwise would emerge only after enormous effort spent on countless tables scattered through many printed volumes" (Selnow

1994, 93). Each TIGER disk covers at least one state and costs roughly $250.

A number of businesses are now selling software to help access and refine TIGER data, including Map Applications, Inc., and Demographic Data Consultants. Some software manufacturers, including Strategic Mapping, Inc., have combined scores of census demographic characteristics, business and consumer data files, and even information on lifestyles with a mapping feature. Atlas GIS for Windows combines seven different data sets, ranging from Census Data, to Marketing/Product Potential, to Crime Risk Assessment files. On top of this, they have included a data base management system and word-processing feature. The ease and power of this package is nothing short of stunning. The only drawback is the somewhat hefty price tag, about $1,200 for a system. All of these packages combine color graphics with the mapping features so that important clusters can be discerned that would not otherwise be apparent in numeric tables.

Census data, stored in a host of different formats, can now be easily exported to other software packages. They also provide "display/retrieval software" to help the download process. A researcher may wish to analyze the statistical relationships between clusters, for example. To do so, he or she need only download the data into his or her SPSS or SAS package. To better manipulate the data, one may wish to use dBase, Lotus, or other data management systems with which they are familiar. Certainly the ability to bring census data into word-processing programs, such as WordPerfect and MS Word, is helpful in preparing reports, as would be the application of graphics programs. All this is now possible.

Certainly every new-style consultant will want to purchase a powerful, newly compiled three-volume CD-ROM reference set. Updated every two years, the set includes the *Statistical Abstract*, *US Counties*, and *County and City Data Handbook*. Instead of hefting around stacks of printed reports and searching out this information for each new race, this set contains key data from the census, as well as from other federal agencies and private organizations, for states, metropolitan areas, counties, and places with a population of over 2,500. There is even a built-in mapping feature and database management system. The cost is currently $300.

Perhaps most important, the computer revolution in census data allows for easy integration of additional attributes. One sure application is to combine the mapping feature and population characteristics with prior voting information. As will be seen in Chapter 5, many states now provide prior election data in computer format. By combining this information with census data, two critically important contextual ingredients are pulled together. Even if not provided in computer format, a modest amount of data entry would complete the task. Recall that TIGER allows for precinct-level analysis—precisely the level of voting data available from the county or state government. It is certainly possible, for instance, to discern the demographic profile of split-ticket voters, or the propensity of older people in the district to vote solidly Republican.

It is possible to merge census information with scores of other federal and state government data sets, such as the FBI Uniform Crime Reports, the U.S. National Center for Health Statistics, the U.S. Bureau of Economic Analysis Statistics, state and local chamber of commerce information, and so on. As long as the data sets contain at least one common information characteristic, they can be joined. Some of this information will be available on computer files; in other instances, it will have to be added manually. It may also be somewhat difficult to find such data on a block or precinct level. Often the lowest geographic unit will be county or city. In any event, this upgrade capacity adds a new dimension to aggregate data research.

Finally, census data have been put on the Internet. By simply clicking on the Census Bureau's "Home Page"(http//:www.census.gov), the user is offered a list of options—including files on Population and Housing, Economy, Geography, and the Market Place, among others. The Economy draw contains key economic features like current industrial reports, state and local government finances, income and poverty data, and agriculture data. Thankfully, TIGER has also been incorporated into the system and these data can be downloaded. Not only is this a quick and easy way to access demographic information, it is perhaps the best way to find out about the data files available from the Census Bureau. By clicking on "Market Place," the user gets a complete overview of the CD options and other Census Bureau products. "Data Access Tools" does much the same for alternatives for accessing and manipulating data. There is even an "Ask the Experts" file to get the e-mail addresses of regional and national specialists.[3] Other sites on the Internet containing U.S. Census data are Census State Data Centers, CIESIN-US Demography, and Microelectronics and Computer Technologies. These are excellent places to find information on state- and congressional-level demographics, but they may be of modest use for block- and precinct-level analysis. Clearly, Internet data will be the next wave of demographic research. In only a few years, campaign professionals will look back on CD ROMs as we now look back to hard copy.

In brief, the computerization of census data, combined with the mapping feature and ability to add new data sets, today allows for countless updates, expansions, and refinements of demographic information. Modern campaigns are computer driven. And while much of this discussion of CD-ROMs, overlaying data bases, and Internet access may seem highly technical to some readers, it will invariably become second nature to the campaign hacks of the twenty-first Century.

BEYOND AGGREGATION AND INFERENCE

As powerful a tool as this may seem, the reader will recall that census demographic information relies on aggregation and inference; it goes no lower than the block level. We still can not know precisely who is of German descent and who makes more than $100,000 per year. Yet, because the computer revolution has made data management possible, it is now feasible, and indeed highly beneficial, to add individual-level information to these files. Much more will be said about the creation and maintenance of voter files in the pages to follow, but several points can be noted here in relation to demographic overlays.

The first step in this process is to add raw voter files from the registrar of voters. This addition, at a nominal expense, allows the campaign to merge block-level demographics. This information will be critical in putting together mailing lists and for fine-tuning targeting. Many residents who are included in the census enumeration are not able or registered to vote. Our concerns are, of course, only with voters. After adding voter names, we can go even farther by combining numerous "enhancements." Here, other public information tapes, such as those from the state motor vehicle department, the state fish and game commission, and the county assessor's office, can be combined to create a much deeper profile (Beiler 1990, 33). From the motor vehicle tape alone, for example, we can learn which voters own expensive cars, two or more vehicles, mobile homes, and recreational vehicles.

Another source of data are "in-house data sets." Nearly every campaign maintains lists of voters, contributors, and volunteers. Data might also be compiled from lists of newspaper clippings, letters sent to the candidate, attendance at candidate forums, prior campaigns, and so forth (Selnow 1994, 75). In-house lists might also be garnered from parties, interest groups, and other campaigns. Furthermore, most elected officials will have a list of voters who have expressed an interest in one topic or another while serving in office. One cautionary note is in order here, however, in some states the use of lists acquired during official hours or in the conduct of official duties cannot be used for campaign purposes.

List vendors offer an impressive array of data sets—ranging from mere zip code sorts, to consumer lists, to club membership data and magazine subscription lists. In today's world, the list development enterprise is a big business, and campaign professionals have joined the act. Campaigns can rent these data sets (selling them would put the vendor out of business), and they can be again overlaid with census demographics. Much related, list *brokers* have sprung up. These business entrepreneurs, similar to real estate brokers, help campaigns search the market for the best available lists to suit the campaign's needs, acquire the lists, handle billing, and test the data (Selnow 1994, 80–84). Because of their high cost, most campaigns rely upon list brokers only for fund-raising activities, but it may be worth the expenditure to create a highly targeted database.

Another possibility is to create an individual-level data set. California consultant Wayne Johnson suggests pulling together a team of walkers and telephone callers to disperse throughout the district in search of voter-specific data. Information on the passions of specific voters is compiled and then returned to the headquarters where it is keyed into the larger data set. This process is much different than polling because the goal is not statistical inference, but rather precise information on specific voters.

No doubt, such a process is time and resource intensive. It may be overly optimistic to presume a congressional or even a countywide campaign team would be able to garner information from more than a fraction of the overall electorate. Nevertheless, a list of voters and their specific concerns would, in and of itself, provide a powerful targeting tool. Campaigns are won and lost at the margins and, as Johnson notes, "We are already making direct contact with actual voters. Why shouldn't we be collecting data in the process" (Johnson 1992, 52). By combining this expanded set of individual-level data with demographic information, we also gain the ability to discern better the interest of numerous subgroups. The reader may recall the problems of breaking down survey results into numerous cells. Even a survey of 1,000 respondents produces statistically meaningless results when overlaid with just three or four variables. By drastically expanding the issue-specific information in our data set, say to 15,000 voters, and then crosstabbing it with census material, we get a solid hold on a much larger set of subgroups. In a way, this process lies somewhere between individual-level research and aggregated data. We might also suggest that it is a move in the direction of Claritas Clusters, but in a more refined level of analysis.

BRING THE PIECES TOGETHER

By now the necessity for the mindful use of demographic research should be apparent. Modern campaign management, at its core, is a process of presenting the appropriate message to each voter, and demographics help in this regard. A logical query is how a budding campaign team might bring the pieces together. How might these data be readied for use?

One approach would be to assemble a demographic research team. This group might also be part of the computer or database squad, as much of the work will be computer-assisted data manipulation. Obviously this group should be up to date on the latest computer technologies—including data format conversion procedures and the process of downloading CD-ROM information to software programs. A first step should be to define clearly the geographic area covered by the district. Next, inquires should be made to the U.S. Bureau of Census to look over the information available on both floppy disk and CD-ROM.[4]

After accessing the census data, the process of merging other data files can begin. As noted above, there are few limits here and, generally speaking, the more the better. A careful record should be kept of the files added and the variables (characteristics) contained in each. A master "code book" should be compiled with a listing of all the available characteristics and sort options.

The next step should be to get a "feel" for the district. By this it is meant numerous runs over the data, starting with a district-wide examination. What is the percentage of blue- versus white-collar workers in the district? How many African Americans live in the district? How many crimes occur in the district each year? After looking at the overall statistics, the next step should be to examine the data progressively moving to smaller and smaller geographic divisions, again using scores of characteristics. Although 9 percent of the citizens are unemployed district wide, what is the percentage in X County or in Y Township who are out of work? What is the ethnic background of most residents in the west side of Z City? How many veterans live in Block A verses Block B? This investigation should be open-ended, in other words, done without any specific criteria or goals in mind.

Once the overall "feel" investigation is complete, a meeting should be organized, where the demographic team presents its findings—with the use of visual aids, such as bar charts and graphics—to the campaign strategy team (along with the candidate). Nothing definitive regarding strategy, tactics, or message should be discussed at this point. The objective of this presentation should be to begin the process of knowing the voters of the district.

The next steps are systematically to examine the benchmark survey and begin the process of overlaying this information with the demographic data. We may find, for example, that college-educated voters strongly favor tough-on-crime legislation. This finding would be of little help if we did not know where these voters live. Thanks to our demographic research we have little trouble finding them. Again, the idea is to proceed from the largest geographic area to the smallest.

After this, prudent attention must be given to prior electoral data. It may be enough at this point to note that this information is critical to know, for instance, where the Democrats and Republicans are, where there exists a high density of split-ticket voters, and where turnout is especially high. Very much related, the mapping feature must be accessed at this point in order to create electorally relevant divisions—that is, geographic divisions based upon the criteria deemed relevant, not simply the legal subdivision. Recall, the smallest denominator here is the precinct. Together, demographic research, survey data, and prior electoral data merge to form a powerful targeting weapon.

Downloading and manipulating the sets of data and turning this information into relevant fodder for a campaign is no simple task. The best way to understand this process is to do it. It would be fantasy to expect anyone to become proficient with new computer software without using it. The same is true for demographic data—the more it is transformed and overlaid with other data sets, the better the researcher is at doing it. One will also find that this process is as much an art form as it is a science. Two researchers may seek the same information but go about it in a much different way.

A second approach to accessing demographic data is to pay to have it done. For campaigns with limited time and staff, there are data based management companies, such as Map Applications, Inc., the Tarrance Group, CACI, Claritas, and TRW, who can help with the job. The campaign team simply provides the company with a voter list on computer file, and they match the names with their master file. The campaign instructs the company about what types of variables they require.

Data vending companies provide two types of characteristics. The first, and most readily available, is again based upon aggregation statistics. They simply have all the census data at the block level and overlay it with the voter file; if a person lives in an high-income area, they are assumed to be wealthy. A second type of overlay involves individual-level characteristics. Perhaps much more than we would like, these companies have a massive amount of information on most Americans—club memberships, home ownership, vacation tendencies, credit information, hobbies, and spending habits. CSS-Direct, a Midwest-based marketing service, for example, offers the ability to match voter files with scores of consumer and business listings. This information can be detailed, which greatly aids targeting activities such as direct mail (Selnow 1994, 85–92).

The advantage of database companies are their speed and accuracy. A vast amount of up-to-date information can be acquired nearly overnight. The companies might also be able to produce mailing labels, making the entire process of moving from demographic targeting to voter contact a two- or three-day activity (depending on the mail process). Often, campaigns will use these services at the end of a close race, when all the stops have been pulled out.

On the negative side, the cost of using such a service can be high, and it goes up drastically as the campaign seeks greater detail. Another drawback is that the data are out of your hands. As noted above, it serves the campaign well, in numerous subtle ways, to understand the voters in the district. One good way of doing this is to pursue carefully the demographic profile of the district. It may also be handy for different elements of the campaign team to sit together with voter database information at their disposal in order to hash out their strategy, tactics, and resource allocation. This is not possible when mere lists are provided from a vendor. Finally, although database companies can provide information in a few days, much campaigning takes place in the wee hours of the night and over the weekends. Having this targeting data at your disposal can be a considerable help.

In summary, no campaign should move forward without an accessible demographic-oriented database. It may prove advantageous at points to buy lists and upgrade information, but this information must complement rather than replace demographic research.

CONCLUSION

This chapter began by posing the question of why Gene Hackman, in the movie *Power*, would make such a fuss over "demographics." We now know that of all the things he might have requested, few elements are more useful in a modern campaign.

An obvious strength of this form of aggregate data is our improved ability to convey an appropriate message to each voter. A campaign that moves in the direction of personalized appeals, moves in the direction of victory. Because demographic characteristics do a fairly good job at discerning various "types" of voters in a district, and survey research can help us understand the concerns of voters in these groups, we can infer that any person with these characteristics will also hold these interests. While not perfect, demographic information allows us to make informed decisions at a relatively nominal cost. As with other forms of contextual material, these data not only help with targeting, but with the development of a suitable theme and issue platform.

The data also help furnish an appropriate style for the campaign. If, for example, the district is made up of predominately blue- collar workers, we would certainly want to use a different tone and style than we might if the district were composed of academics or business executives. Much related, this information helps discern appropriate tactics. Understanding that the district is primarily a bedroom community, for instance, may suggest attention to train stops, bus depots, and other places where commuters might assemble.

In brief, demographic research aids in the development of message, style, and tactics. Accordingly, it also says a good bit about resource allocation. Each of these components are key ingredients in any race.

Thankfully, the way in which consultants can access and manipulate demographic information has drastically improved over the years. New-style campaigners now purchase census data on CD-ROM and overlay it with scores of other data sets. It can be taken a step further by adding individual-level material. Another possibility is to secure the services of one of the many burgeoning data vendors or mapping software packages. There is no excuse not to have state-of-the-art demographic data as a fixed corner of the contextual foundation.

NOTES

1. For a more complete description of the files, see Selnow (1994, 92-99). One may also seek information from: Customer Service Office, U.S. Department of Census, Washington D.C. 20233, (301) 457-4100.

2. This information was secured from the author's interview with Mark Weaver, formerly of Wilson Communications, in September of 1995.

3. To request information on the Census Internet services, call 301-457-4100, or send e-mail to webmaster@census.gov.

4. Customer Service Office, U.S. Department of Census, Washington D.C. 20233, (301) 457-4100.

Chapter Five

Prior Electoral Targeting

Upon his death, Richard M. Nixon might have looked back on his long political career with fond memories and surely some regrets. Most could predict some of his remorse: Watergate and so forth. But much of the disdain that will underscore the Nixon presidency centuries to come might never have happened if he had won his first race for the White House in 1960. Herein lies one of his greatest regrets.

It was during the early part of the campaign that Nixon, on the advice of his aides, vowed to visit every state. When the pronouncement was first made it seemed to make sense—why not be "a president for all the people?" Even the smaller states had important media markets that reached tens of thousands of voters. Near the end of the campaign, however, several of the states had not received a visit from the GOP candidate. Upon being reminded of this pledge, Nixon was forced to spend critical days during the final stretch traveling to electorally insignificant parts of the country. Many of the states he went to were already in his back pocket and in others he had no chance of winning. In the end, Nixon was defeated by John Kennedy in one of the closest presidential elections in American history.

Nixon's campaign might be contrasted with Bill Clinton's 1992 effort. In that race, the Clinton team saw fit to sort states into three categories: ones they could never win, ones they would win, and toss-ups. No effort was spent on states in the first two categories. Conversely, all the stops were pulled out in the marginal states. Whereas voters in New York and Indiana rarely saw Clinton or his surrogates, voters in Ohio, California, Florida, and a few other "leaning" states were inundated with Bill, Hillary, Al, and Tipper. Clinton won.

To this point in our discussion of the list of givens, close attention has been placed on elements that help craft the right message. It has been repeatedly argued that each person has buttons, and the task of modern campaigning is to find them and push them. While this is a critical piece of the contextual pie, an important component has been missing. Do all voters receive the same level of attention during the course of the campaign? Put a bit differently, should the campaign actively seek out the interests and concerns of each voter? Should the campaign cast its net as wide as possible, as Nixon's advisors argued in 1960?

The answer to each of these questions is a resounding, "No!" It is a common, but no less grave, mistake that candidates and beginning consultants look at the entire voting population as if it is one pool of potential voters. Like Nixon, they plan their activities and allocate resources in order to reach *all* voters. The logic seems to be that, if all voters are approached, as opposed to say two-thirds of them, it would be easier to get 50 percent plus one. While this might seem straightforward, nothing could be farther from the truth.

Sophisticated campaigns amass a clear understanding of the prior voting history of a district, and from this information strategic decisions are made—not the least of which are the areas to concentrate on and the areas to leave alone. This information can highlight areas with highly partisan voters, those likely to oscillate between Republicans and Democrats, and those with high levels of expected turnout. In brief, prior electoral data give us critical information about the voting habits of the electorate and help the campaign allocate resources in the most efficient manner. We now know that it is a serious mistake to campaign equally hard in all areas of the district, even if there are unlimited resources (a rarity, indeed).

This chapter reviews the logic behind prior electoral targeting, many of the calculations and statistics needed to understand the data, ways of storing and accessing it, and how it can aid in the development of strategy. Prior election data which are readily available and critically important, are often the least understood aspect of modern campaigning. This chapter is thus one of the most portentous of the book. Nixon's team made a grave error in 1960, an offhand mistake that changed the career of a rising politician and the history of American politics. No new-style consultant would dare follow the same path.

HOW DOES PRIOR ELECTORAL TARGETING WORK?

In the study of campaigns, there is an important distinction between *individual-level behavior* and *aggregate behavior*. Some elements of this distinction were addressed in the preceding chapters, but a bit more elaboration is in order. Individual-level behavior includes the numerous complex forces that lead to a person's actions. For many decades, scholars and students of elections have struggled with the antecedents of vote choice. What makes a person vote for a particular candidate? Partisanship was found to be a solid predictor in the 1950s, but today this influence seems to have taken a back seat to other forces. Even so, it is no less than pretentious to suggest that any variable, or even a small set of variables, accurately describes why a person votes the way he or she does. Perhaps some people make their decision based upon the breakfast they had that day. Conceivably, others cast their lot because they are trying to impress a friend, or because they were taught by their parents to despise all candidates with beards. Scholars will always be frustrated by the multifarious nature of human behavior. Any effort to understand the idiosyncratic character of individual-level voting behavior will run into serious obstacles.

The story is a bit different at the aggregate level, which is the combined result of numerous individual actions. It is a fascinating phenomenon that the sum of the parts is often different than the parts themselves. An example here would be our discussion of the coattail effect in Chapter 3. It was noted, that while voters do not cast ballots for lower level candidates based upon the popularity of those at the top of the ticket or the state of the economy, there does appear to be a relationship between these variables when election results are added up. An individual-level relationship does not exist, but an aggregate one does.

This is precisely the assumption behind prior voting statistics. That is, we may have a difficult time discerning how individuals behave in an election, yet we can make rather startling predictions about the outcome of the election without polling data. Just because a voter cast a ballot for candidate Y in one election does not mean he will vote for the same candidate in the next election. Yet, if a neighborhood provides strong support for a candidate in one election, chances are great that they will support him or her in the next—that is, unless something exceptional has changed.

Another interesting and surprisingly accurate assumption is that, while a great number of Americans move each year (the Census Bureau estimates one in five), the voting predisposition of any given area remains roughly constant. If a precinct had a high level of turnout in 1994, it is likely that it will have a high turnout in 2002—even though a large number of its residents turned over.

The logic behind prior electoral targeting is thus twofold: (1) while we have a difficult time understanding the motivations behind an individual action, in the aggregate we can make accurate predictions and (2) the best predictor of future aggregate voter behavior is past aggregate voter behavior. With these two assumptions, campaign strategists can look deep into the vote history of a district. By combining and sorting prior aggregate statistics, and by calculating new ones based on contemporary information, we can target which voters to approach. Prior electoral targeting is thus a method for approximating reality. It creates a model of what is expected to happen in a given election. From these data an "audience" is defined, leading to a more efficient allocation of time and resources.

What kinds of things can aggregate voter information tell campaign strategists? Many statistics and calculations will be presented below. Overall, however, there are three basic types of information available from prior election data: (1) how many people will vote in the election, (2) the partisan predisposition of the electorate, and (3) the volatility of the voters in the district.

We can get a good idea of the number of people likely to vote in *our* election. As noted in Chapter 3, the number of likely voters wavers. In some areas 40 percent of the eligible voters will come out, and in others 80 percent will make the effort. A clear understanding of the overall projected turnout, as well as expected levels throughout the district, aid strategy considerably. If Summit County, Ohio, for example, had a 61 percent turnout in the 1988 presidential election, and a 59 percent turnout in the 1992 presidential election, we can assume that the 1996 turnout will be roughly 60 percent. By a similar process, we might discern that neighboring Portage County has an expected turnout of only 46 percent. All things being equal, we might best spend our time and money in Summit rather than in Portage County. (The voting population of each county will also play a factor here, as noted below.)

We can discern the partisan predisposition of the district. Invariably, in some areas Republican candidates do well, while in others Democrats win. Examining prior election outcomes gives us this information. How have the candidates from our party done, in each area of the district, in the past? In any state or district, some areas will be solidly behind a candidate even before the race begins, and others will be hostile. The task is to discern the strong, weak, and swing areas. The campaign can, of course, lose voters in strong areas, and win in places they had not foreseen. Yet, few would wish to ask someone for a date without having some indication of the likelihood of that person saying "yes." If we discern that the answer would be "no," would we still ask? Perhaps, but in a much different way than if we believed it was likely. Electoral targeting is no different.

The third broad type of information available from prior electoral data concerns the volatility of the electorate. By this it does not mean the chance that voters will erupt into violence, but rather their propensity to vote for Democrats *or* Republicans (and to a lesser extent for third-party candidates). It is a measure of probability that voters in any given area "have it in them" to vote for candidates for *both* parties. Electoral permeability can occur between elections years, where voters support the candidate of one party in one election year, and a candidate of the other party the next. Or, it can occur in the same election, where voters support a Democrat for one office and a Republican for another. In some areas the propensity to shuffle back and forth is high, suggesting an erratic electorate (some would say a discerning, thoughtful group of voters). In other areas it is low, suggesting predictable outcomes.

For new-style consultants, electoral volatility is conceivably the most weighty piece of data they might have at their disposal. Only a few years ago, most voters either stuck with Democrats or Republicans. It was indeed rare to find someone casting a vote for Harry Truman as well as a Republican governor. Today, strict party loyalty guides fewer voters. Divided government, where the president is of one party and Congress is of the other, is a recent development and a direct manifestation of weakened party loyalties. This is not to say electoral volatility has taken hold evenly throughout every state and county. We find in some areas that voters continue to vote straight ticket, year after year, while in others they are much more inclined to jump around—some might say "vote for the candidate instead of the party." The task of the campaign strategists is to discern where these two very different types of voters live.

Electoral volatility, at first glance, would seem to challenge the idea that electorates act predictability. In other words, does it make sense that districts can be predictable and inconsistent? In actuality, some neighborhoods are always unstable—that is, election after election, they demonstrate a high level of electoral volatility. Voters might, for instance, give 55 percent to the most popular Republican on the ticket, but just 27 percent to the least popular Republican. We might observe this behavior year after year, suggesting this area is consistently volatile. Conversely, some areas are consistently stable. The most popular Republican will get 55 percent, and the least popular GOP candidate will still receive 51 percent. There is little variance in election outcome. If this pattern occurs year after year, as we would expect, this area would be deemed electorally stable. As will be seen below, there are several ways to calculate this behavior.

Understanding the volatile tendencies of an area greatly aids the efforts of a campaign team. It makes basic sense, for instance, to assume that candidates down in the polls would more efficiently spend resources in "swing" areas than in ones with little variability. Campaigns are won and lost at the margins and understanding where toss-up voters live can make all the difference.

It is important to note that each of these three basic statistics are very much interrelated. Alone, they provide part of the story, but combined they form a powerful tool. One area may be highly volatile, but also have a low turnout. What difference would it make if the area is considered "swing" if few voters go to the polls? Similarly, one area may be modestly Republican, but have a high turnout level. It may be more important to a Republican candidate's chances than an area with a higher Republican performance, but lower turnout. Much more will be said about the interplay of these sets of information below.

Every candidate and most consultants are often lulled into the idea that they can change the electoral tendencies of a district. The candidate may say, "Turnout has been just 47 percent in the last three elections, but I am running this time and will work hard, so we should assume it well be ten points higher."

Or they argue, "The average Democratic performance has been roughly 62 percent, but if we push the right buttons and use the right strategy, we can bring that down to under 50." Unfortunately, more often than not, efforts to alter drastically the electoral tendencies of a district fail. Indeed, it would be presumptuous to presume that the last campaign did not also try to kick up turnout. Districts are not fixed in stone, nor is the die cast before the campaign begins. On the other hand, the electoral history of the district is a strong predictor of future behavior, and deviations are rare. Where we find upsets, it is generally the product of swing voters, instead of the reversal of long-standing trends. Turnouts can be improved or reduced, Republicans can win in Democratic areas, and oscillating voters can stay the party line. Yet these deviations must be seen as unlikely. The campaign would be much better off working within the givens, rather than optimistically believing they can change them. There is generally enough room in the givens to win; the trick is to figure out how.

Finally, like many elements of modern campaigning, the analysis of prior electoral data is as much an art as it is a science. It can also be very exciting. There are endless possibilities for data manipulation and the creation of new, more telling statistics. The colors of the spectrum are provided and the canvas is blank. Some ideas as to what might be painted are provided below, but the readers should keep in mind that there is much leeway for innovation. The goal of the researcher is to squeeze all relevant information from the raw data.

RAW VOTING DATA

What Data Should Be Collected?

The first step in conducting prior electoral targeting is to compile a complete list of voters in the district. When thinking about who might go to the polls, several possibilities should be understood. In any district there are, by virtue of simply living within the borders, residents. Some residents are not citizens and therefore cannot vote, so this group is of little interest. Neither are all citizens, as many will be under eighteen years of age and not able to vote. Nor are we concerned with simply voting-age citizens, although these folks are legally allowed to participate in the election, many will not register in advance and, as such, will be unable to cast a ballot on election day. All we are concerned with are the *registered voters* in the district. This will prove not only useful for targeted activities, such as direct mail, but also for the foundation for election targeting statistics. *None* of the targeting measurements outlined below will rely upon groups other than registered voters—"population" statistics play no role in electoral targeting.

Voter registration lists will change as the election progresses. The exact group of people able to vote in March will be different than in late October. The campaign must get the full list as soon as they begin contextual research (most likely in the spring prior to the election) and make monthly updates. We might expect roughly a 10 percent adjustment over the course of the election. Information contained on voter registration lists consists, generally speaking, of name, address, telephone number, date of birth, and gender. Some of the other possible bits of data are social security number, race, criminal record, and place of birth.

Unfortunately, not every state provides voter registration lists to the public. In some, such as Nebraska, they are granted only to political parties. In others, such as South Carolina and Indiana, a user may inspect the information, and perhaps write it down, but photocopies are not possible. For the most part, there are few limits and the costs for these lists are reasonable, about $.50 per 1,000 names.

Twenty states currently require voters to declare party enrollment on their registration form, and another nine make this optional (Selnow 1994, 88–91, citing Hancock 1992). This information, when available, is critical, as self-declared party enrollment says as much about projected voting behavior as any other single characteristic. Once acquired, handy lists can be made of Democrats, Republicans, independents, and third-party enrollees, as well as breakdowns based upon geography.

The second step is to amass as much election data as reasonably possible. This means that all the results for the smallest unit possible for the last eight to ten election years. In other words, results must be compiled by precinct—or what are termed election districts in some states—for each of the last two presidential, five House, two U.S. Senate, two gubernatorial, five state house and senate, and three mayoral races. Particular attention should be paid to the results of prior elections for the office currently being sought. If a candidate is running for county auditor, for example, the results from at least the last three county auditor races should be compiled. In all, results from about thirty races should be gathered.

When analyzing prior election data, it is profitable to have a pool of prior elections to choose from. It is better to have some races gathered, but never examined, than it is to rely upon races for explanatory statistics that do not fit, simply because they are the only ones available. The collection and compilation of the results from thirty races would seem to be an arduous task. On closer inspection, it might not be so difficult. For example, there are roughly 100 election districts in state house districts in New York State. One hundred precincts by thirty races is only 3,000 pieces of data entry. This project could be handled in one or two days. Congressional races are about five times as large, but the chore is still very manageable.

One final piece of information is the voter registration *totals*, again by precinct, for each of the last ten to twelve years. In other words, how many people were registered to vote on election day in each of the last ten elections. Where possible, it would be handy to have party enrollment totals from these elections as well.

In sum, three sets of data are needed for prior election targeting: current voter registration lists, prior race results, and prior registration totals.

Collecting and Organizing Prior Election Data

There are several ways to compile raw voting data. The best option is to gather this information from the state or county government agency responsible for compiling it. In some states this is the state or county board of election, and in others it is the office of the secretary of state or the county or town clerk. Either way, one government office is responsible for compiling these data, and the first step is to find out which one it is and where it is located.

If at all possible, the researcher should travel to the office and ask for the data. Prior election data can be requested over the telephone or by mail, but often these requests are put at the bottom of a pile. Another reason for personal visits is that there are a number of options to consider when requesting data, many of which may not be adequately described over the telephone. In some instances, tabular reports will be compiled in advance, such as the 1994 congressional elections results by county, or the 1992 gubernatorial results by town. They may even include percentage results as well as the raw numbers. Obviously, these should be collected. More likely, results will be provided by raw total for each of the races.

Fortunately, some states are now compiling results on computer data files, making copying much easier. Ohio, Texas, and Illinois, for example, provide computer accessible data for the last ten years. A shortcoming, however, is that, although most are *now* compiling results on computer disk, past races remain in hard-copy form.

Another place election results might be gathered is the local newspaper. To get complete results, go to the edition following each election. Local party organizations will generally save election results, particularly for the last few years. Still another possibility is the library. For county and local races, the municipal library will normally have files on recent elections. There may even be bound volumes. For congressional and statewide races, most libraries will carry *America Votes* (Congressional Quarterly Press), *The Election Data Book* (Brenan Press), *America at the Polls* (Congressional Quarterly Press), *Congressional Quarterly's Guide to U.S. Elections* (Congressional Quarterly Press), and other reference works. While these volumes can be handy—some, for instance, provide maps and vote outcome overlays with demographic data—the lowest geographic unit is generally the county. This is simply too large a unit of analysis. These books also highlight only presidential, U.S. Senate, House, and gubernatorial outcomes.

A final possibility is the Internet. Similar to library reference guides, the shortcoming of this source is that it goes only to the county level and the types of races are limited. It is not possible, for example, to get outcomes of state legislative or mayoral races, or even congressional races at the town or precinct level. No doubt this is coming, but it may be several years down the road.

The first step in organizing prior election data is to define a unit of analysis. It should be small enough to render precise estimates, but not so small that the compilation process and analysis become arduous. For most state legislative posts, municipal campaigns, or countywide offices, the unit of analysis should be the precinct (election district). There may be, for example, 250 precincts in a citywide race, or 175 in a state senate district—depending on the city or state. Some states will allot more or less voters per polling place than others, but a rough estimate is about 800 per precinct.

It may be difficult to use the precinct as the unit of analysis in gubernatorial and other statewide races; there may be from 10,000 to 20,000 per state. Compiling and analyzing results for such a large number of units may not only be difficult and time consuming, but the appreciation of patterns might become difficult. A better option might be to use towns, cities, or other municipal boundaries—with additional breakdowns for highly populated areas. An even better choice might be state legislative boundaries. In New Hampshire, for instance, there are 400 state house districts, and in Georgia there are 180. Not only are these manageable, but each has *roughly* the same number of voters. Also, results by state legislative district are compiled by the state board of election or secretary of state office. In some states, such as Connecticut with only forty-one state house districts, legislative districts may be too large.

The choice of the unit of analysis may also be a function of the resources available to the campaign team. Campaigns particularly flush with volunteers or money may have the option of choosing a smaller unit of analysis because they can afford the extra data input time and have the computer sophistication to merge units to better discern patterns and trends. Again, the guide is to select a small enough unit to be precise, but not so small as to bog down the process or unduly complicate the analysis.

As with any data set, there are two options for organizing prior electoral figures: hard copy and computer format. New-style campaigns should look to computer data management systems for the answer. Computer data sets are quick to create and vastly easier to sort and refine. There are scores of traditional spreadsheet software packages available, many quite modest in price, and, as noted below, only basic mathematical compilations are necessary. More sophisticated systems, such as Excel and LOTUS are obviously excellent, yet any spreadsheet package on the market will suffice.

There are also numerous software packages specifically designed by campaign professionals to help sort and analyze prior election results. Aristotle Industries, Campaign Advantage, Ace Computer Solutions, Telescript, and dozens of other companies now market software for campaigns. Any of the packages allow the novice to understand quickly how to create and maneuver through a prior election database.

It is certainly possible to compile and analyze prior election statistics with a calculator and a pencil. The first step is essentially the same as with a computer: a complete list of the units of analysis and the corresponding results must be compiled. This time, instead of making keyboard entries, the researcher must note this information on hard copy—preferably an accountant ledger sheet.

In any data set a distinction must be made between the rows and columns. The rows of the data signify the unit of analysis, and the columns are the various election results. Some of the columns will be actual vote totals, while others might be the number of registered voters, turnout percent (if provided), election result by percent (if provided), and so forth. The idea is to fill in as much information as possible, allowing different columns to be combined and sorted for different tasks. There is little harm in adding columns that are never used. At the very least, they provide options when developing statistics, as noted below. In all, it is entirely likely that forty or so columns of data will be entered (approximately thirty columns of various race results, ten for enrollment data). Once all the data have been entered, time should be spent going through the set, checking for accuracy. These numbers will form the basis of a vast amount of campaign activity and resource expenditures. It is important to make sure they are reliable.

PRIOR VOTING STATISTICS

This section reviews many helpful election statistics. It starts with the most basic, and ends with several more sophisticated measures. The reader should keep in mind that these are offered as suggestions. The precise measures used for understanding the voting tendencies of any district are as much a product of the ingenuity and artfulness of the researcher as the needs of the campaign strategy team. Very much related, it is essential that the logic behind each statistic be understood. Mistakes about how to calculate one statistic or another often stem from a misunderstanding or a disregard for the logic behind the measure. When confused, the best approach is to put down the calculator or mouse, and ask, "What am I trying to figure out?" Very often, this simple task brings the steps of the calculation into focus. Finally, all of the statistics, unless otherwise stated, should be calculated for the smallest unit of analysis in the data set. Turnout, for example, will vary greatly from one precinct to another.

Who Can Be Expected to Vote?

Size. The most important single characteristic of a given unit of analysis, such as precinct, town, or state legislative district, is how big it is. Here we are not concerned with geographic size, but rather the number of possible voters. To determine the size of a precinct during any given election, simply note the total registered voters. This number, as noted above, varies from year to year, and even within one election year. To determine the size of a given unit of analysis in prior elections, the number of registered voters on election day is used.

Prior Number of Voters. As simple at it may seem, the calculation of the number of voters often baffles researchers. Not only does the number of voters change from election year to election year, but also between races in the same year. In Chapter 3, *drop-off* was discussed; it is nearly always true that the number of voters in an election declines as one moves from the top of the ballot to the bottom. The number of people going to the polls is the same, but the number of people casting a vote for each office varies. Some researchers describe this as "voter fatigue," where their attention span and interest decreases as they proceed through the ballot. The proportion of drop-off is usually only a few percentage points from the top of the ballot to the bottom, but this can be pivotal when devising precise election estimates. Accordingly, the first step in determining the number of voters, in a past election, is to look only at that election, paying no attention to the totals for races above or below on the ballot. If, for example, one is interested in the number of voters in the 1992 congressional election, it is necessary to look only at the voters in that election.

The second step is to combine the vote totals for all candidates for that office. It would be a mistake to combine the vote totals for only the Democratic and Republican candidates, if minor party candidates ran that year. Again, a minor party candidate might receive only a few percentage points of the overall total, but precision is the name of the game in prior electoral targeting. Simply put, then, the number of voters in a past election is equal to the sum of the votes casts for all the candidates running for that office.

Total Votes = Democratic Candidate Vote Total +
Republican Candidate Vote Total + Minor Candidate Vote Total

Prior Turnout (Percent). The most rudimentary statistic to devise for any campaign is turnout. *Prior turnout* is simply the proportion of registered voters who actually voted in a given election. If, for instance, we are interested in knowing the turnout in a 1988 state house campaign, we would calculate the number of people who voted in that election, divided by the number of registered voters that year. To determine the number of voters in an election, combine the vote totals for all candidates running for that office, as noted above.

Turnout = Total Vote Cast for That Office ÷
Total Registered Voters on Election Day (that year)

A note of caution should be made: It is critical that the number of registered voters used to determine prior turnout correspond to the election in question. It would be a grave error to use 1994 registration numbers to calculate the turnout for a race in 1988. What we are interested in is, given the number of possible voters, what portion of them cast a ballot for the office of interest. If registration totals from one year are applied to an election in another, the logic is distorted and the statistic becomes meaningless.

Projected Turnout (Percent). A statistic that a campaign must pay special attention to is the projected turnout. Based upon the assumption that past trends predict future behavior, this measure tells us the proportion of registered voters likely to vote in the election. There are several steps in calculating this measure.

Two like races must first be selected as a basis of comparison. By "like", it is meant elections in the same district, for the same office, and, more important, during the same type of election year. Turnout during presidential elections is often ten to twenty percentage points higher than in off or odd election years (see Chapter 3). Accordingly, it is critical to pick races from similar years. For example, if running a congressional election in 1996, House races from 1992 and 1988 are preferred (each are also presidential election years). If running a state senate race in 1998, state senate races from 1994 and 1990 are the best choices (each are off election years). The same holds true for municipal races (usually odd election years). It would be a serious miscalculation to rely upon an on year election race to predict turnout in an odd year election campaign.

Another item to keep in mind is that "like" races imply roughly the same level of competition. One should never rely on election results derived from races where a candidate runs unopposed—that is, unless your candidate is also unopposed. Turnout in noncompetitive elections is usually lower than in hard-fought ones. This does not mean only identical races should be used, only *roughly* the same type of race is necessary.

If no races fit this criterion perfectly, logic dictates picking the next best thing. One should never mix election years when calculating turnout, but swapping a state senate race for a congressional one, if necessary, is not a tragic flaw—especially if the second race used in the calculation is congressional. Swapping a gubernatorial election for a U.S. Senate race would not drastically alter the outcome. Briefly stated, given as much information as reasonably possible, select two like races.

Prior turnout percent should then be calculated for each of the two like races. Again, prior turnout is a function of the total number of people casting a ballot in that election, divided by the total number of registered voters during that election year.

Taking the mean of the two prior turnouts represents the final step. The two figures are added together and divided by 2 (or multiplied by .50). This provides an average prior turnout, or the projected turnout percent. Although one race can suffice to calculate prior turnout, many times there are out-of-the-ordinary factors. By using two races to calculate this measure, atypical swings in any given year are minimized, thereby yielding a more uniform estimate.

Measuring projected turnout percent is therefore a process of selecting prior like races, calculating turnout, and averaging these figures. When consultants or media commentators speak of "turnout," they are referring to this statistic. This is the projected turnout.

Projected Number of Voters. There is yet another way of calculating who will come to the polls. Instead of using a percentage to describe the level of voter activity, a more refined approach is the actual number of people expected to vote in the election.

It makes sense that what we really care about is the number of voters, not some abstract percentage. To calculate a projected number of voters, simply take the projected turnout percent and multiply it by the most recent voter registration total available. For instance, if we determine the projected turnout to be 63 percent, and there are 3,000 registered voters, than 1,890 voters are expected to come to the polls for our election (.63 x 3,000 = 1,890).

As noted above, registration rolls change as the election calendar progresses. Generally speaking, more people are registered in October than in March. One way to take such changes into account is to revise your estimate as new registration figures become available. Another option is to examine past registration trends, estimate the size of growth between the current date and election, and multiply this to the current registration figure. For example, assume it is March 1 and the current registration total is 3,000. By looking carefully at past registration trends, we might discern an average increase of 5 percent between March and November, during *similar* election years. The next step is to multiply 3,000 times 1.05, yielding a projected registration of 3,150 on election day. This figure, combined with the projected turnout, can be used to calculate the projected number of voters. So long as the core logic behind the statistic is adhered to, there are always ways to fine-tune and improve prior election statistics.

Relative Weight. Once the number of expected voters has been calculated, it is a good idea to figure out the relative weight of each precinct (unit of analysis). In other words, given registration totals and past turnout, which of the precincts have the largest number of voters, and which have the fewest. The first step is to combine the expected vote totals from each of the precincts. This is the *total* number of voters you expect to vote in the election. Second, take the number of voters expected in each precinct and divide this by the total number of expected voters. This, of course, yields a fraction, or a relative weight measure—sometimes referred to as percent of effort. If, for instance, we expect 310 voters from Precinct X, and we expect 6,200 voters district wide, the relative weight of Precinct X would be .05 (130 ÷ 6,200 = .05). If Precinct Y has 155 expected voters, its relative weight would be .025 (155 ÷ 6,200). The larger the fraction, the larger the relative size of the precinct. When this process is completed, all the precincts can be rank ordered; they will also equal 100 percent.

Relative Weight = Expected Voters in Precinct ÷
Total Number of Expected Voters District Wide

Votes Needed to Win. Another statistic a campaign will wish to figure out is the votes needed to win. Unlike nearly all the other prior election measures, this need not be calculated for each unit of analysis, but rather for the district as a whole. We need not win every precinct in order to win the election, and it would be a mistake to think otherwise.

When it is a two-candidate race, deriving this statistic is straightforward: take the total projected number of voters (see above), divide it by two, and add one.

Votes Needed to Win = Total Projected Voters x .50 + 1

With minor party candidates in the race, this figure is somewhat more difficult to estimate and more tenuous. The best approach is to determine the percentage of votes similar third-party candidates have received in the past. A percentage of the vote total will suffice, suggesting that third-party candidates from any election year will do. By adhering to the notion that past elections say a good deal about future ones, we can assume X percentage of voters will again cast their lot with the minor party candidate(s). This percentage is then multiplied by the projected number of voters in the election. The remaining figure is then divided by two, and one is added.

Votes Needed to Win with Third Party Candidate =
Projected Third-Party Percent x Projected Voters x .50 + 1

Measures of Partisan Leanings

One of the most important contextual elements to understand is the voting predisposition of the electorate. That is, all things being equal, which party will the voters of the district go with? Does the district lean toward Democrats or Republicans? Although the voting stability of the electorate has declined, and election outcomes are becoming harder and harder to predict, each state and district can be labeled "Democratic," "Republican," or "swing." Numerous measures can be used to evaluate the partisan leanings of a district, with three outlined below: base vote, average party performance, and races won.

Base Vote. Base vote is an uncomplicated, telling statistic. It suggests the worst a candidate of your party will do in each precinct. It can vary quite a bit; in some areas this figure may be 20 percent, and in others it may be 40 percent of the total vote. The base vote indicates how even the worst candidate of a given party will do. More to the point, it suggests how many voters will stick with a candidate, even though he or she is a dud.

To calculate base vote, select any race from any election year in which the candidate of your party was soundly defeated, using districtwide totals. The only criterion here is that unopposed races are not useful. The vote percent this candidate received in each precinct should then be calculated.

To move beyond a base vote percentage, simply multiply the current registration total (or projection), times the expected turnout percent, times the base voter percent. This will yield total base voters.

Average Party Performance. Average party performance (APP) reflects the proportion of the vote candidates of each party generally receive. Put a bit differently, it is used to determine the normal percentages of party strength in a precinct (Beaudry and Schaeffer 1986, 30).

To calculate the APP, first select three typical races. By typical, it is meant races that are competitive and have few outstanding strikes for or against one of the candidates. Often presidential races are used. It makes little difference which election or election year the races come from, only that they be "typical." The second step is to calculate the vote percentage for your party's candidate in each of these races, for each precinct. As noted above, third-party candidates may need to be factored in.

Next, add each of these percentages together, and divide by three. This figure is the average party performance percent.

To figure what this percent implies in actual votes, simply multiply the average party performance percent by the current registration totals, and then by the expected turnout percent.

In all, average party performance (voters) entails:

1. Picking three typical races and calculating percent vote for candidates of your party for each;
2. Adding these percentages together, dividing them by three;
3. Multiplying this figure, the average percent, by current registration totals;
4. Multiplying this number to expected turnout percent, to yield the average party performance (voters).

In the end, the APP suggests the number of voters expected, all things being equal, to support a candidate. Of course, the inverse of the party performance for one candidate is the party performance for the other. If the average Democratic performance is found to be 47 percent in Precinct X, the average Republican performance will be 53 percent in that same precinct—that is, unless third-party candidates skim off some of the vote.

Races Won. Many times a campaign team will calculate average party performance and be disheartened to find they are on the short end of the stick. The average party performance may be only 43 or 45 percent, implying, again all things being equal, that your candidate will lose. And indeed this is precisely what the figure implies. Nevertheless, this statistic is only an aggregate estimate, and it may not clearly reflect possible outcomes. Another way to examine the partisan disposition is to choose a large number of normal races, perhaps fifteen to twenty over the last ten or so years, and inspect how often candidates of your party have won. Again, this should be calculated by the smallest unit of analysis. Instead of calculating a percentage, this time use a dichotomous measure—did your party's candidate win or lose each election? Merely add up and note the number of times they won. You may find, for instance, that out of eighteen races, candidates from your party won seven times in Precinct X, nine times in Precinct Y, and twelve times in Precinct Z. This dichotomous tally will generally parallel average party performance, but it may also shed new light. You may find that, although the average performance is below 45 percent, candidates from your party have won more than half of the elections in the last ten years. On the other hand, you may discern that, although the APP is 45 percent, candidates of your party rarely win. With the latter scenario, a campaign team would surely have its job cut out for it.

Measures of Persuadability

As useful as measures of partisan leanings are, they tell only part of the story. Another set of invaluable measures deal with the level of electoral volatility, or what is termed the persuadability. Here we are not concerned with the typical winner or losers, but rather the extent to which voters in the precinct move from candidates of one party to candidates of the other between election years, or within the same election: in other words, the degree to which voters in each area have it in them to vote for candidates of *both* parties. In statistical terms, it is a measure of the standard deviation of election outcomes.

Recall that average party performance is the mean of three race outcomes. Average party performance for Precinct A may be a function of 50 percent + 52 percent + 54 percent. For Precinct B, it may be 35 percent + 52 percent + 69 percent. Both have the same APP (52 percent) and even the same number of races won (two). Yet, they are vastly different in their levels of volatility. In the first precinct, the outcome is generally stable, with most voters "fixed" in their vote choice, while in the second they are considerably more inclined to move from candidates of one party to the other—to play both sides of the fence.

In the recent past, voters generally cast their lot with one party or the other. Areas were "solidly Democrat" or "fixed Republican." Terms like "yellow dog Democrat" (or Republican) were used to describe the inclinations of voters in a given state or district: "They'd sooner vote for a yellow dog, than they would a Republican." Accordingly, elections were highly stable and predictable. Today, fewer voters use party labels to help decide their vote choice. The extent of this "independence," however, varies from state to state, from neighborhood to neighborhood. It is essential that a campaign understand where voters are "fixed" and where they are "loose." Three statistics are suggested to help in this regard: swing factor, split-ticket factor, and an aggregate base-vote analysis.

Swing Factor. Swing factor is a statistic used to measure the electoral volatility *between* election years. It is designed to measure the number of voters who will support a Democratic candidate one election, and a Republican candidate the next (or vice versa).

The first step is to pick a race in which a candidate from your party did well, and then calculate the percentage of his or her vote for each of the precincts. Next, choose a race during a different election year in which a candidate of your party did poorly, again calculating the percent for each precinct. Swing factor is simply the difference between each of these percentages. For instance, if the Democratic candidate received 63 percent in a 1992 congressional race, and 48 percent in the 1994 presidential campaign, the swing factor will be 15 percent (63 percent - 48 percent).

Swing Factor = Strong Democratic Outcome (percent) –
Weak Democratic Outcome (percent)

Three points regarding this calculation become apparent. First, it makes little difference which race is noted first or second in the computation; the absolute difference is sought. Second, the swing factor is identical for both Democratic and Republican candidates; unlike average party performance, there is only one measure per unit of analysis. Finally, a precise definition of "strong outcome" and "poor outcome" is nonessential, so long as the same two races are used to calculate swing factor throughout the district. In other words, one should not agonize over the selection of races, as long as a candidate of your party does well in one and poorly in the other. Swing factor provides a measure of relative electoral volatility—which precinct or county is the most likely to vary, and which is the least. As such, the most erratic precincts discerned by using races in which the winner captured more than 65 percent of the total vote will be the very same precincts found by using races in which the winners netted 55 percent. The idea is to pick races with different outcomes and examine the relative fluctuation from one race to the other. In fact, the relative volatility would, in all likelihood, be the same even if your party's candidate won both races, as long a there is some variance in outcome (they both did not receive precisely the same percentage of votes).

After the percent swing factor has been determined, it is necessary to turn this figure into an estimate of swing voters. To do this, again multiply the total registered voters, times projected turnout percent, times swing factor percent.

In all, calculating the projected number of swing voters is rather a straightforward task:

1. For each precinct, subtract a strong Democratic outcome from a poor Democratic outcome—this is percent swing factor.
2. Multiply percent swing factor by the current registration total, again for each precinct.
3. Multiply this number times the expected turnout percent, to yield the projected number of swing voters per precinct.

Split-Ticket Factor. The split-ticket statistic provides information similar to swing factor, only it is based on intra-election volatility. In other words, it measures the extent to which voters will switch from party to party within the same election.

To calculate the split-ticket factor, simply find a race in which a candidate of your party did well and a race in which a candidate of your party did poorly in the same election. The split-ticket factor is determined by subtracting the difference. For instance, if Bush received 57 percent in 1992, and the Republican candidate for governor netted 47 percent that same year, the split-ticket factor is 10 percent for that precinct. In order to add precision, this may be done for several elections, with the results averaged together.

Once again, it is necessary to turn this percentage into expected split-ticket voters. To do this, multiple split-ticket percent by the current registration total, then by the projected turnout.

Aggregate Base-Vote Analysis. A final measure of persuadability is derived by combining each party's base vote. Simply stated, the smaller the combined total of each party's base vote, the greater the number of independent thinking voters. Conversely, as the combined percentage of each party's base vote increases, the number of persuadable voters diminishes. This is also a relative measure.

First, find the base vote for each party (see above). Second, add these percentages together to yield each precinct's base-vote composite. In order to calculate the number of "fixed voters," simply multiply this composite score times the number of registered voters, times the projected turnout. The number of persuadable voters is the inverse. For example, if Precinct X holds a 27 percent Republican base vote, and a 24 percent

Democratic base vote, the percentage of fixed voters is 51 percent, and the percentage of "accessible" voters is 49 percent.

Rank Ordering of Precincts

The measures noted above are only the tip of the iceberg. There are scores of other statistics one might uncover, conveying new subtleties and telling findings. Or, perhaps just a few key statistics will be calculated. Is it necessary to calculate each of the persuadability measures, or simply the swing factor? These and many other judgments await the researcher and strategists.

One process must be undertaken. In order to understand and utilize prior election data, each unit of analysis should be ranked according to the category of information sought. After the calculations are completed, there must be a ranking of precincts based upon size (which is a function of registration and expected turnout), performance, and persuadability. The strategist must be able to put his or her finger on a list of the precincts (counties or towns) with the greatest number of likely voters, the ones in which candidates from each party can count on, and the ones with voters amenable to your candidate's appeal.

Order ranking is a function of the statistic at hand, registration totals, and the expected turnout in each precinct. It is misguided, for instance, to assume that a 26 percent swing factor places one area ahead of one with a 20 percent swing, without first examining the size of the district and the projected turnout. The same is true for each of the measures. Campaigns are concerned with voters, not some abstract percentage. How many voters can we count on? How many voters are persuadable? How many voters represent our base?

One approach is to adhere rigidly to a ranking. That is, establish a rank order of all precincts for persuadability, performance, and other measures. Here, there would be a first ranked, second ranked, and third ranked precinct, and so on for each category. While there are some advantages to this system, namely its precision in selecting precincts for certain activities, these lists are often somewhat cumbersome. For example, is the 41st precinct all that much more important than the 48th, or are they essentially the same? Where are the cutoffs made?

A second approach is to create an overall ranking and then break the list into a number of sections, perhaps "high," "moderate," and "low." There is clearly some precision lost with this approach, but minute distinctions need not weigh down strategy decisions, particularly in the heat of the campaign. This process allows the campaign team quickly to label each precinct and move ahead with strategy and allocation decisions.

A final approach is to break down the rank ordering into sections, but this time overlay the information on a map of the district, using a color scheme to denote "high," "moderate," and "low." Prior election data cannot stand alone; other contextual information must be incorporated, not the least of which is the shape and breadth of the district. By combining findings with geography, a more comprehensive picture is provided. For instance, perhaps the 1st and 2nd ranked persuadable districts are hundreds of miles apart, but the 2nd, 3rd, and 5th are closely coupled. The campaign might be better off forgoing its efforts in the 1st precinct, to concentrate efforts in the latter group. In brief, prior election data must be merged with other contextual pieces, and a graphic display aids in this effort.

USING PRIOR ELECTION DATA

In one sense, prior election statistics will mean the same thing to every consultant. By calculating the relative weight of each precinct, areas of the district with the most voters come to light. All things being equal, the campaign would spend more time in the big precincts, than in the small ones. Average party performance tells which areas can be counted on, and measures of persuadability indicate where voters are fixed and where it is likely they will cross back and forth. Deciphering prior election statistics can often be a straightforward task.

On the other hand, much of the "art" in modern campaigning comes from the creation and use of this information. There is tremendous leeway here, and consultants are limited only by the extent of their own ingenuity. These statistics do not stand on their own, but are merged with each other to enhance their meaning and produce improved strategic choices. Also, each campaign offers a unique set of contextual and campaign-specific constraints which greatly affect the use of prior election data.

One consideration, when using average party performance, is the position your candidate holds in the race. If he or she is ahead in the polls, and by all estimates should win the race, the best strategy might be to hold your own. This could be efficiently done by discerning the best areas in the district for candidates of your party, and combining it with the relative weight of each precinct. This would yield the best, most electorally rich areas, which could then be reinforced. The goal here would be to find, and get to the polls, loyal supporters.

If you are down in early polls, and are not expected to win, conceivably the best strategy would be to find the faithful and give them a dose of reinforcement. Next, look to highly persuadable areas. It might be a serious mistake to campaign in areas were your opponent has a lock. Not only would this be a waste of resources, but it might also kick up interest in the races in an area not likely to go for your candidate. Why wake up sleeping dogs? The goal would be to concentrate on *potential* supporters, rather than reinforcing a base.

Conceivably the best way to highlight several potential uses of prior election data is with an example. New York's 111th State Assembly District is, by all counts, a Republican area; nearly all local elected officials in the district are Republican, and voter enrollment is roughly 2:1, Republicans to Democrats. Nonetheless, the assemblyman from the district, William MaGee, is a Democrat. MaGee was elected in 1990, defeating a ten-year incumbent.

MaGee's 1990 campaign team confronted two difficulties: the district had strongly favored Republicans, and their campaign would be modestly funded. The race would have to be funded on a shoestring budget. The solution seemed to be a finely tuned targeting plan, combining prior election statistics with polling data.

The first step was to discern the "yellow dog Republican" areas. Of the 105 election districts, roughly 25 were deemed solidly Republican. The average Republican party performance in these areas was over 60 percent; few Democrats had ever won in them. No effort whatsoever was promoted in these areas. Although MaGee was chided by the media and local politicos for not working in these areas, no campaign activity was directed toward the voters in these election districts during the entire campaign.

Second, the strategy team sought to uncover those few areas considered "solidly Democratic"—roughly twenty election districts were found. Because resources were tight and MaGee was seriously down in the polls, it was decided to make little effort in these areas. The logic was that, if MaGee could not count on these voters, he was sunk anyway. Instead of cultivating these voters, the team was forced to assume that they were already in the bag, and need only be reminded to vote on election day.

This left those election districts which might, by some optimistic criteria, be labeled swing. Yet the campaign still did not have enough resources to "work" the voters in all of the remaining sixty election districts. A concerted effort was made to find those districts with the highest propensity of persuadable voters and to rank order these areas by their relative weight.

This information was combined in a series of calculations, using a "votes needed to win" estimate as the goal. In other words, a series of estimates was drawn, based upon the weight of each election district, swing factor, and each candidate's estimated base. For example, considering his base of support, and his opponent's base, how many swing election districts were needed in a target group if MaGee was able to win them all by 52 percent; by 55 percent; by 57 percent; by 60 percent? In the end, roughly forty election districts formed the principal target group. If he could win more than one-half of these precincts by at least 55 percent, and break even in others, MaGee stood a chance.

The campaign proceeded aggressively to court the voters only in this group, sticking closely to the issues and themes discerned from survey research. The most appropriate way to reach these voters, given their dispersion throughout the district, was a fine-tuned direct-mail program, carefully constructed literature drops and canvases, and an ambitious telemarketing operation.

MaGee won the election by a fraction of the vote. As expected, his base had come through and, more important, he had captured over 55 percent in most of the targeted election districts. The campaign had successfully tackled a deficit in resources and voter support, and had done so with use of prior election statistics. Not only did they push the right button, they did so among the right group of voters!

CONCLUSION

This chapter was designed to acquaint the reader with the logic behind prior election research, how this information might be collected and organized, and the many statistics that might be drawn. A few suggestions were also offered regarding its use. The overall goal of the chapter was to highlight another means of targeting campaign activities. This time, however, it was not the message that is to be fine-tuned, but who should receive it. It is a grave error to assume that each voter must be approached and solicited, even if the campaign had the resources to do so. Richard Nixon learned how serious a mistake this was in 1960. No modern consultant dare suggest such a broad-based strategy. Prior electoral targeting is but another tool consultants should keep nearby.

Chapter Six

Opposition Research:
Let's Look at the Record

Bill MaGee's efforts to win the election for New York's 111th State Assembly District were aided by careful attention to prior election data and polling results. The campaign team was able to push the appropriate message to a limited group of swing voters, thereby overcoming a serious party enrollment deficit with finite resources. They also had at their disposal a vast pool of painstakingly compiled information on the opponent, Jack McCann. Having served in the state assembly for ten years, and as a town supervisor for fifteen years, McCann had amassed a significant public record. The team scrutinized the details and presented to the voters a less than flattering profile.

One particularly effective discovery is worth reviewing briefly. In many ways, New York State is best considered two states: the greater New York City area (including Long Island), termed "downstate"; and everything north of Westchester County, termed "upstate." Downstate is heavily Democratic, as are most members of the state legislature from this area. Conversely, most elected officials from upstate, including McCann, are Republican. Political and cultural animosity between the "two" states is keen and longstanding, stretching back to the turn of the century. Even today, one of the worse things you might suggest of an upstate politician is that he is a pawn of downstate interests, and vice versa.

In the state assembly (the state house), the majority party has been Democratic since 1932. Among other things, they control the flow of legislation, budget appropriations, committee assignments, office space, and pork-barrel allocations. The minority party (the Republicans) is left to nip at the edges and do the best it can to frustrate and stall. Numerous games are played out during each legislative term when both sides posture, harass, and embarrass each other.

The Democrats in the assembly, accordingly, have nearly complete control over the budget process. One technique used by the Republicans to stonewall the process is to offer amendments, knowing full well that they will not pass. These phoney measures can embarrass the Democrats. For example, the Republicans might suggest adding $500 million to "fight youth crime," leaving the Democrats to vote against the project because the budget agreement had been struck with the state senate and the governor. The Republicans would then claim that the Democrats are "soft on crime." They also use such tactics to make themselves look good. They tell voters: "You see, we tried to get more money to fight youth crime—because we know you're concerned about it—but those damned Democrats voted it down!"

When they discovered this trick, the MaGee campaign was able to turn it around to their advantage. It seems that, in 1988 the Republicans made a pledge to vote *as a team* to support their amendments. During that year, a *few* of the Republicans were from downstate (mostly Long Island). These members, like the rest of the minority, offered amendments seeking funds for roads, bridges, rail stations, parking lots, ferry ports, and many other projects helpful to downstate residents. McCann, being a team player, voted for these amendments even though his district is 200 miles to the north.

The MaGee team had found their silver bullet. They put together a direct mail piece with a large picture of New York City Mayor Ed Koch on the outside and a caption asking, "What Do Ed Koch and Jack McCann Have in Common?" Upon opening the mailer, the reader was informed, "They Both Work for New York City!" Below was a list of downstate projects for which McCann had voted, including their staggering price tags. At the bottom, the figures were compiled, and a final caption read, "At a time when *our* roads, bridges, and schools are falling apart, Jack McCann is pushing for over $1 billion for New York City. Who is he working for, Ed Koch or us?"

The mailing caused an uproar in the race. Newspapers throughout the district picked up the story, as did many of the television and radio news programs. The notion that McCann was a "pawn of downstate interests" quickly spread. He was forced to react and defend the amendment votes, distracting attention from his modest record of accomplishments. This single mailing, sent early in the campaign, turned a longshot into a neck-and-neck race. It was possible only because meticulous care was given to opposition research.

Only ten years ago, aggressive opposition research—termed "oppo" in the trade—was viewed as a specialized type of campaigning. Few knew how to compile and organize this information, and even fewer knew how to use it. Today, new-style consultants agree that it is one of the most important contextual ingredients and plays a lead role in nearly every race.

This chapter is designed to acquaint the reader with opposition research. The first section will present a discussion of the many ethical issues surrounding its use, followed by a review of why this type of campaigning is especially effective in the second section. The third section looks at the many different types of opposition data, the fourth where it can be found, and the fifth will discuss how it can be organized efficiently. The chapter will end with speculation on how oppo not only provides fodder for attacks, but also helps prepare for them.

ETHICAL ISSUES IN OPPOSITION RESEARCH

Opposition Research as a New Development?

It is a common misconception that aggressive opposition research is a recent phenomenon. Nothing could be farther from the truth. In fact, oppo has been around since competitive campaigning started. During the presidential election of 1800, the Federalists dug up information that Thomas Jefferson had several slave mistresses, and may have had a child with one of them. Things got especially ugly in the election of 1884, when Grover Cleveland was charged with fathering a child out of wedlock with Maria Halpin. The Blaine forces devised a short chant: "Ma, Ma, where's my Pa? Gone to the White House, ha, ha, ha." The Cleveland team retaliated by disclosing that Blaine had used his office in Congress for financial gain. Personal correspondence supporting these charges surfaced and were printed in the press. The Democrats coined their own chant: "Blaine, Blaine, Jay Gould Blaine! The Contentional Liar from the state of Maine." One of the more interesting outcomes of the 1884 race was that Cleveland admitted to his ethical shortcoming, and he turned it around to win the election. On election night, Cleveland supporters chanted: "Hurrah for Maria, Hurrah for the Kid. I voted for Cleveland, and I'm damned glad I did!" (Johnson-Carter and Copland 1991, 6–7).

At the same time, most commentators and students of campaigns will argue things that are "different" these days. There are several possibilities as to why modern campaigning seems especially suited for attacks—or what some consultants term "comparative advertising."

First, the computer revolution has drastically altered the means of collecting and organizing opposition data. As will be seen below, campaigns now have at their fingertips literally tens of thousands of bits of information. If the opponent makes a statement, it can be checked for accuracy and contradictions in seconds, and the findings can be faxed to reporters just as quickly. We are in an era of instant candidate retort, made possible by computer technology. Moreover, on-line services, such as *Lexis/Nexis*, *Data-Times*, and *Time Nex* allow for rapid media searches. Everything a politician has said to a reporter can be pulled up on a CRT in seconds. There is simply nowhere to hide in today's political world.

In the past, oppo was conducted by college students or by the candidate's spouse at the kitchen table; today scores of consulting firms specialize in this field. For a fee, campaigns can get much of what they need, not unlike survey information. Opposition research need not be an arduous task.

Consultant Dan Hazelwood suggests that another factor fueling the demand and use of opposition research is the laziness of most reporters. He suggests that issues are rarely covered because of their complexity and that politicians are able to spoon-feed reporters. The result is a hunger among the voters for issue-oriented information; opposition cues help fill that void (Persinos 1994, 21). Larry Sabato (1989) suggests that the media have, since the rise of investigative journalism in the aftermath of Watergate, become fixated on gossip and character issues—feeding into the hands of campaigns that are ready and willing to push these buttons. Linda Fowler echoes this sentiment, "Changing standards in the news media about what constitutes investigative reporting has broadened the scope of activity that is now subject to scrutiny [during campaigns]" (Fowler 1995, 205).

Finally, the opposition research craze may be a function of its effectiveness. It is used more these days because new-style consultants understand *how* to use it effectively. As media consultant bigwig Bob Squier notes, "I love to do negatives. It is one of those opportunities in a campaign where you can take the truth and use it like a knife to slice right through the opponent" (Luntz 1988, 72). So one answer to the question why oppo has become a fundamental piece of modern campaigning is that it works.

A Code of Ethics?

Because something is effective, does that mean it is appropriate? One of the pivotal issues facing the modern campaign profession is the ethical use of opposition data. Is it right, for example, to tell the voters about something that happened ten or twenty years ago? Is all public information fair game? And what about the private lives of candidates? Is it acceptable to manipulate figures to cast the worst possible light on the opponent's record, so long as it has a factual basis? What about taking quotes and statistics out of context? Finally, do the standards of fairness differ for incumbents and challengers—for candidates ahead or behind in the polls?

On the optimistic side, many practitioners argue that opposition research is good for the democratic process—not only during elections, but while officials serve the public. It moves campaigns away from style and imagery, and pushes them toward issues. It makes elected officials and candidates accountable for their actions. In other words, it keeps them in line, and those with defective records might best look for another line of work.

Many would argue that far too many corrupt candidates were elected to office in the past, and that opposition research leads to a cleaner, more accountable system. In tandem with the media, aggressive comparative campaigning serves a watchdog role. "This is particularly true," writes scholar Linda Fowler, "when one considers how difficult it is to monitor and evaluate the performance of politicians in office" (Fowler 1995, 203).

Advocates of opposition research would also suggest "the more the better." Short of outright lies, full information on the public and private lives of candidates serves the democratic process. It is elitist, they argue, to limit the information available to voters because it is assumed that it should not matter. Does it make a difference that the opponent was tagged for drunk driving twenty years ago? Conceivably, it should be left to the voters to decide—if it does not, it will be discarded. If a potential candidate is concerned about protecting his or her privacy, he or she should stay out of public life.

Others say that aggressive opposition research brutalizes politics by making it too personal and mean-spirited (Persinos 1994, 20). While there is certainly nothing wrong with disclosing factual information about your opponent, particularly if it deals with official duties, it is quite another to resurrect decades-old personal issues bearing little relevance to the responsibilities of office. By making everything fair game, modern campaigning can drive good people, who fear being dragged through the mud with their families, from seeking office. It is well known that charges, no matter how fraudulent, which require vast resources and time to counter, can seriously damage reputations. Moreover, personal attacks and the misrepresentation of public records alienate voters and lead to personality-based elections instead of a debate over policy. This group would argue that the steady decline of voting is directly linked to the mean-spirited nature of modern campaigns.

Where one lines up on this issue is a personal matter, and many superb consultants can be found on both sides of the fence—even if few dispute its effectiveness. At the very least, there is general agreement on three standards: the information must be true and reasonably verifiable, legally obtained public information, and relevant to the race at hand.[1] Within these parameters there is significant leeway. Much of the skill and art of comparative campaigning is to paint one's opponent in the worst possible light given these restrictions.

Honest information means an accurate description of the event. Did the opponent receive a DUI ticket in 1965? Did he or she miss 127 votes during the past three legislative sessions? Was the candidate divorced? How much money did he or she secure for projects in the district? If it is true, then it can be used. For instance, if 127 votes represents one-fifth of the total number of votes, and state legislators make $50,000 a year, it can be argued that the voters lost $10,000 worth of service. If an opponent was convicted of drunk driving fifteen years ago, but is now running on a "make our roads safer" platform, is this person a hypocrite?

Opposition research must be obtained through legal measures. In other words, for it to be proper, someone "off the street" should be able to find the information as well. As outlined below, many legal data sources are available. Prior traffic tickets, for instance, can be found in police blotters and city or county crime statistics. Public service activities are all public information, as are legislative records and voter registration information. Did your opponent fail to vote in six of the last ten local elections? This is public information. Certainly media stories are public knowledge, and any government official, particularly one in office for some time, has made a mark in the media. Furthermore, anything said to the media can be considered not only public, but truthful—so long as the campaign does not know it to be false.

Relevance is a bit more subjective. For some, there need be only one voter who cares about the issue. Others might use standards such as "discernable impact," and still others would mandate that it have a bearing on the candidate's ability to perform the duties of the office. By any of these precepts, most information is usable.

Do personalities have a significance? This is an arbitrary question, but many would argue that it does; character issues say a good deal about one's view of government, one's capacity to govern, and how one might handle the job. If an official spends his or her day in a series of carnal calisthenics, perhaps he or she is not doing her job representing the people. If he or she is divorced, maybe this says something about a candidate's view of family values. A few areas practitioners deem extraneous include a candidate's race, religion, ethnic background, sexual orientation, and the activities of family members.

If the standards regulating opposition research are, more or less, subjective, are there any checks? What stops overzealous consultants from presenting false, illegally obtained, and irrelevant information?

Because new-style campaigning is a recent profession, there are few regulations on unethical behavior. A consultant might receive the scorn of his associates, but to date there are few ways of officially condemning a consultant's misuse of opposition data. In January 1994, the American Association of Political Consultants (AAPC) passed a "Code of Ethics" by-law. Among other things, it states that members of the association shall not make appeals based upon racism, religion, or gender; shall refrain from false and misleading attacks on an opponent or on his or her family; and shall document accurately and fully any criticisms of an opponent. Clearly, this is a step in the right direction. Yet there does not seem to be any disciplinary mechanism, and there is certainly no guarantee that those running campaigns are members of the AAPC; there are no licensing requirements for campaign consultants.

Newspapers, thankfully, are increasingly keen about the truthfulness of campaign advertising. Most spend time checking out the accuracy of charges; and several, such as the *Washington Post* and *New York Times*, run features detailing the authenticity of radio and television spots—primarily, however, in presidential elections. There is hope that local newspapers will follow suit. Several states have adopted "tell-a-lie, lose-your-job" laws, designed to take the profit out of dishonest campaigning. A 1984 California law, for instance, strips a politician of office if a jury finds that deceptive claims were the major cause of victory. It applies to all local, state, and federal offices (except the presidency). Unfortunately, these laws have, for the most part, proved to be hollow—it is exceedingly difficult to prove a deliberate distortion was the cause of success.

Other proposed regulations on deceptive campaign advertising include a mandate that candidates appear in all attack ads, state or federal funding made available to candidates who are unfairly attacked, free media time given to respond to attacks, and the creation of bipartisan commissions to review the truth of all charges. Whether such measures will succeed may have more to do with public outcry than the action of elected officials. As with all campaign reform measures, it may be overly optimistic to expect elected officials to change the system under which they were elected.

Perhaps the best check on the misuse of opposition research is the voters themselves. The public has grown increasingly offended by false, misleading, and distorted charges. If an attack is found to be untrue, more damage can be done to the accuser. False accusers are scorned for "lying," and it is exceedingly difficult to recover from such a tag; voters and the media will take all future claims with skepticism.

In sum, opposition research need not be conducted in the bushes with trench coats and cameras. There is a great deal of legal information on every elected official and even on those who have never run for office.

WHY OPPOSITION DATA WORKS

Precisely what goes on in the minds of voters as they struggle to decide which candidate to support has confounded scholars and practitioners for ages. One thing we might agree upon is that they are rational; they are concerned about the outcome of their choice. Voters speculate as to what will happen if candidate X is elected rather than candidate Y. From this core supposition, scholars have assumed two broad possibilities: *prospective* and *retrospective* evaluations.

Prospective evaluations about candidates are based upon futuristic assumptions. The voter looks at the candidate—qualifications, party label, personality, and platform—and guesses what kind of job he or she will do down the road. When candidates talk about their plans, they are attempting to push the voter's prospective button. When Bill Clinton promised "a new covenant between the government and the people," he was asking voters to look ahead.

Retrospective evaluations are just the opposite. In order to make accurate estimates about a candidate's future behavior, past activities are evaluated. In other words, voters look backward to make a better guess about the future. When Ronald Reagan asked in the 1980 presidential election; "Are you better off now than you were four years ago?," he was leading voters to recall the problems of the Carter administration. Retrospective evaluations are believed to be an efficient way of forecasting the future.

Because prospective evaluations require a good bit of study (the voter has to know a candidate's plans, which are often complex), retrospective evaluations are believed to be dominant. Most voters evaluate what will happen in the future by examining what has happened in the past; and why not, it seems to be a logical, cost-saving technique. Often, the candidates themselves are external to this conjecture. It may be that the Republican party has done well of late; therefore, the voter will decide more Republicans in office is a good thing no matter who they are. Or they say to themselves that female legislators have let them down in the past, so no female candidate will get their vote. There are an infinite number of criteria a voter might use for his or her retrospective evaluation. Both types of evaluation are subconscious—most voters do not choose which model to employ.

Opposition research taps into the retrospective process. It is an attempt to convey to the voter the perils of selecting the opponent by pointing out the shortcomings of past behavior (see Fiorina 1981, ch. 1). Because retrospective evaluations seem to be the principal evaluation process, messages of this sort are very effective. Because is it simple to understand, retrospection requires little work on the part of voters. In a sense, voters are confronted with two choices: either look at each candidate's plans for the future (a speculative, time-consuming chore) or examine what they have done in the past (a quick, "factual" process). If the backward-looking cues are unflattering, the evaluation of the candidate will be likewise.

It is fair to that say more college students choose their school based on the recommendation of a friend who had attended it in the past, rather than what school officials suggest the next four years will be like. People choose to return to the same restaurant time and again because their last meal was good, not because different items have been added to the menu. The hardest part of a marketing campaign for a new product is to get the consumer to try it.

It is because of the power of this process that fewer and fewer candidates can afford to neglect their past shortcomings or to uncover their opponent's. The more comparative information is used, the more accustomed the voters will become to it. And the more voters become accustomed to this type of evaluation process, the less likely they will be to return to the chore of prospective estimates. It is no wonder that opposition research has become an important specialization in the campaign profession.

TYPES OF OPPOSITION DATA

As is by now apparent, numerous types of opposition data are available. Five areas are outlined below: (1) public service information, (2) media derived data, (3) prior campaign details, (4) business and career data, and (5) personal information.

Public Service Information

Public service information pertains to activities undertaken while serving in an elected or appointed public position. Many of these activities will be overt—for public consumption—and others will have been done behind closed doors. No matter how thoughtful, careful, and attentive to the public's needs an official might be, there are always acts that can cause damage during campaigns. Politics is, after all, the struggle over the allocation of scarce resources. There are winners and losers in every political debate. The task of the opposition research team is to find the past activities that will be viewed as offensive to a significant number of voters. If the opponent has never held public office, this section would not apply.

Floor Votes. The 1994 midterm election was not a good year for Democrats, as scores of gubernatorial, state legislative, and U.S. Senate and congressional candidates went down to defeat. While many of these defeats shocked the political pundits, at least one race surprised few. Marjorie Margolies-Mezvinsky (dubbed "MMM" by the media) was elected to Congress in 1992 on a "fiscally responsible Democratic" platform. She pledged to be a "different kind of Democrat" and even went so far as to promise not to raise taxes. Shortly after her arrival in Congress, however, she was confronted with the volatile debate over the 1993 budget. Included in the bill were significant reductions in federal spending, but also modest tax increases for some taxpayers. Bending to the powerful arm twisting of her Democratic colleagues, and even President Bill Clinton, she voted "yea" for the bill. It took little time for her opponent to point this out to the voters. Margolies-Mezvinsky was quickly returned to private life.

First-term Democrats were not the only ones to be thrown out of office in 1994 because of bad votes. Ten-year incumbent Buddy Darden of Georgia was knocked off by Bob Barr because he was perceived to be out of touch with the district (Shea 1995). Among many of Darden's votes highlighted by Barr was his support of the

1993 Crime Omnibus Act. Even though the bill provided funds for more prisons and police officers, it also banned the sale of certain assault rifles. This aspect of the bill became the rallying call for the numerous gun advocates throughout the district. He also voted for Clinton's budget bill. In the end, Darden was dubbed a "liberal" (certainly not a term of endearment for politicians in Georgia) and was defeated, shocking most political observers.

Perhaps the hardest task of an elected official is to make decisions regarding proposed legislation. Many times they would prefer to stick their heads in the sand, knowing their decisions will likely upset voters no matter which way they decide. Controversial bills can also often be played both ways. If Darden had voted against the crime bill, he might have been labeled "soft on crime." For the opposition research team, voting records can, at times, be like shooting fish in a barrel.

Congress, as well as most city councils, county legislatures, and state legislatures, confront literally thousands of measures each session. Many of these bills are technical, and may be of little importance to the voters, but many are hotly debated. It is imperative that the research team have a record of all these votes, spanning the official's entire career, no matter how insignificant some may seem.

How does the campaign later determine whether a vote matters? The first step is to understand the contours of the legislation; in other words, really know what it is about. One way to do this is to consult lobbyists or staffers familiar with the vote. Second, as will be seen below, presumed "bad votes" should be presented in plain language to respondents in a survey or focus group. If they suggest it is important, it is important.

Simply discerning on which side of the issue the opponent voted is only the beginning. Another gaffe is the "flip-flop." This is when the official changes his or her vote or position over time. The candidate may have voted for abortion rights in the early 1980s but switched and voted against it in 1994. Voters not only disdain a breach between their views and the official's vote choice, but the sincerity of the official as well. Nothing is worse than a pol who panders to the whims of public opinion.

In 1990 U.S. Senator Carl Levin (D-Mich.) visited troops stationed in the Persian Gulf, beaming back photo footage from the deck of the battleship *Wisconsin*. His opponent was quick to remind voters that, in 1985, Levin had voted against reactivating the *Wisconsin*. This change of heart was a sour point to the voters—particularly to the many veterans in the state.

A third item to look for is patterns of group voting. Legislators often vote along party lines, or with some other cluster of legislators based upon ideology, geography, or a demographic characteristic. For instance, a state senator might vote 99 percent of the time with his or her Republican colleagues, and another might stick with the Black Caucus 97 percent of the time. This activity, if carefully approached, can be used to suggest that the opponent is a "follower instead of a leader" or "is more concerned with partisan pals than the voters back home." Voters today scorn pure partisanship and value independent thinking. Consistent block votes suggest otherwise.

Finally, many groups and organizations rate public officials based on their votes on issues of concern to that organization. These rating scores can be used against the opponent in and of themselves, and also to highlight potential gold mines. If the Association of Manufacturers, for instance, rates the opponent at the bottom 10 percent of the entire legislature, perhaps the opposition team should look closely at why this is the case and how the voters might react to an "antibusiness" candidate.

Committee Votes. It takes little experience or training to know that an official's voting record should play an important role in opposition research. Equally significant are committee votes. Many measures, often controversial ones, never reach the floor for action but are instead killed in committee. Yet, if the official voted for or against something, it makes little difference where it took place. Keen attention to committee votes can highlight numerous problem votes. It may show flip-flops not only from year to year, but also from committee action to floor action. Occasionally, a legislator will vote for a bill in committee and later on—when the public becomes involved in the debate—against it on the floor. When this is found, the opposition researcher should sit up and take notice; the opponent can be attacked for pandering or for his or her position on the issue—there are two sides to chose from.

Absenteeism. Nothing carries more weight in politics than evidence that suggests that a public official is lazy—that he or she is not fulfilling duties or looking out for constituents. A sure way to suggest that an official is not "working for the people" is to point out missed votes. In the 1984 Kentucky U.S. Senate race, challenger Mitch McConnell (R) was able to upset incumbent Dee Huddelston (D) by highlighting scores of missed votes. In an especially powerful and humorous television spot, a man, led by four bloodhounds, frantically searches for signs of Huddelston in his Washington office—but he is nowhere to be found. The narrator states that Huddelston missed numerous important votes in Congress and did so while collecting money for giving speeches in exotic places, such as Hollywood and Puerto Rico (a reference to collecting honoraria when addressing interest groups).

Again, in nearly every legislative body, there are hundreds, if not thousands, of votes each session. Most legislators are bound to miss a few. The number of missed votes can be added together, for either a session or a series of sessions (which ever is more damaging), and highlighted as a sign of laziness or neglect. In 1992 Oklahoma congressional candidate Dan Weber (D) made hay against his opponent, Frank Lucas (R), by pointing out that Lucas had missed 140 votes in the state legislature. On top of this, it was noted that these votes were missed because Lucas was campaigning, "including 40 that had transpired while the Republican was fund-raising in Washington" (Beiler 1994d, 48). In 1980 Bill Richardson (D-N.M.) discerned that his opponent had missed 11 percent of the votes while in Congress. He then calculated how much 11 percent of the congressman's salary was and had buttons printed which read, "Where's my share of the $35,000?" (Persinos 1994, 22). Nearly all legislators miss votes, and adding the number up can give one a powerful tool. If, nothing else, it forces the opponent to explain the absences.

A second approach is to highlight the issue covered by a particular missed vote. A legislator may have been very attentive to floor votes, but just one that was missed may have been important to the district. Harley Staggers was defeated in 1992, in part because he missed a key vote funding a new FBI center in his West Virginia district. This can be a two-pronged attack. First, the legislator neglected his duties, and second, he was insensitive to the needs of the district.

Just as committee votes are important, so are committee absences. Again, these votes are only a slightly different sort, and missed ones suggest malfeasance, laziness, a disregard of constituent needs, or all three. Close attention should be given to any pattern of missed votes. Do the absences occur primarily at the beginning or end of the week, suggesting the opponent was fast and loose with three-day weekends?

A note of caution should be made at this point. It is imperative to have an idea why the official missed the vote(s) before the information is used as an attack. There may be a good reason for the absence. Woe to the campaign that charges an opponent with neglect, only to hear, "Yes, I missed seventeen votes. It was because my daughter was in the hospital undergoing a liver transplant. Little Katie means the world to me and I had to be by her side."

Bill Sponsorship. Another aspect of an official's record is the extent and type of bill sponsorship. On any piece of legislation there are sponsors and cosponsors. In other words, numerous people are anxious to be viewed as creating and pushing through a particular piece of legislation. In some instances, a bill will have only one or a few sponsors; ,in others dozens of members will "sign on." In some bodies, forms are circulated that allow the legislator simply to sign his or her name to become a cosponsor. Accordingly, it is likely that the opponent will take credit for being a cosponsor of hundreds of bills.

There are several ways to approach this. First, if the legislator fails to sponsor legislation important to the voters, he or she can be attacked for neglect. On the other hand, if the legislator sponsored a bill that did not become law, he or she can be charged with ineffectiveness. A third possibility occurs when the member has a tendency to cosponsor many bills and most of them never become law (as most bills do not). Here the legislator can be charged with wasting taxpayer money, particularly if the measures are defeated by a large margin.

Another item to examine is the relationship between bill sponsorship and voting record. Occasionally, legislators will vote against measures nearly identical to ones they are sponsoring. It is also sometimes found that they will sponsor bills that contradict their stand on prior votes or even prior bill sponsorship.

Committee Assignments. Committees and subcommittees have jurisdiction over a limited set of issues. An official's committee assignments, ergo, indicate their priorities. What is more, some committees are simply more prestigious than others and deal with more portentous topics. The current and past assignments of the opponent must be carefully examined.

Another piece of ammunition at Bill MaGee's disposal dealt with Jack McCann's committee posts. It seems that, during much of his tenure, McCann served on the Agriculture Committee. This made sense because the primarily rural district boasts numerous family farms. One year prior to the election, however, he was bumped as ranking minority member of the Agriculture Committee to the ranking minority member of the Racing and Wagering Committee. Not only was this new assignment less prestigious, but it was quickly found that there were no race tracks in his district.

MaGee effectively spread the message that McCann was "more interested in gambling than the survival of family farms."

Scholars have understood for some time that committee posts serve different member goals (Fenno 1973). Some committees, for instance, help members become more respected and powerful within the institution, and others are better suited for reelection concerns. The important point here is to assume that committee assignments indicate member preferences and juxtapose this with the needs of the voters. A member of Congress from Iowa who serves on the Merchant Marines and Fisheries Committee might well have some explaining to do. Look for contradictions with the voting record, bill sponsorship, and unexplained changes. If the member wallows in insignificant committees, this too can be used.

Leadership Posts. Similarly, the leadership position a member holds, or does not hold, says a good deal about his or her status and effectiveness in that body. Voters generally expect officials who serve for a length of time to become more knowledgeable and respected within the institution. In time, they should become a committee chair, a minority or majority leader, a whip, and so on. If they do not move up the leadership ladder, this may indicate a host of problems, namely ineffectiveness or simple apathy.

Member Items. A mainstay of incumbency reelection aids are member items, also termed "pork-barrel projects." Each year city, county, state, and federal budgets are carved up for specific projects. These projects, termed by one scholar "particularized benefits" (Mayhew 1974), are rewards to officials so that they can take credit back home. Officials report their success in securing these funds in the media and in the mail, leading the voters to believe that they are effective legislators and are concerned about their needs. There is considerable variance in member item allocation. Favored members of the majority might receive, for instance, ten times the amount garnered by a weak minority member. Therein lies an opening for a challenger.

The first step is to compare the claimed acquisitions of one's opponent with those of members in neighboring districts. Discerning that another official was able to get twice the amount would be an interesting piece of information. It would suggest, at the very least, that the opponent is less effective at bringing home the bacon and that the voters are getting shortchanged. If the opponent is a member of the minority party and if the adjoining districts are controlled by majority party members, it should be easy to find a contrast. The opponent may counter by suggesting, "It is not my fault, that's the way all Democrats are treated." The comeback would be, of course, "Well, then, perhaps it's time to elect a Republican—someone in the majority—to get our fair share!"

Another item is the extent to which funded projects are really the result of one's opponent's efforts. Anytime the government does something good, there is no shortage of pols willing to take credit. If two or more suggest that they were the driving force, as will nearly always be the case, someone must be stretching the truth. It is common to find both the state house and state senate candidates taking credit for being *the* person to bring home the same project. Officials from neighboring districts might also join the act. Often a state or local official, such as a mayor, will try to take honor for a federally funded project for which they deserve absolutely no credit. Member items and other projects are a way for officials to brag about their accomplishments, and more times than not they are stretching the truth.

Official Mailings. Much related, public officials make great use of mailings to keep the voters "informed." This process is often referred to as franking. Those with an overly ambitious mail program should be called to task over the misuse of public funds. In Congress and in some state legislatures, it is common for members to send out hundreds of different mailings each year.

In the 1990 Indiana U.S. Senate race, Barron Hill (D) made mileage against incumbent Dan Coats (R) by highlighting Coats' overly ambitious franking. In a television spot, a homeowner stands in front of his open roadside mailbox watching a gusher of letters jet from it. The flood of mail continues as the announcer states, "Dan Coats has dumped 13.1 million pieces of junk mail on Indiana." The message is powerful; Coats is wasting taxpayer money.

Public officials also get sloppy with the content of their mailings. On careful inspection, contradictions between mailings, between the member's voting record and statements in the mailings, and between public statements and claims in the mailings can be found. While franking can be an official's best way to reach voters systematically, it can also come back to haunt him or her.

Office Staffing and Expenses. The only thing voters despise more than wasted taxpayer money, is taxpayer money wasted on public officials. Although she was ultimately successful, 1992 California U.S. Senate candidate Barbara Boxer was stung by charges that her office payroll was exceptionally high. Many other candidates have been similarly charged, with opponents underscoring luxurious offices, padded payrolls, no-show employees, lavish equipment, nepotism, and so on. Certainly Dan Rostenkowski's (D-Ill.) fall in 1994 can be attributed, in part, to his publicly funded office that was used only for reelection campaigns. Voters expect their taxes to be used efficiently, and when pols are found to be doing otherwise, it can prove to be the kiss of death.

One technique is to compile payroll and office information on the opponent and compare it to members in neighboring or similar districts. If, for instance, the mayor of a city with 100,000 residents has an administrative overhead three times the size of a similar-sized city, the voters may be interested. One might also inquire as to why the opponent has three district offices and the neighboring legislator has only two. In brief, one way to attack the office-spending issue is through a comparative lens.

Another approach is to conduct an analysis of what the voters "get for their money." Here the researcher would add up all the taxpayer funds used to support the opponent's operation including pay, office expenses, travel, postage, and so on. Then an analysis is done on what the opponent has accomplished. It might be found, for instance, that although it cost $698,765 to support the member and his or her staff each year, the member was unable to pass any legislation. A comparative element might be included as well. For example, if the neighboring member spent less, and did more, there would seem to be a strong case for waste and neglect. Close attention should be paid to whether the opponent had ever voted for a pay increase, for obvious reasons.

Official Travel Information. Finally, it is wise to pay special attention to the travel records of the opponent. Elected officials often travel to conduct business. These trips, often referred to as junkets, can be a treasure chest of dubious information.

In the recent past, members would travel with their spouses and staff to attend "conferences," "seminars," "study sessions" and the like. It just so happens that most of these events took place in exotic, sunny places. In reality, these trips were paid for by lobbyists attempting to cozy up to a group of legislators. This can certainly be labeled a conflict of interests and draw voter scorn.

In his 1990 reelection race, Democratic congressional candidate Ben Nighthorse Campbell (Colo.) was attacked for having accepted a trip with his wife to Alaska, paid for by Chevron Oil (*Congressional Quarterly*, January 16, 1993). Joan Kelly Horn (D) hammered away at incumbent Jack Buechner's (R) excessive travel budget in the 1990 Missouri 2nd District congressional campaign. One of her more powerful charges was that Buechner missed a critical vote on the savings and loan crisis because he was attending the Paris Air Show (*Congressional Quarterly*, October 13, 1990). As noted above, Dee Huddelston was hit not only for missing votes, but also for doing so while attending events in romantic places. And Stephen Solarz (D-N.Y.) was knocked off in 1992 partly because of his frequent trips abroad; he was painted as more concerned with partying with foreign leaders than attending to the concerns of his constituents.

Many times "official" trips take place at the taxpayers expense; often these are called "fact-finding missions." The researcher should discern not only the frequency of these expeditions, but also the extent to which real work was done. Attention should be paid to the per diem expenses legislators often collect while traveling on official business. In 1988 a state legislator in New York was found to have filled out a day-long travel expense voucher to be in Albany (the capital), the same day his picture was taken at an event in the district.

Media-Derived Data

An equally powerful source of opposition data is the media. Candidates cherish attention and struggle to get themselves in the paper and on the six o'clock news. Because of this, it is common to find a multitude of quotes, statements, positions, and pictures even for those who have never held a public post.

The Gaffe. It is an interesting paradox in today's campaign environment that candidates need the media to win, while at the same time the media are poised to uncover any miscalculation that could destroy a candidate's chances. Because they are forced to seek media attention, candidates spend much of their time with reporters and in front of cameras. It is generally a matter of time until something damaging is said or done; and the media, of course, highlight these gaffes.

New York's 1992 U.S. Senate race was a case study of negative campaigning. Linda Fowler has called it "one of the nastiest campaigns ever visited on the state" (1995, 206). During the waning days of the general election, challenger Robert Abrams (D) made a mistake that most observers believe cost him the election. He was campaigning in a small upstate city when, in the heat of a rally, he dubbed his opponent, Al D'Amato (R), a "fascist." Little was made of the comment at first, but, as the story made the wire service, more and more outlets carried it. Though the campaign had been hard fought, this choice of words was seen as over the line, and perhaps even a shallow attempt to play the religious/ethnic card. Abrams, a Jew, was scorned for implicitly linking D'Amato (an Italian American) with the Fascist movement in Europe in the 1940s in order to garner support from the downstate Jewish community.

As part of an outreach program, Representative Martin Hoke (R-Ohio) taped a series of media interviews in the spring of 1994. During one of these sessions, Hoke, not realizing that the microphone pinned to his chest was on, commented on the physique of the female reporter. The gaffe was quickly picked up and became front-page news back home.

Everyone in politics for some time will have said or done something they would wish they had not have. Often these are trivial mistakes when made, but, if they are carefully approached, they can become the focal point of attack. After an all-night negotiation session, a New York state senator was asked by a reporter how much money he was able to secure for local projects in his district. Because the member was in the minority, it was not surprising that his share was modest. In answering the reporter's query, the Senator made a ring with his thumb and index finger, suggesting "0." Unfortunately for him, this gesture was captured by a reporter, and several years later a crafty opposition research team resurrected it. Using the picture, mailings were sent out: "This is how much influence your State Senator has!"

Contradictions. Another way in which media stories can be useful is to compare statements with actions. In many instances, candidates or elected officials will say something to a reporter that contradicts a prior stand—or even better, some type of past activity, such as a speech, vote, or bill sponsorship. This form of mistake parallels the flip-flop, discussed above.

In an attempt to hold on to his West Virginia congressional seat, Harley Staggers repeatedly told the local media that he was disgusted with Washington politics and never voted for a congressional pay raise. His opponent, nevertheless, was quick to list the bill numbers and dates on which Staggers voted in favor of pay increases. "Facts don't lie," argued his opponent, "Do you want a congressman who does?" (Persinos 1994, 23). It need not be as conspicuous as a pay raise vote. Many times the comment will be a broad policy statement that contradicts a prior position. Candidates are anxious to be all things to all people. Fortunately for their opponents, the media are often there to record these statements.

Investigations. Occasionally the media will make it easy. One of the biggest upsets in New Jersey's 1992 state senate election was the defeat of the Republican majority leader, John Dorsey, who had held the post for eighteen years. The media painstakingly uncovered, among other things, that "Dorsey had been retained as an attorney by four local governments, and that his billings to them had totaled more than a million dollars in the previous year—fully 6,000 hours of claimed work" (Beiler 1994c, 45). An editorial in a lead paper noted:

While Dorsey gets rich off his political friends, he uses his position to ruin political enemies. After 18 years in the Senate, Dorsey acts like he owns the place. He is a walking argument for term limits. (Beiler 1994c, 61, citing *The Daily Record*, October 24, 1992)

Another upset was the 1992 reelection defeat of Martin Luther King III for Fulton County Commission Chair. King's powerful name and high positives led most believers to conclude that the race would be little contest. Notwithstanding, a number of negatives quickly emerged. One of the most robust was the media disclosure, one week before the election, that he had paid off $200,000 in tax liens to the IRS and did not own any property in the county. Since the position called for careful attention to the county's tax roles, "King had virtually no rebuttal," commented Emory University scholar Merle Black (Joyella 1994, 45).

Scandals are somewhat different than investigations. They are ethical shortcomings that can often include numerous politicians. The most recent national exposé to prove damaging was the "check-bouncing scandal." It was discovered in the spring of 1991, that members of the House of Representatives were able to write "rubber" checks on their House Bank accounts and to have these overdrafts paid without penalty. It had been a long-standing custom and hundreds of members regularly bounced checks, only to pay them off at some later date. While it is true that none of the money used to cover the checks was at taxpayer expense, voters were enraged over the "abuse." A list was published, detailing the precise number of checks each member had bounced in the last ten years.

The check-bouncing scandal became the rallying cry of the anti-incumbent, "change" bandwagon during the 1992 election. Members who had written large numbers of bad checks had a good deal of explaining to do. Many of the real abusers, such as Stephen Solarz—who had bounced 743 checks—were asked to find another line of work. Thomas Downey, a promising Democrat from Long Island, and Mary Rose Okar of Ohio were both defeated after bouncing roughly 175 checks each. Still others, knowing their reelection would be difficult, decided to retire.

The exact import of the check-bouncing scandal in the minds of voters is difficult to discern; there are conflicting arguments among social scientists (Ahuja et al. 1993; Alford et al. 1994; Dimock and Jacobson 1995). In fact, a large number of members had bounced scores of checks but were reelected. Bill Goodling (R-Pa.), for example, bounced 450 and was easily reelected. Perhaps voters are willing to forgive transgressions seen as partisan bickering or symptomatic of politics in general.

For the purposes at hand, it is enough to suggest that large scandals can play a significant role in an election even if they do not directly lead voters to make a different choice. Local media may pick up on the issue and draw attention from other themes. It can also force the opponent to respond. Many would-be contributors and volunteers may be attracted to the opposition candidate because of the transgression. Finally, a "theme" of dishonesty, corruption, contempt, or neglect may be built by using the scandal as a foundation.

Prior Campaign Information

A third broad source of opposition research is past campaign activities. There is possibly no greater truism in electoral politics than the propensity of candidates to promise the moon. In their scramble to win office, candidates will exaggerate their accomplishments and experiences, ensure certain support or opposition on policies, and guarantee the success of programs once in office. By collecting and analyzing past campaign literature, commercials, and media reports, the opposition team can garner an abundance of useful information.

Mindful attention should be given to the nexus between pledges and behavior. If the opponent promised never to vote for an increase in local property taxes, but later voted for such a measure, some explanation is in order. These contradictions can show up in bill sponsorship, floor votes, committee actions, and amendment votes. If the opponent makes broad promises to, for instance, clean up crime and fix the schools, but little changes during his or her term of office, this could indicate the candidate's ineffectiveness, uncaring, or distraction. The discrepancy need not be from one election to the following session; instead, opponents should be called to defend promises made at any point in the past, generally speaking. Does it matter that the opponent pledged to protect the environment in 1988 but voted for industrial deregulation in 1994? To some voters it may be insignificant, but to others it could be a serious matter.

Another possibility is to scrutinize promises made in the campaign literature. The opponent may contradict himself or herself in the same race, or between campaigns. Candidates will often fine-tune their messages to different groups, as suggested throughout this book. Thoughtless candidates and consultants can make pledges to one group that contradict promises made to another. This is a sign of a campaign without direction and conviction, and it is an indication to voters that the candidate will say anything to win. Again, voters disdain this type of pandering.

Contradictions need not be the only source of potential information garnered from campaign material. Often statements are made contrary to the views of most voters. The opponent may have had his or her picture taken with an unpopular figure or group. In 1994 Democrats across the nation were scrambling to explain past campaign literature containing "buddy-buddy" shots with Bill Clinton—the president was very unpopular at this point in his term. Furthermore, they may have backed a measure that was popular at one time but turned out to be a disaster.

Exaggerated resumes can also spring up in campaign literature. In 1992 Rep. Campbell (D-Colo.) ran into trouble when he had to correct an embarrassing mistake made in his campaign material. It seems that several of his mailings noted that Campbell was trapped behind enemy lines in Korea for five weeks. In actuality, he was a member of the Air Force police and never got closer to enemy lines than nine miles away (*Congressional Quarterly*, January 16, 1993).

Still another potential gusher of opposition data is the examination of contributions from past elections. All federal office candidates must make detailed reports to the Federal Election Commission containing, among other things, all individuals and Political Action Committees (PACs) who contributed more than $100 to their campaign. Nearly all states have similar disclosure requirements. In other words, this means a list of all past contributors. The opposition team should scour this information.

Extremist groups or very unpopular individuals can sometimes be found on disclosures as "backing" one's opponent. Martin Luther King III was not helped in his race for Fulton County Commission chair by the discovery that one of his contributors was a suspect in a murder case. Money is always needed, and in the hurry to fill war chests, many candidates will pay inadequate attention to who is giving the money.

Sometimes the appearance of a conflict of interests can be found in disclosure reports. If, for example, one's opponent accepts huge sums of money from labor unions, and then votes consistently to aid their cause, this might suggest that the money was used to influence votes. Scores of U.S. Senate and congressional candidates have had to explain their acceptance of contributions from savings and loans institutions, while, at the same time, voting to deregulate that industry.

If one's opponent's campaign is perceived as overly negative, this too can prove helpful. Not only will the media pick up on it, but "below the belt" campaigns are scorned by voters—particularly less partisan ones. Campaigns that spend exorbitant sums of money are seen as "buying" the district. Much related, candidates who not only spend a great deal of money, but have not lived in the district for a long period, can be tagged as "carpetbaggers"—living in the district only to win political office. Michael Huffington (R) was attacked in his 1992 congressional bid for either being a carpetbagger or not paying California income taxes by maintaining a home in Texas. Democrat Steve Orlins was vigorously challenged by his opponent, Peter King, in a 1992 congressional contest for being "a carpetbagging millionaire who is trying to buy the election." Apparently, Orlins grew up on Long Island, rented a home in Manhattan, and in July before the election rented a house in Queens (*Congressional Quarterly*, January 16, 1993).

Business and Career Data

Running for and serving in public office are not the only ways your opponent can amass a record. Prior business activities and career information can provide a powerful stockpile of inauspicious material. This information can be grouped into three broad areas: resume inflation, questionable practices, and questionable associates.

Resume Inflation. Few of us do not stretch the boundaries of honesty when putting together a resume. It is perhaps only natural that the best possible light be put on past experiences, and candidates are certainly no different. When the line between stretched honesty and an outright fib is crossed, the opposition team should be ready to pounce. Voters expect boasting from pols, but they do not anticipate lies.

Ken Bensten's (D) 1994 upset victory over Eugene Fontenot (R) in Texas' 25th congressional district was not only an example of fine-tuned spending (Fontenot outspent Bensten four to one), but a superb illustration of carefully conducted opposition research. Throughout most of the campaign, Fontenot had used his impressive resume to call attention to his professionalism, integrity, and character. Among other lofty claims, he was billed as a practicing physician and a lawyer. To undermine these claims, the Bensten team focused on Fontenot's resume. Under persistent pressure, Fontenot was forced to admit that he had not practiced medicine in a decade and had never practiced law. The resume collapse did not end there. As consultant Craig Varoga notes:

Prompted by Bensten's TV and mail showing $3 million in IRS tax liens against Fontenot's hospital, Fontenot said he hadn't run the hospital during the years in question—contradicting his official biography. (Varoga 1995, 35)

In the end, Bensten was successful in defining his opponent, essentially stripping him of his professionalism/character theme. Fontenot had crossed the resume inflation line.

Uncovering the exact truth about one's resume is a difficult, often sticky business. Terms used to describe past activities are often subjective; rarely are the boasts as glaringly misleading as Fontenot's. It is up to the skill and ingenuity of the oppo team to bring this information to light.

Questionable Practices. Precisely how your opponent has spent his or her professional years may be important. If an opponent has engaged in dubious activities, then the voters should be made aware of this. The opponent may have run a business later found to be responsible for creating a toxic waste dump, or have served on a board of trustees found to be evading taxes. Many doctors have malpractice suits to hide, attorneys have poorly run cases, business owners have had tax problems, union officials have scandals, and so forth. The opponent may have been a school principal or a superintendent in a district where student test scores declined or a district attorney in a county where the crime rate increased.

In the race for the 1994 Ohio state attorney general's office, Betty Montgomery repeatedly reminded voters that her opponent had never prosecuted a criminal case—even though he was the incumbent attorney general. She argued that he lacked courtroom experience, precisely the skill needed to be an aggressive attorney general. To the astonishment of the Ohio political community, the voters agreed.

It is also possible that the opponent is (or was) a stockholder in an unethical business. There are an infinite number of alternatives for investments and how one chooses to invest may say a good deal about his or her judgment and character. Presidential hopeful Phil Gramm (R-Tex.) found his investing in a company that produces pornographic films, even though he had no knowledge of or role in its activities, was deemed by many to be a serious misjudgment—particularly by voters in more conservative states.

Questionable Associates. Guilt by association may be unfair, but it is no less influential in today's political world. Another area of business-centered information is the conduct of associates. If the opponent is in a business firm in which one of the members was accused of tax evasion, this may be of interest to the voters. Perhaps the opponent was a deputy in an office riddled with scandal. It may even be as simple as being a member of a party in disfavor with the voters. The opponent may have had little to do with the problem(s), but as an associate of the same business or member of the same group, he or she should be called upon to explain the circumstances.

One should, nevertheless, be cautious here. Voters are generally reasonable, and overly aggressive charges based on mere association may backfire—and rightly so. As a last ditch effort to save his campaign, Eugene Fontenot responded to Ken Bensten's charges with his own silver-bullet spot. The television ad claimed that Bensten, as a member of the board of trustees of a progressive arts agency, helped obtain federal money for violent pornographic works. Bensten quickly shot back with a list of other Texans who supported the group, including the Houston Police Department, Republican business leaders, prestigious corporations, and even Fontenot's own campaign treasurer (Varoga 1995, 34). Needless to say, the silver-bullet turned out to be a dud.

Personal Information

A final broad type of oppo is personal information. As noted above, it is unethical to find or use information that is not readily available to everyone or is untruthful. In other words, it is unscrupulous to hide in the bushes with a camera or to present gossip as if it were fact. On the other hand, as will be seen below, a good deal of personal information can be obtained from the media, court records, the local recorder of liens and taxes, the board of elections, and even the opponent. Even if it is available to the public, the strategy team should proceed carefully with personal information, as voters are keen to low-blow attacks. Of course, much of this depends on the voters in each district. Whereas, in some areas, Representative Barney Frank's hiring of a male prostitute may have been his downfall, in his district the voters were willing to look the other way.

One area that seems to haunt some candidates is their recreational and social affiliations. Richard Fisher was damaged in his efforts to secure the 1994 U.S. Senate nomination in Texas by charges that he had dropped his membership in a country club that included no black or Jew during an unsuccessful 1993 special election campaign, only later to get his membership reinstated (Beiler 1994b, 50). Many other candidates have had to confront similar problems.

Certainly any criminal record is fair game. This is not to suggest that anyone ever convicted of a crime is unfit for office, only that they should be called to explain their acts. Driving while intoxicated arrests, no matter how far back, should be brought to light. We might also put in this category any sort of lien against the opponent. Many of us have had financial troubles, but we are not asking to oversee the public purse.

Whether the opponent has lived in the area for some time and whether he or she has missed voting in elections are important facts. It is common to find candidates living in the district only a short time prior to the elections. Occasionally, it is found that the opponent has voted haphazardly.

Carol Mosely-Braun (D-Ill.) ran into trouble in her U.S. Senate bid when it was disclosed that she accepted, with her siblings, a $28,750 inheritance from her mother even though her mother was being supported by Medicaid and Illinois state law required that the income be applied to her expenses. To save her neck, Mosely-Braun voluntarily paid $15,000 in back medical expenses (*Congressional Quarterly*, January 16, 1993).

While the sexual proclivities of candidates may have once been fodder for opposition research, today it seems to be less so. A divorced candidate raises few eyebrows, as does one's active social life. Delinquent child support payments, on the other hand, certainly do draw interest. Few candidates will find their way to public office after not living up to their child-rearing obligations.

There is a good deal of new research to suggest that, as party identification becomes less meaningful, voters increasingly rely upon personalities to make their decision. As they do, candidates will be more inclined to use character-based appeals and to paint their opponent as morally corrupt. Playing the character card can be quite effective. Once again, even though voters use personality-based information to help make up their minds, they are also sensitive to overly hostile and undocumented charges. A campaign should, at the very least, proceed slowly when using this type of opposition research.

WHERE TO FIND OPPOSITION DATA

As is by now apparent, there are numerous possibilities when it comes to highlighting the deficiencies of your opponent. Where can the opposition research team legally obtain this information?

Public Service Information

Every government agency, branch, or office provides public information about its members and activities. The first step is to find a government "blue book" or "red book." Among other things, these reference manuals provide biographies. For executive offices, such as mayor, county commissioner, or governor, periodic reports are often published. By contacting the public relations officer for that branch, mounds of information—such as budget actions, vetoes, measures signed into law, agency orders, staffing decisions, and so on—can be secured. Another vault will be local media outlets. By carefully scanning through clippings at the local newspaper, for instance, a good deal of material can be compiled. The local library will have a section or file devoted to the city/county/state government.

In some ways, it is easier to explore the actions of a legislator. Nearly all legislatures, save only the smallest town, city, or county councils, will have public information offices (in some instances, they are called the house or senate clerk's office). These offices serve as the data archives on the actions of the entire legislature (or legislative branch) and of each member. They will provide information on bill sponsorship, amendment votes and sponsorship, voting records, committee assignments, committee actions, and so forth. They can also grant copies of specific bills.

Fortunately, the public information offices of Congress and nearly all of the state legislatures are now computerized. In Colorado, for instance, voting records, bill sponsorship, committee assignments, and the like have been on computer for the last ten years. In Oklahoma, it is for the last five. In some states, computer access is only a recent development; North Carolina, for example, is "up," but only with information since 1994. In still other states, such as Georgia, journals are printed and published every week and are accessible at libraries throughout the state.

An advantage of computerized legislative information is the ability to search quickly and list relevant information. Within an instant, a print out can be obtained. On the negative side, while this information is, by law, open to the public, that does not mean it is free. Most public information offices charge a fee for computer runs and print outs. In New York, researchers can get nearly all they request but have to pay $.25 per page for the information. Another modest drawback is that, in some states, such as Ohio, one must provide very specific requests; they will not print out a blanket, session-long voting record.

Privately operated data services, which monitor the actions of the executive or legislature, can also be used. *Legitech*, for example, provides daily updates of actions on bills, sponsors' memos, members' voting records, campaign contribution reports, and a host of additional information on each member of the New York State Legislature. *Indiana Issues* does much the same for its state. There are several for Congress, including *Government Information Insider*, *Legislative Information Group*, and *Congressional Quarterly Washington Alert*. Keenly interested in the progression of bills, lobby firms and special-interest groups often subscribe to these services. If the campaign is working closely with one, it may be possible to use their service as part of an in-kind contribution; otherwise, these data services are generally expensive.

As surprising as it might seem, another source of information is the opponent's office. By simply requesting information on bill sponsorships or committee assignments, for example, detailed information can be obtained. The same is true for member items. If interested in the amount of money that an official secured for various projects in the last few years, asking the office for the information can work. Public officials realize the importance of keeping in touch with concerned citizens, and anyone requesting information is promptly given consideration. Of course, if they know that the information may be used against them in the coming election, the chances of getting such help declines precipitously.

The local party organizations or library are good bets to find out about one's opponent's franking. There may even be someone in the community who has collected a large portion of the mailings. It is again possible to call or write to the opponent's office and have past newsletters or other issue-specific mailings sent to you. In Congress and in several states, records of each member's frank account is kept, which allows public inspection. The office of the secretary of state is the best place to find this material. Unfortunately, other than the total franking budget, specific mailings are generally not kept for local-level officials.

Regarding office and travel expenses, in most states this is public information. It may require a series of letters, copying charges, and a bit of waiting, but vigilance and patience should prevail.

Media-Derived Data

The best place to collect media-based material is from the outlets themselves. Newspapers generally create files on public officials, or at the very least an index of stories. Only a copying fee is required. As for local television and radio stations, they too index stories and interviews. They may provide copies, but again for a fee.

Local party organizations sometimes save clippings on public officials, as do certain associations and interest groups. For higher level office candidates, such as those for governor or the U.S. Senate, large papers in the state will be indexed and can be found in libraries. A quick way of finding articles is to use one of the many CD ROM indices, such as the *National Newspaper Index* or the *Newspaper Abstract Ondisc*. Here the researcher simply types in the name of the opponent and instantly receives the citation of every article in which he or she is mentioned. Unfortunately, these indices contain a limited number of papers, usually the larger and most prestigious ones, and go back only a few years.

A final possibility is to use an on-line database, such as *Lexis/Nexis* or *Data-Times*. This can be a powerful, cost-efficient alternative, and the full text of many major newspapers is now available. The community library should subscribe to one of these services. "For a fee, the librarian will input your opponent's name and print out any articles, columns or even public notices that contain the name" (Farinella 1992, 43).

Campaign Information

The best place to start when collecting prior campaign information is again the local media outlets. A full set of campaign-centered stories should be amassed. The library, too, will contain these stories, as well as a good deal of your opponent's past campaign literature.

As for prior radio and television spots, the local party should have some. Another bet is a friendly political scientist or communications professor at the local college or university. It is unlikely that the stations themselves will have saved copies and even more doubtful that they would provide them.

Contribution and expenditure information will be provided by the Federal Election Commission, which is located in Washington, D.C. They produce an on-line file, published by *Time Nex*, for an access fee of about $15 per hour. There are several other sites on the Internet, including *Lexis/Nexis,* where this information can be found. State or county boards of election (secretary of state office in some states) will provide this material for local-level races. Many times, however, the disclosure forms are in disarray and expensive to reproduce.

Business and Professional Data

There are a growing number of options when collecting business-related opposition data. A starting point would again be an on-line service. This time, instead of just searching under the opponent's name, the candidate's business or organizational affiliations should be scanned. Checking the *Directory of On-Line Data Bases* may suggest a clear path. A number of publications will also be helpful, including trade journals, regional business journals, chamber of commerce reports, biographical directories, corporate annual reports, and so on. The local newspaper or community library may have files on the opponents business.

Data on liens, which indicate whether your opponent or his or her business failed to pay their taxes on time can be useful. There are various places to look for this information, including the local recorder of deeds, the district courts, or the county or city courthouse where one can inquire where lien information may be found. It is also possible to pay a title insurance company to conduct a lien search (Farinella 1992, 43–44).

If the opponent runs or has run a business regulated by a state or county agency, requesting information from the agency may work. Each state has an employment office, which compiles information on the creation and loss of jobs. Calling the local chamber of commerce may prove to be fruitful, as might the business's public relations office, if they have one. It is even possible to get modest information on a candidate's military record by writing to the National Personnel Records Center in Saint Louis, Missouri. It is necessary to supply the candidate's social security number (Farinella 1992, 43–44).

Personal Information

Much of what has been noted above could be helpful in collecting personal information. Local media outlets and libraries will have some good material. A second step is to check if the opponent has ever been a party in a court action. Unfortunately, there are scores of possibilities here—including municipal civil courts, local criminal courts, family courts, and several levels of state courts. Each should have its own defendant index. If one's opponent has lived in several locations, this process can be very time consuming.

The local board of election should always be checked to make sure that the opponent has voted in elections. This can also indicate how long he or she has lived in the area prior to the campaign.

CREATING AN OPPOSITION DATABASE

Once this mountain of information has been compiled, the next logical step is to organize it so that it can be used quickly and accurately. In the old days of opposition research, including the 1970s, filing cabinets were filled with folders of different information. There might be, for instance, a thick file on news clippings. As issues arose during the course of the campaign, different files would be pulled and sorted through to find the counterattack. Carefully segmented hard-copy information was seen as the cutting edge—that is, in its time. Once again, computer technology has changed everything.

Like most other new-age campaign technologies, computerized opposition research was pioneered by the Republicans during a presidential contest. In 1984 the Republican National Committee (RNC) doled out $1.1 million to create the Opposition Research Group. Their first task was to collect detailed information about each of the eight Democratic candidates running for president. They pulled together a staggering set of facts, using over 2,000 sources and 400,000 documents. Next, a staff of readers sifted through the documents looking for direct quotes, quotes attributed to the candidates, and quotes about the candidates by others. The information was then coded and entered into a massive computer database. In the end, the system contained approximately 75,000 items and 45,000 quotes (Bayer and Rodota 1989).

By the time the Democrats had nominated Walter Mondale, the Republicans were ready. For starters, they produced *Vice President Malaise*, a 200-page analysis of the Mondale record, and sent it out to every party official in the nation. Second, the data set allowed quick, pinpoint accuracy. Each time Mondale opened his mouth, Republicans were ready to point out contradictory actions or comments. While Mondale campaigned from location to location, they were equipped to tell the voters about his positions and statements harmful to their community. The data set was also instrumental in preparing Ronald Reagan for debates. When all was said and done, the project was viewed as the "secret weapon" of the race (Bayer and Rodota 1989, 25).

Today, computerized opposition databases are essential in any mid- to high-level race. Overnight analysis has been replaced by immediate follow up. Campaigns must be prepared to counteract charges and minimize damage by beating the opponent to the punch. As veteran consultant Averell "Ace" Smith notes: "When your opponent calls you a jerk, you should be equipped to show that JERKPAC is one of his biggest contributors simply by punching a button" (Smith 1992, 51).

There are two routes to use in organizing opposition data: creating your own database or paying to have one compiled. If you create your own, it is essential to start early. The first step is to select a database management system. As noted in previous chapters, there are many to choose from. The next step is to gather all the information in hard-copy form, which is then coded using established and extensive criteria—including categories based upon the source, when it took place, where it took place, the subject area, the action taken (including any quotation), and a brief description of the item. Care should be taken here, as the coding process forms the bedrock of the accurate, timely analysis.

Next, the items should be entered into the database. Depending on the number of items and the team of keypunchers, this stage can take a considerable time. The master file should be copied into several subject files, such as those by subject or type of action. The master-file will be the most frequently used, but the smaller ones will afford a bit more in-depth investigation when needed. A final step, as with any data set, is to run a series of mock tests.

In all, setting up an opposition database is an arduous, time-consuming process. It can be less expensive, and if the candidate is working on the process as well, at least in the early stages, he or she may become better acquainted with the opponent and better able to think fast on his or her feet.

The other option is to hire a professional opposition research team to set up the database. "Not surprisingly, most consultants advise that research be conducted by pros like themselves" (Persinos 1994, 56). Not only is oppo time consuming and costly, many argue it takes a trained eye to fit the pieces together. Consultants provide a base of information; for congressional, gubernatorial, and state legislative races, they will arrive with a detailed data set on the opponent's official activities. They either keep up-to-date data themselves, or they pay a service to do it for them. They also provide user-friendly software, allowing the strategy team to do some updates themselves. Finally, they lend a big hand in complementing the file with all the additional information.

A drawback is the fees collected by these professionals, which can be quite large, and also by relying on an outside firm to organize the database, the campaign loses some of the creative tools. In the process of collecting, sorting, and inputting information about the opponent, the campaign team gets a better understanding of what they are up against and how to proceed. Some of this is lost when outside consulting firms do the work.

HOW TO USE OPPOSITION RESEARCH

It is of foremost importance to remember that opposition research is not merely used to attack, but to highlight the negative. Another critically important use is to emphasize the opponent's strengths. Just as good lawyers will never ask a question of a witness on the stand without already knowing the answer, candidates should never claim to be better in a particular area without knowing how strong the opponent is. A candidate may have a solid platform on the environment, but if the opponent has been past president of the Environmental Defense Fund and has had the best environmental rating in the legislature ten years running, perhaps another issue should be stressed. Opposition research is not negative research. Rather, it is used to know the strengths as well as the weaknesses of the opponent.

Although some consultants will debate this issue, it is a solid idea to establish your candidate's creditability before going on the offensive. Voters consider the source as well as the information. If they are unfamiliar with the source, the effect of the charge may be negated. Along similar lines, it is often helpful to have supporters of the candidate echo any charges, particularly if the candidate is not well known. A respected community leader may effectively do this.

Attacks should not be haphazard but in tune with the overall message about the opponent and your candidate's theme. If, for instance, you are attempting to paint the opponent as "old news" and aloof, all attacks should be directed at his complacency in office. Every charge must also be carefully investigated and documented and checked by someone other than the person who did the research. Carelessly compiled information can backfire, painting the candidate as a liar. The media will also put greater stock in your material if they have documentation in their hands to support it (Ridder 1994, 57).

Do not expect one charge about the opponent to change the course of the campaign. There are few silver-bullets in campaigns. Instead, opposition research should be used repetitively and should begin early in the campaign. By the end of the election, voters will be inundated with charges and countercharges and in all likelihood "tune them out" (Ridder 1994, 57).

Another important tip, suggests consultant Rick Ridder, is that, when a powerful piece of information has been found, it is a good idea to build up your candidate in this area before the attack is leveled. When you drop the final "atomic bomb," your candidate will then have more creditability (1994, 57).

Turning the Tables: Researching Your Own Candidate

Of all the advice consultants might provide regarding opposition research, none is more universally agreed upon than the need to know your own candidate equally well. In a prudent campaign, all of the steps outlined above should also be undertaken for your own candidate. Opposition research is not a one-way street; the opponent will conduct the same type of research on his opponent—your candidate. The only way to be prepared for the upcoming onslaught, and it will surely come, is to know the weapons they have at their disposal. If your candidate missed 157 votes, you had best start working on an explanation. It may even be a good idea to preempt the attack with an explanation—get it out in the open before the opponent chooses the most damaging point in the race.

Second, nothing is more harmful to a campaign than to level a charge only to find that your own candidate is also guilty of the offense. The media love such blunders. In order to make creditability charges stick, the candidate must be free of them, too.

Finally, a campaign team should never assume that their candidate has either perfect memory or perfect candor. When asked to recall their problems, candidates often have selective memory. The only way to understand your strengths and liabilities fully is to research your candidate carefully. This does not imply that it should be done behind his or her back, only that it should be comprehensive instead of based on the candidate's memory.

CONCLUSION

How opposition research is collected, organized, and used has come a long way since Grover Cleveland was charged with having a child out of wedlock. In a sense, however, much is the same. It is a campaign activity designed to know the strengths and weaknesses of your opponent. It is a contextual element that can, if properly used, change the course of a race. And there is little reason to expect that opposition research will become less powerful or accessible. The more candidates push voters to their retrospective cues, the more effective these cues will be. Added to this is the burgeoning maze of on-line options helpful to researchers.

To many, the movement toward fast-paced opposition campaigning is a plus for the democratic system. It keeps out, they argue, would-be candidates who have something to hide. Others argue that it is a prime culprit in the ever-increasing meanness of modern campaigns. Perhaps a new wave of consultants will devise and enforce a set of ethical guidelines regarding the use of candidate research. Either way, new-style consultants should pay close attention to these new technologies, as they are rapidly changing the way in which candidates run for and win office.

NOTE

1. This three-pronged approach parallels John F. Persinos' suggestion that opposition be "honest, legal and relevant to the race" (1994, 22).

Part Two

STRATEGIC THINKING

Chapter Seven

How to Become a Wise Consumer of Campaign Polling

Jesse Marquette

The 1990 Texas lieutenant governor's race between Democrat Bob Bullock and Republican Robert Mossbacher was a toss-up going into the final weeks of the race. The Bullock team decided to conduct a tracking poll two weeks before election day. The results suggested that his support among women was sagging. The decision was made to include a female announcer and emphasize education on his last round of television and radio commercials. Not only did Bullock win the race by a slight margin, he carried the women's vote as well (Dowd 1992).

A political poll is a public opinion survey conducted to gather information useful in the conduct of a political campaign. The campaign may be a run for elective office, or a referendum, bond issue, or initiative, but in each case it is necessary to get information about how people feel about the issue and how they are responding to the events of the campaign. Since political polls are a special case of public opinion surveys, the purpose of this chapter is to demonstrate how one can become an *informed consumer* of survey research for political campaigning. It is not intended to teach how to conduct surveys—that would require an entire volume by itself.

Since political polling has become such a tremendous component of modern political campaigns, it is necessary to understand the characteristics of a good poll. Armed with this knowledge new-style consultants will be able to judge whether the survey information provided is of the quality needed to make decisions. For example, polling is a critical factor in making choices about the allocation of resources, the kinds of positions the candidate will emphasize, and the order in which various events are staged or advertising is scheduled during the course of a campaign.

WHY CONDUCT POLLING?

A political campaign is an attempt to influence public perception in order to achieve a victory by one candidate or proposition. In order to run an effective campaign, it is necessary to understand the current distribution of and potential changes in opinion within the constituency. The primary reason to undertake a survey is usually because it is not possible to find *up-to-date* information about perceptions in any other way. All surveys are expensive, including political surveys, no matter how narrowly focused. Surveys that are properly run also take time, which in a campaign is usually at a premium. Given both the expense of surveys, and the fact that they are time consuming to administer and analyze, it is always best to answer as many questions as possible with nonsurvey data. Other chapters in this book look at aggregate data to develop campaign themes, both from existing documentary evidence and from such materials as prior election results and demographics.

Once it has been determined that a survey is the only way to acquire individual-level data, it is important to ensure that any surveys conducted on behalf of the campaign are done for a reasonable fee and in a timely manner. Remember that, during the course of many campaigns, information from other surveys may become available without having to pay for it. Depending on the scope of the campaign being conducted (congressional, statewide office, large city mayoral races), other organizations, especially the mass media, may conduct surveys that are appropriate and, to a greater or lesser extent, usable in your race. For example, during most statewide campaigns in the United States, a variety of surveys are conducted throughout the course of the campaign on behalf of one or another media outlet. These surveys are usually quite well done because they are commissioned either from well-respected commercial polling operations, or run as a consortium between the media and university survey research centers. The kinds of questions asked are usually germane to the flow of the campaign, and such "free" data should not be overlooked in your planning.

The most frequent type of poll conducted during election campaigns is the privately commissioned poll, either purchased from a professional or run by campaign volunteers. Assuming that you will be working with such resources, then the question becomes, what can you find out using a poll? The most obvious question is whether anyone has heard about your candidate—what is his or her level of *name recognition and standing?*

Individuals who choose to run for public office have often been members of various civic organizations or have held positions that have put them in the public eye to some degree. They hope that this prior visibility will be of significant help in a race for elective office. While such service may be of benefit in fund-raising and campaign organization, visibility in terms of civic or other service does not necessarily translate into recognition among the mass electorate. The basic question of whether an individual is well known among the electorate is therefore one of the first and most frequent topics in political polling.

In many races neither candidate will be well known, yet one candidate will have a distinct edge in public preference. Since elections are decided only by the votes cast, monitoring the distribution of preference between declared candidates is another major aspect of political polling. This comparison of candidate standing is one of the major uses of political polls by the mass media and constitutes the central component of "horse race" journalism. While knowing who is ahead and who is behind is obviously of interest to a campaign, the major use of polls is to find out how to maintain or change a candidate's name recognition and standing, not merely report it.

A second major use of political polling revolves around the identification of *issue preferences*. One of the major functions of polls conducted prior to, or early in, a campaign is to understand the distribution of issue preferences among the electorate in the relevant constituency. At the beginning of any campaign, candidates will have a series of issues they believe are significant and wish to pursue as the race proceeds. Choosing which of these issues are likely to make effective campaign themes depends on the beginning distribution of preferences in the electorate. It makes no sense to campaign on an issue about which no one cares or one in which the distribution of opinion is so inflexible that no amount of effort will change it. Resources are always tight, so the effective campaign will focus on those topics for which there is a potential audience.

A third broad type of information to be gathered is the distribution of *knowledge* or *belief* about particular topics or events among the potential electorate. For example, is an opposing candidate vulnerable because the public is aware of his or her inappropriate behavior? The extent and distribution of such beliefs can be determined using a survey. Armed with this information, strategies can be designed to maximize the visibility of that particular impropriety to the relevant electorate.

Underlying attitudes about various social and political values make up another major area to be investigated. For instance, if someone believes that abortion is murder, then no amount of discussion of public policy options, short of an outright ban, is going to satisfy that voter. The difference between issue preferences and underlying attitudes is that an issue preference represents a choice among current policy options. Underlying attitudes toward social or political values exist even in the absence of specific proposals. If your client has a particular preference for a flat tax, a not yet widely discussed proposal, you could investigate potential support or opposition by examining underlying attitudes toward fairness, or taxes in general, as they relate to the initial response to the flat tax idea. This approach allows you to determine whether a particular issue position is likely to resonate with the underlying value structure of the constituency. You might guess that it would probably not be good idea for a serious candidate to run as a socialist in a constituency in which the vast majority of the public characterize themselves as very conservative. Underlying attitudes, such as general ideology, strength of religiosity, and partisan preference, are all clues to the likely behavior of an electorate in particular circumstances, and they can be tapped by using surveys.

To this point we have referred to the "distribution" of opinion or preferences or knowledge without being very specific about how that distribution is formulated. Most political polling will examine the distribution of opinions or information by reference to such *demographic characteristics* as sex, race, age, income, and place of residence (see Chapter 4). Later in this chapter, we will show you how to construct such distributions. For now we will simply note that it is possible to ask such questions as "Do men and women view the day care issue the same way?" or "Is the proportion of self-identified conservatives the same in the northern and southern parts of the district?"

In a similar vein, one can use surveys to *test hypotheses* about particular propositions. If it is believed that a particular issue will appeal to a particular subgroup, let's say for example, a particular issue position is most likely to garner support among Catholics, it is necessary to ensure that the survey include a demographic question on religious preference as well as on the issue question. The hypothesis is tested by creating a cross-classification table breaking down the level of support for the issue among the various religious denominations in the constituency. If the hypothesis is correct, then Catholic voters should respond much more positively to this particular issue preference than other religious groups within the constituency. This is the type of information one would seek in order to target particular groups for special appeals.

TYPES OF SURVEYS

For our purposes we can separate political polls into four major types: focus group, benchmark, tracking, and quick-response or "brush fire" polls.

Focus groups are the latest craze on the survey scene. They consist of a small group of respondents "chatting" about their opinions, beliefs, and attitudes for roughly three or four hours. The moderator is instrumental in helping to "pull" information and opinions from the respondents. The data are carefully recorded by the survey team, usually by a video camera. The idea is to sacrifice concerns related to sample size (discussed below) in order to extract more fully the breadth of opinions—to get the flavor and emotion behind each issue. Although focus groups may appear to be simple affairs, in actuality they are quite technical and must be carefully supervised. Fortunately, they are generally less expensive and much quicker to process than traditional random sample polls. They can be undertaken throughout the race but are most widely used in the beginning—to help set the stage for the benchmark poll.

A *benchmark poll* is a major survey, conducted with a large cross section of the appropriate constituency, that is designed to provide baseline measures on the whole variety of information noted above. Prior to beginning a campaign, one is interested in finding out the level of name recognition of the candidate, the distribution of various issue preferences on the topics the candidate wishes to pursue, the level of knowledge of the electorate of various aspects of either the current political situation or actions undertaken by the candidate in the past, and a distribution of the core underlying attitudes, such as partisanship, ideology, and religiosity as well as standard demographic data. This basic information would be used early in the campaign to design campaign strategy and choose questions to be followed in other polls.

Tracking polls can be constructed in a variety of ways, but the fundamental idea is that they are relatively brief, cover a limited range of issues or information, and are administered on a *regular basis* in order to determine trends. One would normally want to track name recognition, candidate support, issue support, the effectiveness of particular types of campaign events, commercials, and so on. Most tracking polls will be conducted as a series of separate samples taken at regular intervals during the campaign. Depending on the funding available and on the significance of the race, these polls might be conducted on a weekly basis, although that level of activity would usually be reserved for presidential contests and gubernatorial or Senate races in large states. A series of separate surveys make it possible to observe change in the overall distribution of preferences in the electorate, but they cannot tell you much about why someone changed.

Another approach to tracking gathers an initial sample of respondents and then reinterviews them at future points during the campaign. This *panel* approach will tell you more about who is changing than successive cross sections, but it is expensive because it is necessary to keep good records on the respondents, and people become bored and quit participating; the very act of repeatedly being interviewed may change the behavior of some people.

A *quick-response poll* is intended to identify the effect of particular campaign events or campaign commercials a very short time after those events have occurred. For example, if your opponent launches a series of attack commercials, then a quick-response poll would be administered to determine the effect of the ads on your position.

CRITERIA FOR HIGH QUALITY SURVEYS

As already noted, this chapter is not designed to help make the reader a pollster, but rather to become a good consumer of polls and survey data. There are many choices to be made in designing a good survey, and a bad choice at any point can produce useless or, even worse, misleading data. This section will cover a wide variety of topics in the process of conducting survey research and will look at each topic from the point of view of you as a consumer of polls for campaign guidance.

What do we mean by good? In our terminology, "good" means that we minimize what is referred to as total survey error. This idea is relatively simple. Let us assume that there is some actual level of support for your candidate; let's say that 55 percent of the public would vote for your candidate. You are going to conduct a survey amongst that public and you want your survey result to be as close to 55 percent as possible. The difficulty you always face in survey research is that you do not know the actual characteristic in the population. If you knew for certain that 55 percent of the electorate supported your candidate, why would you bother to ask the question?

Since we can only estimate desired characteristics of the population, the conceptual problem we confront is making sure that the survey procedures are designed to minimize error because we do understand the sorts of things that produce errors in surveys. We can divide error into three separate pieces: instrument error, measurement error, and sampling error. The total error in a survey, that is the difference between the "real" population proportion and the result of your survey, comprises these three pieces. Although, oddly enough, much of survey research has concentrated on the issue of sampling error, normally it represents only a small portion of the error likely to be found in a survey.

Instrument Error

Unless we are incredibly sloppy in our sampling procedures, instrument error—the way in which we word our questions and the order in which we ask them—is most likely to produce major variations in the perceived distribution of opinion within the public. In a classic piece of research, Howard Schuman and Stanley Presser (1981), repeated a question order experiment originally developed by H. Hyman and P.B. Sheatsley (1950). They found that the results of questions dealing with attitudes toward freedom of the press are significantly altered when the ordering of two questions are switched. Many others have found similar results.

A second major source of instrument error comes from whether an "undecided response" is explicitly invited. The classic example of this is the question, "If you were going to vote today, would you vote for candidate A or candidate B?" The second form of this question is, "If the election were held today, would you vote for candidate A, candidate B, or have you not yet made up your mind?" The addition of the phrase "have you not yet made up your mind" enables the undecided respondent to reply comfortably, "No, I haven't thought about that topic yet." Given that a respondent has agreed to talk to an interviewer, and given that the question presents him or her with only two choices, many respondents feel the appropriate thing to do is to choose from between the two alternatives given. Only individuals with fairly strong egos will volunteer to say, "Look, I haven't made up my mind," ignoring the fact that they were not given the choice of "undecided."

In the first form of the question, we are actually forcing the respondent to choose between A and B. The logic among survey practitioners has been that we want to force an answer to the question because, after all, in the voting booth the only choice is A or B. In reality, there is always a third choice for voter X: not to cast a ballot in a particular race if they have not made up their minds. For top of the ticket races, such as governor or president, close to the time of the election most people will have made a choice between A and B, even if they are not very happy about it, and can answer our question.

Table 7.1 shows an example of this effect from an experiment conducted in the 1990 race for governor of the state of Ohio (Marquette 1991). As shown, there are major differences in the reported vote intention when the question is asked with, and without, the undecided option in the question. In the "not offered" form, George Voinovich appears to lead by 15 points, but only by 6 points in the "offered" form. What is the real lead? To determine that we must consider such questions as the respondent's overall likelihood of voting, whether an initially undecided respondent can indicate a "leaning" preference, public interest in the race, and so on. When the likelihood of voting was factored in for this race, the "offered" form was off by less than 1 point from the actual result, and the "not offered" was off by 3.4 points. This is actually quite an amazing reduction, since such a large proportion of the original sample reported they were undecided.

Measurement Error

In our terminology, "measurement error" refers to the mistakes that are made by interviewers in asking questions or recording respondent answers, or the mistakes made by coders and keypunchers in translating the results of the interview into an electronic form for analysis. A major source of measurement error results from the failure of interviewers to read questions in exactly the same form to every respondent. If interviewers are not well trained, they may read questions with slight wording variations or, in the worst cases, begin asking the questions from memory. The effect of such variations is that, instead of asking one question of all respondents, the poll asks as many different forms of the question as there are individual interviewers. Given the effects of the wording variations demonstrated above, one can grasp the significance of good interviewer training and supervision.

Table 7.1
Response Form Effect on Vote Intention Distribution

	Stated Vote Intention		
Form	Celebrezze	Voinovich	Undecided
Offered	28.1%	34.1%	37.8%
Not Offered	33.7%	48.6%	17.7%

Even if the question is asked properly, and has been answered clearly by the respondent, it is possible for the interviewer to record the answer incorrectly. New processes of computer-assisted interviewing help minimize these types of errors by checking responses as they are entered by the interviewer.

Depending upon how the survey is actually being conducted, another source of measurement error involves the process of coding and transcribing the data for analysis. In pencil and paper administration, interviewers return from making telephone or face-to-face interviews and provide somebody in the central office with a stack of completed interview schedules. Those interview schedules must be entered into a computer for analysis. Any errors occurring at this point will also contribute to total survey error since, even if the interviewers asked well-crafted questions and were thoroughly professional, the data that will actually be analyzed is what the coders and keypunchers place in the computer.

Sampling Error

The third major type of error in a survey is sampling error. Most surveys are actually best described as sample surveys: only a small proportion of the total population is interviewed, and the information gained from the sample is used to infer the opinions of the entire population. Sampling error results from the fact that each sample drawn from a population will produce a slightly different estimate of major characteristics because not everyone is interviewed. In one sample, there might be a few more wealthy individuals than needed; in another, there might be too many young men; and in another, the sun worshipers might be underrepresented.

If the sample is drawn using proper procedures, then the extent of these errors can be calculated and restrictions placed on our error of estimate. In this case, sampling error is perfectly tolerable because the cost savings of sample surveys are so huge compared to attempts to contact an entire population.

The real problem for survey research is those violations of procedure that result in biases in the sample. For example, telephone interviews have an inherent bias because some people do not have telephones, and those people tend to be poorer than average.   Many people have unlisted phone numbers, and depending on the distribution of reasons for nonlisting, sampling from a phone book may introduce a bias. We will cover some of these issues in the section on sampling.

THE INTERVIEW PROCESS

Conducting a reliable survey entails creating an environment in which the interviewers can have a "friendly conversation with a stranger." Interviewers must be trained, and the questionnaire must be designed, so that the respondent is put at ease, his or her interest level is maintained, and the information is collected correctly, but the respondent never feels as if he or she is being interrogated. A good interview is one that ends with the respondents feeling that he or she had an interesting time as a result of the process. In the following sections we will discuss some basic issues to ensure achieving these goals.

Question Design

Researchers have developed a model with four stages to the process of answering a question: comprehension, retrieval, judgment, and response (R. Tourangeau and T. Rasinski, 1988). *Comprehension* means that the respondent has to understand the question as it was administered.   An obvious means of producing a failure to understand is to ask people questions in a language with which they are not familiar. This is not a trivial issue for election campaigns in many areas of the Southwest, with heavy Hispanic populations, or in many inner-city areas of the Northeast where there are large numbers of immigrants whose command of English is minimal at best. In a more general sense it is possible for questions to be worded in a way in which the respondent will simply not be familiar with the terms used, even if they are in English, and therefore they will not comprehend the question in the manner intended.

The second of the four stages, *retrieval*, requires that the respondent search his or her memory until he or she finds appropriate pieces of information that appear to be related to the question as interpreted. For simple questions, such as "How old are you?," the process will be easy because the answer is readily at hand. For questions, such as "Will NAFTA have a positive effect on the American economy?," the retrieval process will range from quite simple, if the respondent does not comprehend "NAFTA" as a category, to quite extensive, if the respondent has developed multiple assertions about the treaty.

Having retrieved the relevant bits of information, the respondent then renders a *judgment* as to which of those pieces of information are most relevant to the question being asked. How does a belief that "Thou shalt not kill" apply to a question about support for capital punishment? Since many different values may be activated by a single question, the respondent judges which values are most germane to the item presented.

In the fourth stage, the respondents present us with their verbal *responses*, selecting from among the categories they were given in the initial question. It is at this stage that problems, such as the unavailability of a "middle" or "no opinion," will arise. If the respondent has no discernible opinion, but we do not provide that option, what is the appropriate response? If we ask a question such as "Do you favor or oppose capital punishment?," what does the respondent who is in favor of capital punishment only for the killing of police and prison guards do?

Based on these four stages, we can create a general definition of the characteristics of a good question. First, a good question should use terms that are within the realm of understanding of the respondent. Obviously the respondent must be able to comprehend the question.

Second, the question should not bias the respondent toward any particular type of answer. What is retrieved from memory is to a significant extent conditioned by the words that we used to frame the question. Certain kinds of concepts will be called to mind when one word is used, and a different set of concepts will be retrieved from memory when a different word is used. Thus any of the terms we use in the question should not predispose the respondent to retrieve particular concepts because we, either deliberately or unintentionally, biased the question. For example, the classically bad gun control question, which asks, "Do you support your constitutional right to keep and bear arms?," predisposes people to answer "Yes" because the term "constitutional right" will normally call forth a whole range of positive images relating to democratic freedoms. If the question you really want answered is whether the respondent is likely to support some restriction on gun ownership, such as registration, limitation on hand guns, or background checks before purchase, then the question phrased in this biased manner will not address the issues at hand.

Third, a good question will ask only one question. It is often the case that in our eagerness to acquire information we load a question up with multiple parts. It is then not clear which part of the question the respondents are actually reacting to when they comprehend the question and retrieve information about it. In this case, they need to render an extra judgment about which part of the question is most relevant in terms of an answer.

Finally, a good question will have a set of response categories that are appropriate to the range of information that we wish to tap. On many issues it is likely that a substantial proportion of respondents will not have thought seriously about the problem. Constructing a question that does not explicitly permit them to reply they "don't know" or that they have "no opinion" results in the creation of what we referred to earlier as a doorstep opinion. The "opinion" is made up on the spot, by retrieving some material that is at least marginally relevant to the question, based on the words we use in the question, but it does not represent an existing opinion and will promptly be forgotten at the end of the interview.

Types of Questions

We can categorize questions by the kinds of material covered in the question. In this regard we normally would think of four major types of questions: information, knowledge, opinion, and self-perception. (Backstrom and Hursh-Cesar 1981)

An *information* question is one in which we can reasonably expect the respondent to have the material readily available, and it has a factual status, for example, standard demographic items like the respondent's age, sex, race, and income. A *knowledge* question is of factual status but may or may not be known to the respondent, for example, who their member of Congress is and to which voting precinct they are assigned. An *opinion* question asks the respondent for a judgment about some object, such as whether they favor or oppose rules requiring exhaust emission checks on automobiles, whether they favor or oppose particular candidates, their attitudes about abortion, and their attitudes about the space shuttle.

Self-perception questions are also opinion questions, but in this case the respondent is the focus of the opinion; for example, "In politics do you normally think of yourself as a Democrat, Republican, or Independent?," or "Do you consider yourself to be a moderate, a liberal, or a conservative?"

We can also classify questions by the form of response requested. Normally we think of items as having either an open or closed response pattern. For an *open* or verbatim response question, we ask the respondent to answer our question in their own words. In the fixed or *closed* form question, we ask the respondent to choose from among a predetermined set of categories. The major difference between the verbatim and fixed response format is that you need to know enough about the topic area under study to produce a set of reasonable categories from which to choose. For example, it is almost impossible to create an exhaustive list of categories that could be presented to the respondent in answer to a question such as, "Right now, what do you believe is the most important problem facing America?" The range of possible replies is so broad that we cannot reasonably create a set of fixed response categories to present to the respondent.

The virtues of fixed response categories are that they are easier for the interviewer to record, they are easier to enter in a data-processing program, and they do not need the additional step of coding the verbatim responses into a format that can be analyzed. The fixed response question has the disadvantage of forcing the respondent to make a judgment as to which category their opinion belongs. It is not at all unusual for a respondent to believe that he or she has been presented with a set of choices that make no sense from his or her normal perspective on the problem at issue.

Questions may also be distinguished by their purpose within the questionnaire. A major category of question, in terms of purpose, is the *filter* question. Recall that our intention is to have a friendly conversation with a stranger. The filter question allows us to control the flow of the interview so that respondents are not placed in uncomfortable situations, and they get a set of succeeding questions that make sense in terms of their answers to prior questions. For example, it would be both disturbing to a respondent and totally irrelevant to our purposes if we were to ask a series of questions about the current marital happiness of someone who reported that they were divorced. Therefore, marital status, which is an information question in terms of its subject matter, and a closed question in terms of its format—such as, "At the current time are you married, widowed, separated, divorced, or never married?"—could also be used as a filter question. Those individuals who reported that they were currently married would receive an appropriate block of follow-up questions regarding marital happiness; everyone else would branch to another appropriate segment of the interview.

A *probe* is a second major type of question based on its use within the questionnaire. For example, let us assume that we asked the question, "In politics, do you normally think of yourself as a Democrat, an Independent, a Republican, or something else?" If the respondent had replied Democrat to the first item, a standard probe would be to ask, "Do you consider yourself a strong or weak Democrat?" In contrast, those individuals who had responded Independent would be probed to see if they considered themselves to be leaning toward one party or the other. In this case, the follow-up questions probe for the intensity of reported self-identification. The basic party identification question is fixed response in format, self-perception in terms of information desired, and used as a filter to determine which probe to use. The probe has the same format, as it is constructed as a self-perception question, with fixed response categories, which ask the respondent to choose whether they are a strong or weak partisan.

Sleeper questions constitute another major category in terms of their purpose in the questionnaire. This question may be constructed in any form and is used to check on the veracity of earlier responses. A classic use of this question is as follows. At some point in the questionnaire, we ask people whether they voted in the most recent election; somewhere else in the questionnaire we ask a sleeper about where their polling place is located. If the respondent is unable to answer our question about polling place location, then it raises some question about whether he or she has in fact voted. Under these circumstances, it would behoove us to remove the individuals whose answers were inconsistent in one analytic step and see whether their reported behavior on other characteristics is markedly different from those individuals who were reported voters and who were able to inform us about their local polling place.

Wording Problems

Let us turn now to a discussion of some common problems in designing questions. We have already alluded to the idea of bias in questions. We may load questions in a variety of ways, for example, using the names of very popular or unpopular figures or groups such as Communists or using the name of a popular president, in order to condition support for a policy. For example, if you asked the question, "Do you support President Clinton's policy on X?", as opposed to "Do you support the government's policy on X?," you would get a higher proportion of respondents saying that they support the policy if Mr. Clinton were popular at the time the question is asked. In the era of the Cold War, any reference to Communist was guaranteed to push the responses to a question in a negative direction.

Remember, the purpose in conducting a poll is to get accurate information about your campaign. If you are not careful, or if your consultants are not careful, in crafting the survey questions, you might as well make up the numbers yourself and forget about paying for the poll. You must avoid questions that are confusing to the respondent. We have already alluded to the difficulty of having two-part or multipart questions because you try to gather so much information at one time that it is not clear what question the respondent is actually answering.

There are a number of simpler wording problems that also create difficulties. One problem is the use of colloquialisms. The use of vernacular or colloquial phrases in a question creates the possibility of differing interpretations within the overall population. A colloquial, or slang, term is "slang" precisely because the term is used in a nonstandard manner in different segments of the population. This will be especially true when terms are age, or ethnically, bound and may mean significantly different things to different groups.

Indefinite terms, for example, the use of "frequently" or "often," present another problem. What does frequently mean? What does several mean? It is always best to make explicit the comparisons or ranges that you wish the respondent to employ.

Complex words present another kind of problem. By complex words we mean either long, standard English words that are difficult for an average respondent to comprehend or apparently simple words that really refer to a complex concept. In examining public policy opinions, we are tempted to use long words because that terminology is employed by experts in the area. The average citizen is not a policy wonk. If you intend to ask questions about environmental politics, use of "the loss of forest land" is preferable to "deforestation." Try to reduce the question to a series of terms that are comprehensible and explain the issue, rather than using a complex term not familiar to most respondents. "Voter" is an example of a simple word that actually represents a complex concept. If you ask someone "Are you a voter?," and he or she replies, "Yes," does that mean that he or she votes in every election, every general election, every presidential election, or once a decade?

Survey Introductions

One of the most crucial parts of the questionnaire is the introduction. The vast majority of refusals to participate in a survey come at the introductory point, that is, within the first few seconds after the respondent answers the telephone. Good sample administration creates an additional complication in that part of the introduction to the survey will also require the administration of respondent selection questions to determine which person in the household is to answer the survey. We will discuss this idea in more detail when we talk about sampling later in this chapter, but you must realize that you will have that constraint in the process of introducing the survey to the person who answers the telephone. A properly constructed introduction to a survey should tell the person who answers the phone what the purpose of the survey is and then lead quickly into the respondent selection items. The interviewer must be trained and the survey instrument must be designed so that it is easy to identify the respondent within the household and get that person to the telephone.

Modes of Administration

While there are three general modes of conducting surveys—face to face, mail, and telephone—the telephone interview has come to dominate political polling. Face-to-face administration occurs when an interviewer actually goes to the home of a selected respondent and conducts an interview with that person. A mail survey consists of either a sample or a blanket mailing to all possible respondents. The third and most frequently used mode of administration in political polling is via the telephone. Telephone interviewing may be conducted from a single location, where the interviews are carefully supervised, or it may be done by interviewers from their homes, depending on the quality of the contractor used for data collection.

Each of the modes of administration have virtues and drawbacks. Face-to-face interviewing usually gives the best results in terms of data quality and the highest level of cooperation; that is, individuals who are contacted are more likely to cooperate with an interview request if it is a face-to-face interview than if it is by mail or telephone. However, face-to-face interviews are very time consuming and expensive: a large staff of interviewers is needed, their travel time must be paid for, and it takes time to conduct interviews with a sufficient sample of respondents. Currently, face-to-face interviewing is largely reserved for academic and government polling on topics of major interest.

Mail surveys have the virtue of being relatively inexpensive, but they generally have quite low response rates unless one mails several waves to selected respondents. Getting a sufficient return for a mass mail survey may take many weeks in order to allow for these multiple contacts. This time frame is generally too slow for campaign work. For political polling, another difficulty with mail surveys is that the respondents have to be functionally literate. This is not always the case with a general population of voters in an election. Depending on the particular constituency in which you are campaigning, you may actually have numerous voters who are not literate enough to read and fill out a mail survey. In addition, since mail surveys depend solely on the respondent's interest in the topic, they tend to produce bimodal distributions. People who are either very much in favor or very much opposed to a topic or a candidate are more likely to return the survey than those with marginal interest. Since you are likely to have less information about the relatively uninterested citizenry, it is very difficult to plan a campaign.

By default then, telephone interviewing has come to dominate political polling. The telephone produces reasonably high rates of response compared to mail surveys, although lower than face-to-face interviews. It is very inexpensive compared to face-to-face interviews and now competitively priced compared to mail surveys. In fact, the growth of telecommunications technology and competition in the telecommunication industry has driven down the cost of telephone surveys as measured by the actual cost of the telephone call per interview.

Computer-Assisted Telephone Interviewing

For large survey houses, the technology of computer-assisted telephone interviewing (CATI) has become increasingly popular. This mode of administration has an interviewer use a personal computer on which the interview schedule or questionnaire is presented to the interviewer one question at a time. As the interviewer records answers from the respondent, the answer is checked to be sure that it is within the range of acceptable answers. Branching to the next question in the interview is controlled by the computer program. Both the control on input validity and branch sequences result in much higher levels of data quality. A good CATI survey should have the same "look and feel" as any other method so far as maintaining rapport with the respondent.

Interviewer Training and Supervision

If you are going to be purchasing your survey work from a commercial house, you need to have some sense of the issues raised in the recruitment and training of interviewers. Our intention is to have you know what kinds of questions to ask so that you can get a sense of the quality of the interviewing being done. Recruiting interviewers is a fairly difficult process. While almost anyone can be taught to read a questionnaire, good interviewers seem to have the intrinsic personality characteristic of really liking to talk to people. Survey directors will run through lots of potential interviewers before they find one who really stands out. In order to find, train, and retain these high-quality interviewers, the firm must be busy enough to keep their interviewers regularly employed. Ask for the average length of employment of the interviewers who work for the firm you are using.

You also need to know the general method of payment for the interviewers since the training and payment process for interviewers really does condition how they perform. Most good survey shops will use a combination of an hourly rate and some kind of incentive for completing interviews. A reward for a high completion rate ensures that the sample that is drawn is properly administered, a point we will return to when we cover sampling. If interviewers are paid solely on the basis of a piecework rate, so much per completed interview, then they have no real incentive to worry about the number of refusals they get or whether they complete appointments with designated respondents; this decreases the quality of data that you receive. Recontacting appointments, working numbers at odd hours in order to contact hard-to-reach respondents, and other sample quality control procedures are at variance with the primary focus of interviewers paid on a piecework basis: completing as many interviews as possible in as short a time as possible.

If you are working with a commercial firm, you need to ask about their interviewer training procedures. You have a right to look at their training materials, get a sense of how long they spend training the interviewers, what kinds of information they provide to them, and what sorts of behavior they expect of the interviewers. In terms of general principles, interviewers should be trained that they are to act like a sponge; in other words, they are a measuring instrument no different than a thermometer. Administering questions to respondents and properly recording those responses are a means of measuring the temperature of the electorate on a particular topic. This means that interviewer behavior should always be neutral and nonreactive. They are not in any sense to condition the responses given by the person they are interviewing. No matter how obnoxious the respondent may be in terms of their beliefs, or their dislike of a particular candidate or policy, it is important that the interviewer be trained to record that information as reliably as possible.

It is important to find out how the survey house supervises the interviewers. Interviewing is, after all, a job and it is necessary to employ quality control procedures. The most useful form of quality control is for supervisors randomly to hook into the telephone circuit with the interviewer and listen to an interview being conducted. The supervisor should be able to follow along with the interview schedule and grade the interviewer in terms of their performance on such factors as reading the question, correctly recording the answers, maintaining neutrality, and so on. A well-run survey firm will keep records on their interviews taken during various random monitoring sessions. Those forms will allow survey directors to grade the interviewers and control the assignment of a base pay rate, or the kinds of tasks an interviewer is allowed to perform. Interviewers with long experience, who perform well on these random checks, would be assigned to the most difficult survey projects. This type of random supervision is also necessary to ensure that the interviews are actually carried out.

It is not at all unheard of for interviewers to fabricate a completed interview. This is most likely to happen if the interviewers do not work from a central facility. Interviewers who work from their homes can easily generate faked interviews. The survey house should have some mode of checking completed interviews, usually by having a supervisor call back random phone numbers at which interviews were supposedly collected and confirming that an interview was actually conducted.

It is much easier to control interviewer behavior from a centralized interviewing facility because random monitoring while an interview is being conducted can ensure that a real interview is actually taking place. To be perfectly blunt, we are not talking about brain surgery. The kinds of people who are usually hired to conduct interviews need to be reasonably well paid, motivated by various incentive schemes, and closely supervised to ensure that the work is well done. If a survey house, with which you are considering contracting, is unwilling to discuss these procedures and allow you to see their operation while interviewing is actually under way, then it would best to look for another firm to do the work for you.

Volunteer Interviewers

In some circumstances, you may find yourself relying on volunteer interviewers. This is generally not a good practice. The amount of time you spend training volunteers is relatively short—usually they want to "get on with the job"—but the reliability of even the best-motivated volunteers is questionable. Volunteers tend to have other things on their agenda, and often they will not show up for scheduled interviewing times. Under these circumstances, you may have a phone bank scheduled that you are not able to staff.

In addition, volunteer interviewers tend to be committed to your candidate. While commitment is a good thing when you are talking about stuffing envelopes, hanging door knockers, or other campaign activities, it is not a good thing when you are collecting data. The enthusiasm of the volunteer tends to influence the quality of the interview process. Even by tone of voice the interviewer may convey to the respondent the desirability of expressing a positive response for the candidate. Since you really want to know the actual distribution of opinion in the constituency, it does not help to have interviewers biasing the sample in favor of your candidate. During the interviewer training process, you can try to impress upon the volunteers the importance of being neutral, but this is usually an uphill battle.

Costs

Telephone survey costs are a function of several factors, chief of which are questionnaire construction, the number of interviews, the length of the interview, and the extent of analysis of the data. If you want very complex questionnaires, you will have to pay for development and pretest time. Long interviews and large samples consume interviewer and supervisor time and, depending on the project scope, long-distance telephone charges. Large samples also require the purchase of many phone numbers. Because questionnaire development and data analysis efforts are independent of the number of interviews conducted, pricing for surveys is not a linear function of the number of completions. The primary difference among local, state, and national telephone surveys comes from long-distance telephone charges and any incentive pay needed to get interviewers to work the odd hours required to cover distant time zones.

Given the variety of options available, you would normally expect to get several different estimates from a survey house, providing costs for questionnaire development, report generation, and several different sample sizes, representing different levels of precision.

WHOM DO WE INTERVIEW?

A *population* is defined as a set of units of analysis subject to specified defining characteristics. That rather complicated definition is intended to determine very precisely who will be interviewed. For example, if you were working for a candidate who has a great deal of money, you may decide that one activity will be a very intensive get-out-the-vote drive toward the end of the campaign. In this case, you would want to interview eligible voters but not necessarily registered voters. Your benchmark poll would be conducted with individuals in the constituency who are eighteen or older, citizens of the United States, residents of the constituency, and not in jail. These individuals are all potentially able to vote. Depending upon the distribution of preferences identified by your benchmark poll, you could identify groups who are sympathetic to your candidate but have low registration rates and then target a registration drive.

Later in the campaign you may pass the deadlines by which an individual can register in your constituency so your population would become registered voters. In this case, your population has the additional defining characteristic of being registered to vote.

Sampling Procedures

A *sample* is any subset of the population. If your population is registered voters, then you would want to sample individuals from that population. From a scientific standpoint, modern polling works because we draw *random* samples from the population. That is, we try to define our selection processes so that each person who is a member of the population has an approximately equal probability of appearing in our sample. If we manage to achieve that goal, the data we collect will be representative of the broader population. The central idea is that we will use data from the sample we collect to make statements about the entire population.

In a gubernatorial race, we might interview 800 individuals out of a population of several million registered voters. Our intention is to get a sense of the opinions, preferences, name recognition levels, and so on of the candidates in the race based on that small sample of 800 individuals. The accuracy of our results is a function of whether this sample has been drawn at random. If it has, the results will be representative of the broader population.

If the sample has been biased, then the data will not be representative and the conclusions we reach will be misleading. We conduct sample surveys because they are cheap and fast. In large constituencies, there might be a population of several million people. Even congressional districts hold roughly 600,000 residents. There is no way to enumerate them—that is, to conduct a census by talking to all of them—because you have neither the time nor the money. Modern survey research based on random sampling procedures provides highly accurate results from very small samples.

It is crucial that the processes leading to the random sample be followed carefully to minimize sampling error. Since sampling error is one component of the total survey error, it is important to know the sampling procedure employed by the survey house you are employing.

For electoral research there are only really two major ways to conduct telephone interviewing. One approach is to use some variant of random digit dialing (RDD).

RDD is a technique that generates sample telephone numbers based on the known set of area codes and exchanges which describe the constituency of interest. In principle you could draw a sample from a telephone book. However, for large constituencies, that approach is prohibitive. In addition most metropolitan areas have high rates of unlisted numbers, as much as 64 percent in some areas. RDD was developed to overcome the problem of high rates of nonlisted telephone numbers.

While it is possible to draw your own sample using RDD, most survey houses now purchase samples from specialized sampling firms such as Survey Sampling, Inc. These commercial sample houses are able to improve the proportion of working numbers compared to pure RDD, and they are able to screen out many business numbers. The higher working phone rate increases the efficiency of the survey process.

For political polling, another approach is to work from registered voter lists. The problem with registered voter lists is the same problem we have with general surveys: many voters' telephone numbers are not listed. Registration lists are frequently out of date, and their quality depends on the effort of government agencies to purge the rolls or make other efforts to keep the rolls current. Since telephone numbers are usually optional on registration forms, many registered voters will not have telephone numbers listed. You may be able to make up for that lack. For example, you may use one of the CD-ROM telephone directories that are now available for personal computers and match the name of the registered voter to a telephone number if the voter has a *listed* telephone number. But, those computerized directories are only as reliable as the telephone directory information on which they are based. Although registration lists are widely used as a basis for conducting political polls, you should be aware that there are substantial risks associated with using this approach.

Sample Size

When we decide on a sample size there are two factors to consider: how tight a bound we wish to place on the error of estimate, and how confident we want to be in that estimate. Table 7.2 presents sample sizes based on the combination of a choice of precision and confidence for seven levels of precision and two levels of confidence, making a most conservative assumption about variance in the population.

Table 7.2
Errors of Estimates in Proportions Using Different Sample Sizes

	Simple Random Sample Sizes	
Bound	*95 %*	*99 %*
+/- 7%	196	339
+/- 6%	267	461
+/- 5%	384	663
+/- 4%	600	1,037
+/- 3%	1,067	1,843
+/- 2%	2,401	4,147
+/- 1%	9,604	16,587

Precision is the error we can reasonably expect in our estimate of a proportion given a specific sample size. Assume we have drawn a sample of 1,067 respondents. If we estimate from our data that 46 percent of the respondents favor position X, then the true proportion in the population will be somewhere between 43 percent and 49 percent, which is just 46 percent plus or minus 3 percent. This estimate will be correct in 95 out of 100 samples we draw (we are 95% confident). A general rule for survey samples is the larger the sample size, the more accurate the result.

Other decisions we do not have space to cover, such as clustering or stratification, also impact the effect of sample size, but for political polling the rule is the bigger the better—within reason. Is it worth the cost to increase the sample size from 600 to 1,200 respondents? These and other questions await the strategy and finance team.

One thing you will note about Table 7.2 is that there is no reference to the size of the population. A sample size of 600 will give you +/- 4 percent precision in 95 out of 100 samples whether you are studying a congressional district, a mayoral race, a U.S. Senate race in California, or the presidential election—*so long as you follow proper sampling procedures.*

Weighting

Even our best efforts in administering surveys may result in a sample that is slightly unrepresentative compared to known demographics in the constituency. For example, we may end up with more women in the sample than we know exist in the constituency, or we might have too few minority respondents, or the sample might have too few people with a college education. It is possible, after the fact, to weight the sample so that it is representative of the major demographic characteristics of the constituency in question. If you are using a commercial firm, you need to ask them whether they use weighting procedures. If they do, you need to discuss what kinds of characteristics they use to weight and what database they use to determine the demographic characteristics of the constituency.

The most frequent reason for needing to weight a sample results from decisions made about how the interviewing process is actually conducted. For example, if you have a short field period and you collect 600 interviews in a day or two, then the likelihood is that the sample will be older and more female because older women will tend to be at home and willing to conduct an interview. If no effort is made to identify and pursue selected respondents within households, it will be necessary to weight the results to a more demographically representative picture of the population. If, on the other hand, you have a longer field period, then you will identify respondents who are not immediately available and need to be pursued by making an appointment via the person who actually answers the telephone. Calling back the household at the appropriate time to complete an interview with the identified respondent may require several efforts over several days. These efforts will gradually produce a sample that becomes younger, more male, and more representative of the population in question. If the survey house you are using normally produces a large number of interviews in a very short period of time, the probability is that their samples are unrepresentative and must be weighted in some form. If you can afford the time, it is best to use a longer field period to get a representative sample from the actual sampling process.

The weighting of interviews to make a sample more representative demographically relies on the idea that, for example, if you have interviewed 250 males and you actually need 340 males for the sample to be demographically representative, the 250 you interviewed can be weighted to be equivalent to the 340 males you should actually have interviewed. That is not really a very comfortable assumption to make; the males that you find at home might be attitudinally different from the males who were more difficult to locate. They might work night jobs, or be employed at multiple part-time jobs, or enjoy carousing on a regular basis. Thus the individuals you did manage to interview are not necessarily representative of the individuals you did not manage to interview. Weighting those that you did contact may be misleading. Although post hoc weighting is widely used, you need to be aware that there may be a problem.

DATA ANALYSIS—WHAT DID WE LEARN?

Frequency Distributions

Okay, so we have done all this stuff—what do we get out of it? Tables 7.3 through 7.6 display a set of questions asked in a 1994 political poll regarding the Senate race in Ohio. The four questions reported in that figure would have been asked in the order in which they appear, with the computer controlling the presentation of the items and the skip patterns. In the item displayed in Table 7.3, respondents were asked how interested they were in the race.

The results for that question appear immediately below the item itself. In this case, 452 individuals said that they were very interested in the race, representing 42.6 percent of all the individuals polled. Those 452 respondents also represent 43.13 percent of those individuals who were polled and were able to answer the question. As you can see at the bottom of the panel, there is a value reported as Don't Know. These respondents were unable or unwilling to answer the item. The thirteen individuals coded as Don't Know constituted 1.23 percent of the entire sample. For most purposes, individuals who are unable to answer the question are removed from further analyses. We want to know the number of individuals unable to answer a question. Generally, if you have a question with a lot of Don't Know responses, you probably have a badly written question.

Table 7.4 presents reported vote preference, and we can see the breakdown of responses to that item immediately below the question. The results of the question indicate that DeWine was well ahead in the race with 43.2 percent of the vote among those individuals who understood the question well enough to answer it.

Table 7.3
Interest Level Question and Frequency Table

In the election for the U.S. Senate, the Democrat Joel Hyatt is running against Republican Mike DeWine and the independent candidate Joe Slovenic.

Would you say that you are very, somewhat, just a little, or not at all interested in this race?

(1) Very (2) Somewhat (3) Little (4) Not at all (9) Don't know

Value Labels	Scale Value	Observed Frequency	Percent of Total	Percent of Non-missing Cases
Very	1	452	42.60	43.13
Somewhat	2	360	33.93	34.35
Little	3	115	10.84	10.97
Not at all	4	121	11.40	11.55
Don't know	9	13	1.23	

VALID CASES: 1,048   MISSING CASES: 13

STATISTICS FOR NON-MISSING CASES

MINIMUM	MODE	MEAN	MEDIAN	MAXIMUM	RANGE
1	1	1.91	1.20	4	3

Table 7.4
Vote Choice Item and Frequency Distribution

If the election were held today would you vote for Mr. Hyatt, Mr. DeWine, Mr. Slovenic, or would you skip this race?

(1) Hyatt (2) DeWine (3) Slovenic (4) Skip
(5) Undecided - IF VOLUNTEERED   (9) Don't know

Value Labels	Scale Value	Observed Frequency	Percent of Total	Percent of Non-missing Cases
Hyatt	1	343	32.33	33.17
DeWine	2	447	42.13	43.23
Slovenic	3	39	3.68	3.77
Skip	4	109	10.27	10.54
Undecided	5	96	9.05	9.28
Don't know	9	27	2.54	

VALID CASES: 1,034   MISSING CASES: 27

STATISTICS FOR NON-MISSING CASES

MINIMUM	MODE	MEAN	MEDIAN	MAXIMUM	RANGE
1	2	2.20	1.39	5	4

In Table 7.5 we have an item that was administered to those individuals who made a choice among the three declared candidates for the race: Hyatt, DeWine, or Slovenic. The question would be filled in by the computer so that the interviewer would have read, "How certain are you to vote for Mr. Hyatt," had the respondent chosen Hyatt in the vote choice question.

Table 7.5
Certainty Probe and Frequency Table

How certain are you to vote for Mr. ?
Very certain, somewhat certain, or not at all certain?
(1) Very certain   (2) Somewhat   (3) Not at all   (9) Don't know

Value Labels	Scale Value	Observed Frequency	Percent of Total	Percent of Non-missing Cases
	-1	232	21.87	
Very certain	1	521	49.10	63.30
Somewhat	2	273	25.73	33.17
Not at all	3	29	2.73	3.52
Don't know	9	6	.57	

VALID CASES: 823   MISSING CASES: 238

STATISTICS FOR NON-MISSING CASES

MINIMUM	MODE	MEAN	MEDIAN	MAXIMUM	RANGE
1	1	1.40	1.00	3	2

Table 7.6
Leaning Question and Frequency Distribution

Are you LEANING toward Mr. Hyatt, Mr. DeWine, or Mr. Slovenic?
(1) Hyatt   (2) DeWine   (3) Slovenic   (4) Undecided   (9) Don't Know

Value Labels	Scale Value	Observed Frequency	Percent of Total	Percent of Non-missing Cases
	-1	856	80.68	
Hyatt	1	34	3.20	20.36
DeWine	2	27	2.54	16.17
Slovenic	3	4	.38	2.40
Undecided	4	102	9.61	61.08
Don't know	9	38	3.58	

VALID CASES: 167   MISSING CASES: 894

STATISTICS FOR NON-MISSING CASES

MINIMUM	MODE	MEAN	MEDIAN	MAXIMUM	RANGE
1	4	3.04	3.18	4	3

Finally, in Table 7.6, we report preferences for those individuals who indicated that they had not yet made up their minds, or were intending to skip the race, and were asked a "leaning" question.

Obviously, those coded as "-1" had already made up their minds, so it is not appropriate to ask them this question. For the purposes of further analyses, the remaining individuals could be apportioned to the respective candidates, depending on our intentions. Note that in this table the proportion of respondents skipped rises to 80.7 percent of all cases. Most individuals had some preference in the initial vote choice question and so branched around this item.

Cross Tabulations and Contingency Tables

A contingency table or cross tabulation displays frequencies of responses to one item within categories of another item. This breakdown allows us to visualize the effect of the second variable on the first. We will illustrate the use of contingency tables with an example on the problem of turnout effects on apparent vote choice.

As we indicated earlier, social desirability is a problem in the interviewing process. Sometimes individuals will give answers because they believe it is the right thing to do; because they agreed to be interviewed they feel they must report an opinion even if they have no opinion on a topic. We raised that issue earlier when we talked about the idea of inviting an "undecided" or "don't know" response. One of the places this shows up is the difficult problem of determining whether someone is actually going to turn out and vote. If you ask people directly whether they intend to vote, many people will reply "yes," because voting is the right thing to do. The determination of likely voters is in and of itself an art form, and we do not have enough time in this chapter to discuss it in detail. However, how interested an individual is in a race is likely to have an influence on whether they will bother to cast a ballot in the race, assuming they go out to vote at all.

Table 7.7 is a cross tabulation of the respondents' reported candidate preference by their report of how interested they were in the election. If we concern ourselves with the column headed "very," we are looking at individuals who said that they were very interested in the race. In that column, DeWine leads Hyatt by a figure of 54 to 35 percent. In the second column are those individuals who reported that they were "somewhat" interested in the race; here Hyatt closes the gap to DeWine by about 35 to 40 percent. For those individuals who say they are only "a little interested." Hyatt appears to lead in the race by 38 to 34 percent.

A majority of the individuals who say that they are "not at all interested" in the race report that they intend to skip the race. Now, in practical terms, the questions become who is really going to vote in the race, and what will be the effect of different levels of turnout? The actual vote cast will comprise individuals from these different interest levels. Given the breakdown reported in Table 7.7, we can conclude that DeWine will be the likely winner, no matter what the actual mix, because he leads strongly in the two largest categories.

Table 7.7
Cross Tabulation of Interest Level by Reported Vote Intention

CONTINGENCY TABLE FOR: SENHEARD;
                          WITH: SENVOTE;
TOTAL N OF CASES =   1,061
VALID CASES =   1,026

SENVOTE   SENHEARD

Value Label		Very 1	Somewhat 2	Little 3	Not at all 4	Actual Marg.	Value Pct.
Hyatt	1 OF	158.0	124.0	43.0	17.0		
	CP	35.35	35.0	38.7	14.9	342	33.3
DeWine	2 OF	242.0	144.0	38.0	21.0		
	CP	54.1	40.7	34.2	18.4	445	43.4
Slovenic	3 OF	18.0	15.0	3.0	3.0		
	CP	4.0	4.2	2.7	2.6	39	3.8
Skip	4 OF	3.0	35.0	11.0	59.0		
	CP	.7	9.9	9.9	51.8	108	10.5
Undecided	5 OF	26.0	36.0	16.0	14.0		
	CP	5.8	10.2	14.4	12.3	92	9.0
Col. Marg.		447	354	111	114		
Col. Pct.		43.6	34.5	10.8	11.1	N= 1026	

NOMINAL LEVEL STATISTICS
2 CELLS WITH EXPECTED FREQ. 5
    CHI SQUARE   DF   SIGNIF
    281.5588   12   .00000

    CRAMERS V   CONT. COEFF   LAMBDA
    .3024   .4640   .1140

By itself, how you chose to handle the question of determining likely voters is a crucial question and must be considered carefully. If you are using a commercial firm, you need to be sure that you have an extensive discussion with the firm about their likely voter screening procedures and how they are going to interpret the outcomes. In general you will want to have several cuts at the data looking, at least, at the candidate's position among those individuals judged to be very likely to vote, somewhat likely to vote, and not at all likely to vote. You will then be able to compare the positions of the candidates under the various likelihood scenarios. In the best of all possible worlds, your candidate is the leader and he or she leads whether you are looking at likely, somewhat likely, or unlikely voters. Heartburn time occurs when you have a slim lead among those people who are judged likely to vote but lose that lead among the "somewhat" and "not at all" likely groups. Then the question of turnout and the carrying power of the ticket above the race you are running matters a great deal.

CONCLUSION

We have covered a wide variety of questions that must be considered in commissioning a good campaign poll. Since you do not know enough to conduct a reliable poll yourself, the most important question you can ask is: Do I trust my pollster? Hiring a polling service is no different than hiring an accountant, lawyer, or direct mail service. If you are not satisfied that the pollster is willing to give you thorough answers to the major questions we have covered, then find someone else. Just as there are good and bad lawyers, there are good and bad pollsters. Get the best you can afford.

Chapter Eight

Developing a Campaign Theme

New-style campaigning in many ways parallels contemporary product marketing. Indeed, much can be learned by studying how products are introduced to consumers. Campaigns are, of course, different than merchandising computers, cars, or soap. Products do not have core beliefs and rarely put their foot in their mouth. But many of the techniques are the same, including the meticulous care given to the development of a theme. On the basis of these thematic messages, products either do well or vanish. Political campaigns are much the same.

Perhaps one of the most entertaining and informative product marketing "wars" of the last several years has been the one between the long-distance telephone carriers. The battle has boiled down to three companies: Sprint, MCI, and AT&T. Each one of these companies uses a different theme in an effort to enlist more users.

For Sprint, the initial argument was that consumers would be better off with their service because the quality was better. For years, television viewers were inundated with pins dropping in front of a telephone receiver, suggesting that the quality of Sprint long distance was so good that you could hear the finest detail. When fiber-optic technology became commonplace, and the other companies could make similar claims, Sprint's theme shifted to "simple savings." While other companies have cost-saving plans, Sprint argued that their service charge was just a dime per minute, certainly an uncomplicated idea. We are never told if this is cheaper, but at least it is easy.

Pursuing a different line, MCI has reminded us of the advantages of collective action and the perils of "going it alone." By themselves, consumers wander through the telephone maze getting lost and taken for a ride. By joining a group of like-minded consumers—"friends and family"—protection and savings can be found. Of course, in order to find the way out of the woods, others must be convinced to do the same. Big savings await, we are told, but others must also join before the harvest can begin. Whether or not this campaign is ultimately successful, those who conceptualized it should be congratulated for their cleverness.

These themes created a dilemma for the market pacesetter, AT&T. Apparently, it was not possible to match their competitors' low-ball prices, even if they could expand their consumer base, so another theme had to be developed. The first attempt was a not-so-subtle claim that the other companies were underhanded and could not be trusted. As for supposedly big savings, AT&T prompted consumers to "get it in writing." But after the other companies began to do so, the argument seemed moot. (In fact, it may have even backfired.)

Recently they have shifted to a surprisingly simple message. In one television commercial, a middle-aged women is standing in front of her parlor windows talking on the telephone and gazing out. On the sidewalk is the woman's young boy looking anxiously for someone to play with. She is saying that the move had gone well and her son would soon find new friends. The hardest part, however, would be that she would no longer have her best friend (the caller) to talk with. Not to despair, AT&T will be there to bring them together whenever they wish!

American Telephone and Telegraph has conceivably one of the largest marketing operations in the world. The executives who work on it must surely be considered the best in their field—relying upon state-of-the-art techniques to devise their message. And what is their theme in the war among long-distance carriers? An implied notion is that AT&T is like a good friend, always there when needed. Precisely why consumers choose one product over another is complex—much like one's vote choice. Apparently, tapping "feel good" emotions is as powerful an allure as rational decisions regarding the costs or simplicity of service. On the other hand, maybe AT&T chose the only option available.

This short detour into product marketing is illustrative of the pages to follow. This brief chapter confronts the development and use of a campaign theme. A carefully devised theme is the core rationale for choosing one candidate and rejecting the other(s). It is one of the most important decisions a campaign team will make. Races based on an inappropriate theme, the blending of several unrelated themes, or haphazardly skipping from one theme to another generally fail to attract voters. As senior Republican consultant, Joseph Napolitan, notes, "The candidate has a better chance of winning with the right message and mediocre production than he (she) has with brilliant production communicating the wrong message" (1986, 17).

Unlike many of the topics discussed thus far in this book, choosing the right theme is far from a mechanical process—in fact, it is quite the opposite. As will be seen, selecting the right theme represents the blending of numerous components and is yet another way in which modern campaigning is an art form.

WHY HAVE A CAMPAIGN THEME?

It is a serious mistake to assume that voters are paying close attention to your election, or any election. This is particularly true for lower level offices, such as state legislative or municipal. Voters simply have too much to worry about—not the least of which are their families, careers, entertainment, bills, and what's on the tube that night. Even the most experienced consultants are sometimes lulled into thinking, because they live and breathe their campaigns, that voters are paying close attention. Additionally, at the end of the election period, when all kinds of appeals are being made, it is even harder to get voters to take a look at the candidate's message.

A second item to understand is that voters tend to make rational decisions, but are cognitive misers: decisions regarding the best way to achieve their goals are rationally planned, not pulled out of thin air. Means and ends are weighted, and behavior is adjusted accordingly. With regard to elections, voters seek candidates who suit their ends. This does not mean, however, that they sit around the kitchen table studying the positions of the candidates, sorting out which will work best. Rather, voters seek *cognitive shortcuts* that help them make a rational choice with limited effort.

For a long time, partisanship was the shortcut of choice. By simply discerning each candidate's party label, the voter could match this information with their own affiliation and ideology and make a sufficiently informed choice. So long as the candidate adhered to most of the tenants of the party, little more was needed. But, as partisanship began to wane as a meaningful tool by the 1970s (see Wattenberg 1990), voters were left with making their choice irrationally (choosing based on no information), finding out more about each candidate, or seeking new time-saving devices. Scholars, principally Mayhew (1974b), Ferejohn (1977), and Cover (1977), suggest that incumbency stepped in to fill this vacuum. Though it is difficult to test empirically, Mayhew writes, "A logic suggests itself. Voters dissatisfied with party cues could be reaching for any other cues that are available...incumbency is readily at hand" (1974b, 313). Conceivably, it is argued, the shift from partisan cues to incumbency helps explain high reelection rates.

The limits of this line of reasoning are, nevertheless, also apparent. For starters, by implication, voters pay scant attention to a candidate's qualifications, the issues, the national trends, or a host of other forces that may pull them toward a challenger. This perspective demands, as noted by Linda Fowler, "a level of pessimism about democracy that is difficult to accept" (1993, 79). It minimizes the importance of retrospective evaluations of incumbent performances, as outlined in the preceding chapter, and presupposes that weak identifiers and independents are more inclined to support incumbents than are strong partisans, which does not appear to be the case (Kerhbiel and Wright 1983).

Another likely explanation is that voters seek concise messages that explain what the candidate stands for and then relates this information to their own ends. For some voters, party-based appeals might still work; for others, incumbency could be the cue. For still many others, a host of other messages might be more effective.

This suggests the importance of a theme. It is the foremost characteristic that clarifies why the voters should support a particular candidate. It is an easy way for voters to make an informed choice. As Joel Bradshaw notes,

It is the single, central idea that the campaign communicates to voters to sum up the candidate's connection with the voters and their concerns and the contrast between your candidate and the opponent. It answers the question: Why should your candidate be elected? (1995, 42)

If the candidate is a member of majority party in a heavily partisan area, party-based appeals might be the key. If the candidate is the incumbent and voters are found to fancy experience, this could be the theme. An issue or set of issues could be merged to create a powerful theme as well. The important point is that voters do not have the time or inclination to sort through various candidate appeals—how they stand on each and every issue. Yet, voters are not irrational nor do they pull information out of thin air. Many seek limited information that helps them match their concerns with the candidate best able to address them. A carefully constructed theme serves as just such a cognitive link.

Another way of thinking about the importance of a campaign theme is to consider what occurs without one. Often candidates will forgo the development of theme, believing that voters will somehow pull together their policy stands, like fitting pieces to a puzzle. They provide voters with the ingredients for a cake but do not mix them together or bake it. Nevertheless, few voters have the time or energy to do this—and the ones who do, tend to *confirm* the choice they have already made. Whether provided for them or not, most voters will look for a cost-saving cue. Without a theme guiding the message, statements often crisscross, cross, and contradict one another, leaving the voter confused. For example, often novice candidates will make an appeal to "change" but later on highlight their "experience." The voter is left confused and more likely turned off. It is only natural to assume that, if voters cannot *easily* discern what a candidate is all about, they will be more receptive to candidates who do offer such cognitive shortcuts. This is particularly true for nonpartisan or swing voters—precisely the ones who often decide the outcome of elections.

This does not mean to suggest that campaigns are all "fluff", or that issues do not play a role. As seen below, issues are critically important, but they must be presented in such a way that they are consistent with the overall theme.

SELECTING AND IMPLEMENTING A CAMPAIGN THEME

As simple as the logic behind campaign themes may be, the construction and implementation of one is no easy task. At its core, a theme is the merging of voter concerns with elements of the campaign context. Put a bit differently, an appropriate theme is a combination of what the voters want, what the candidate has to offer, what the opponent has to offer, and other relevant contextual issues. Voter concerns are derived from polling data and, to some extent, some contextual elements, such as demographic research. What each candidate brings to the table is determined, of course, from opposition and candidate research. With this said, there are several additional elements to consider.[1]

It is imperative to understand that "what the voters want" is often ambiguous. The benchmark poll, discussed in Chapter 7, may indicate numerous issues and concerns that stand out, with the foremost being noted by just 25 percent of the respondents. There is also a big difference between concerns that are prompted and those that stand on their own. For example, when Americans are asked if abortion rights are an important issue, nine out of ten generally suggest it is. But when asked, "What is the most important issue facing the nation?," abortion rarely comes up. We might say that abortion is on the minds of voters when prompted, but it is not at the forefront of their worries.

The task of the theme development team is to draw from survey research and other indicators, such as past voting trends and demographic research, a message that best summarizes voter concerns. Themes should be *inclusive*. That is to say, what the voters want may be very diverse, and the task is to get to the heart of their distress. Similarly, one's candidate's qualifications may be multifaceted. In most instances, it would be a mistake, for example, to bill a candidate only as the "environmental leader" even though concerns about pollution are apparent and the candidate is well suited to deal with them. Such a choice does not incorporate the interests of other voters. A better option might be to push a more general theme, like "a candidate concerned about the future." Here other salient issues can be fitted into the overarching message.

Another example would be pertinent if the polling data suggest that voters favor stiffer penalties for criminals and more cops on the street. Instead of being the "tough on crime candidate," perhaps a better tactic would be to be the candidate for "a safer community." What the fear of crime suggests, at its core, is the feeling that one is not safe in the community. To make an area secure, numerous changes could be sought—including more cops and tougher sentences for criminals. But it might also mean a better educational system, promotion of family values, reforming the court system, investing in housing and infrastructure improvements, and so on. Broad themes can incorporate several related ideas, thereby appealing to more voters.

One should also understand the difference between *positional* and *valence* issues (Salmore and Salmore 1989, 112–113). Positional issues have defined sides. Should American troops be sent to Bosnia? Is welfare the responsibility of state governments or the federal government? How should health care be reformed? Valence issues are concerns about which everyone can agree, for example, a strong national defense, decreased crime, the elimination of pollution, the creation of jobs, trustfulness, and leadership. Obviously, campaign themes should, whenever possible, be centered on valence issues. Positional themes oust all those voters on the "other side" of the issue. Conversely, valence-based themes can be more inclusive.

Obviously, when one issue engulfs the concerns of nearly all of the voters in the district, a theme narrowly tied to it is proper. We might label such concerns *referenda issues* (Salmore and Salmore 1989, 113). In many cities, voters are being asked to "invest" in the acquisition of a professional sports team. Often this means footing a massive bill for building a new arena or stadium to be paid for with future taxes or user fees. Even though successful sports teams can mean big money for a city and its businesses, leading to more jobs, supporting one can also mean less revenue for roads, bridges, and schools. Needless to say, this issue can divide a city, forcing candidates for city posts to run nearly exclusively on one side or the other.

Careful attention should be paid to the *office sought* and the *candidate's status*. As outlined in Chapter 3, voters may well expect different things from different candidates for different offices. Candidates for executive posts—such as governors, county executives, or mayors—might wish to focus on leadership and competence. Rather than merely responding to the needs of particular interests, they are expected to lead the state or city government forward. Candidates for legislative posts, on the other hand, might make more hay out of stressing their ability to deliver along with their constituent services. Even U.S. Senators, once expected to stress foreign and national policy, are today resorting to service-based themes. New York's junior Senator, Al D'Amato ("Senator Pothole") is a good example.

Incumbents face more restrictions when developing a theme than do challengers. Judith Trent and Robert Friedenberg suggest that candidate status is a key element in developing a candidate style—an important, yet overlooked, element in an overall communications strategy (1991, 63–68). For one, by definition, incumbents cannot stress messages related to "change" or they will be out of a job. More likely, themes such as "stay the course" or "getting the job done" must be used. They can use the symbolic trappings of the office: strength, integrity, competency, and legitimacy. They also have a record to which they can draw attention, but from which they cannot hide. Instead of attempting to push a theme that is inconsistent with their record, simply because the voters are concerned, it is much wiser for them to find positive aspects of the record. Incumbents can generally amass a "record of accomplishment," no matter how ineffective they might be in office.

In one sense, challengers have a more open slate when it comes to choosing a theme—they do not have a record that limits its selection. However, they must convince voters to *change* their voting behavior. In other words, it is nearly always necessary to contrast the challenger's qualifications with the incumbent's—some would say to attack the incumbent (Trent and Friedenberg 1991, 78–85). As scholars Barbara and Stephen Salmore note: "Most challengers must simultaneously erode the favorable reputation of the incumbent and build a positive case for themselves" (1989, 128). Without a contrasting element, voters have little impetus to "change the course."

As noted in Chapter 3, *national trends* must also be considered. Even though crime may not appear to be a serious issue in your district, it is a "hot" political button in the 1990s. Government "downsizing" is another national trend of late, and candidates who stress bigger and better government, regardless of the ideological leanings of their electorate, will have a long row to hoe. Of course, the state of the economy and the popularity of the president should have a bearing on theme selection. If the president is doing poorly, as Bill Clinton appeared to be doing in the 1994 midterm election, candidates of the other party can turn this to their advantage. Congressmen Jack Brooks (D-Tex.) was defeated in his reelection bid in 1994, in part, because his opponent was able to link him to "Clinton's liberal team."

The theme should be *simple* and easy to understand. Voters are much more likely to tap easily distinguishable cues, than they are complex ones. Messages such as honesty, integrity, experience, concern, change, working hard, family values, and other valence issues are easily understood and have almost universally positive meanings. It takes little effort, for instance, to appreciate what "honesty" implies. In his successful 1990 challenge for the Minnesota U.S. Senate seat, Paul Wellstone developed a straightforward theme: "A man of ordinary means." This was in subtle contrast to his opponent, who was exceedingly wealthy and ready to spend $6 million on the race. As most voters are also of ordinary means, Wellstone's theme was easily understood.

The best themes are often the most *emotional* ones. It should convey a sense of urgency. Throughout an election, voters will be bombarded with candidate appeals. The ones that stick often tap an emotional cord. Jimmy Carter's 1976 message, "I will not lie to you," was of this sort, in light of the Watergate scandal that proceeded it.

Themes should, whenever possible, be *contrasting*. The greatest area of candidate strength is often the opponent's weakest. When possible, the theme might serve to pull voters to one candidate while pushing them from the other. In a 1992 Georgia U.S. Senate race, Paul Coverdale successfully portrayed himself as like most Georgians, while painting his opponent as an extremist. In one powerful television spot, an elderly woman tells voters that Coverdale is "like us," while Wych Fowler the opponent "is just like Ted Kennedy." This theme was easy, emotional, and certainly contrasting.

A critical, yet often overlooked, element in the development of a theme is the *core beliefs of the candidate*. Many candidates run for office because some issue or issues compel them to do so. Devising a theme that does not incorporate these convictions will generally backfire because the candidate will necessarily resort to them during the race. When this occurs, the candidate's message will seem either insincere or, at the very least, unfocused.

Finally, an important element to consider when merging the concerns of voters, the candidate's qualifications, and the opponent's background into a theme, is that the end result must be *credible*. Although voters may not spend a large amount of time thinking about elections, they are also not fools. Outlandish themes are quickly discarded as unacceptable. In 1992 Patty Murray successfully ran for Congress as an outsider to politics, even though she had served several years in the state legislature. You might say her theme bordered on the "creditability limit." Murray won the election, but even her own consultant admitted afterward that most candidates are not so lucky (Shea and Brooks 1995).

Implementation

If a carefully constructed theme can prove so powerful a tool, why not develop and implement several at the same time? By now it should be apparent that only one campaign theme should be developed. "Theme is not a word that should have an 's' on the end" (Bradshaw 1995, 42). The whole idea behind a theme is to provide voters with a cognitive shortcut. If there are many paths to choose from, the voter will either head down several, only to become confused, or refrain from taking the journey altogether. The theme is the core reason why a candidate should be elected, and if it is the foremost reason, it should rarely change.

Once the contours of the theme has been established, it is necessary to formulate a *thematic statement*. This should be a simple, clearly worded answer as to why voters should select a particular candidate. Once this is done, a shortened version should be fashioned, termed the *thematic tag*. If the answer to the first query is "because the opponent represents the issues and policies of the past, and our candidate represents the future," the tag might be "looking forward, not back!" Devising a thematic statement and tag is often an arduous task, and one should not expect to do it quickly. Remember, this core message will guide what information the voters receive from your campaign.

To be effective, the theme must be repeated frequently. In a sense, once the cue begins to take hold, repetition serves to reinforce its effect. Each time it is conveyed, the message is fortified. Product market specialists have long been keen to the power of repetition. Regardless of the exact content of the spot, Coke always lets us know that it is "the real thing." Everyone knows Pepsi is "the choice of the next generation" and that Chevy trucks are built "like a rock." This does not mean a tag should be found in every candidate appeal, only that it should be repeated often.

BRINGING THE PIECES TOGETHER:
THE CASE OF LEE FISHER AND BETTY MONTGOMERY

To conclude this chapter on the importance of developing a theme and sticking by it during the course of the campaign, an illustration is offered. It occurred in the 1994 Ohio attorney general's race, between Republican Betty Montgomery and Democrat Lee Fisher.

Montgomery certainly faced an uphill battle. Fisher was the incumbent and by most counts considered the only "safe" Democrat in the state that year. On top of this, he had amassed scores of endorsements, a massive war chest, and five times the early name recognition, and he was far ahead in the polls. Montgomery's base of support was the northwest corner of the state, generally considered a Democratic stronghold. She had never run for a statewide post, and few pundits gave her much of a chance of success.

Knowing that the fight would be a hard one and that voter interests would be strained among scores of other races that year, the Montgomery team sought the appropriate theme. They carefully examined survey research for the concerns of the voters, what Fisher had to offer, and what their candidate would bring to the table. The result was a simple, yet powerful, message that echoed loudly throughout the race.

Through opposition research it was found that, although Fisher was a practicing attorney before he entered public office and had led the state's highest law office for four years, he had never tried a criminal case. As odd as it may seem, to most insiders it made perfect sense. The Attorney General's Office tries thousands of cases each year, utilizing the services of numerous assistants and deputies. Few would expect the attorney general, the head administrator of the agency, to try a case personally. To the Montgomery team, however, this carried little weight. The "facts" were that the highest law officer in the state of Ohio had never tried a criminal case.

Montgomery, on the other hand, was a former criminal prosecutor for Wood County. It was her job to try criminal cases and, in fact, she had done so for eleven years. Her success rate was not perfect, but it was solid. Most important, she knew her way around a criminal trial courtroom, unlike her opponent.

It was also found that the voters in Ohio, like most voters in 1994, were concerned with crime and the deficiencies of the court system. In poll after poll voters scoffed at "the system" for not being tough on criminals and making their communities safe.

The disparity between Fisher's and Montgomery's criminal prosecution experience, and the concerns of the voters about crime, were pulled together. Their theme statement became: The voters are concerned about crime, and while Montgomery has real experience putting criminals away, Fisher has little. The thematic tag was "make a criminal prosecutor attorney general."

The campaign proceeded to pound this message home. Along with a solid direct-mail program, they moved ahead with scores of television spots. These commercials began by highlighting the need to do something about crime. After letting viewers know she understood their fears about crime, Montgomery highlighted her experience. In one spot, a set of mug shots flashed across the screen while the announcer spoke, "There are a lot of people who won't be voting for Betty Montgomery—the convicted felons she put away as criminal prosecutor." At the end of each spot, Montgomery was featured in a courtroom, looking straight into the camera. "Lee Fisher has never tried a criminal case. If we're really serious about crime, we need a criminal prosecutor as attorney general." This message was flashed across the screen and repeated by the announcer: "Betty Montgomery. Make a criminal prosecutor attorney general."

As the message began to take hold and Montgomery started her ascent in the polls, Fisher responded with perhaps the only course he had, minimizing his lack of experience by discrediting her background. One commercial highlighted Montgomery's plea bargain of a "child molester." The message was that she was soft on even the most wicked criminals. The Montgomery team was ready and immediately counterattacked. The very same day the Fisher ad was aired, Montgomery responded with a spot containing the following:

Lee Fisher says Betty Montgomery let a child molester off easy. Lee Fisher is wrong. No prosecutor was tougher on child abusers than Betty Montgomery. She formed the Child Prosecution Abuse SWAT Team. But Lee Fisher has never even tried a criminal case. Betty Montgomery. Make a criminal prosecutor attorney general.[2]

A second counterattack was even more powerful. It was a comparative ad that asked voters to look at the "facts." Several topics were addressed, each related to the core Montgomery theme. Regarding the number of criminal prosecutions: Montgomery 2,000, Fisher 0. On the years of criminal court experience: Montgomery 11, Fisher 0. And concerning the number of murder cases personally won: Montgomery 100 percent, Fisher 0. After this rather stark comparison, Montgomery was again featured in the courtroom, reiterating the tag of "making a criminal prosecutor attorney general."

A number of forces might have propelled Montgomery into the Attorney General's Office in 1994. Clearly a Republican tide was sweeping the nation and Democrats were taking a pounding across Ohio. There was also an antiestablishment sentiment, and Fisher was a consummate "insider." But many believe that her dramatic upset was the result of a carefully constructed theme that allowed voters quickly and easily to distinguish why she was a better candidate. Voters wanted something done about crime; Montgomery had real experience, and Fisher did not. Sometimes good campaigns are just that simple.

NOTES

1. This list in some ways parallels Joel Bradshaw's (1995, 43) discussion of theme characteristics, and Salmore and Salmore's review of "what shapes a campaign theme" (1989, 126–135).

2. This narrative was transcribed by the author from a marketing "case study" distributed by Wilson Communications, the firm that ran the Montgomery campaign in 1994.

Chapter Nine

Devising a Campaign Strategy

By all indications, the odds were stacked against Milton Marks in his 1992 reelection bid to the California State Senate. Voters in his San Francisco district, and for that matter the nation, were disheartened with "business as usual" and anxious to oust career politicians. Only a few months before, San Francisco Mayor Art Agnos felt the wrath of voter discontent when he was asked to find another line of work. Having served in the state legislature for over thirty years, Marks made an inviting new target.

Marks had been arrested (but not convicted) of drunk driving a few years before, and he had been rated near the bottom of a list of "effective" senators by a leading California political magazine. In the previous session he had missed 838 votes, and he was part of a leadership team in the Senate in which three of his colleagues were found guilty of corruption. On top of all this, his health was rumored to be poor, and redistricting had placed his home outside the district boundaries—adding 30,000 new voters to the electorate (Sheingold 1993, 40; Clarence Johnson 1992).

Early polling indicated that his support was tenuous, even though party enrollment was in his favor. The strongest aspect of Marks' record was seen as his ability to bring projects to the district. (Having served in the majority party for most of his career, his pork-barrel record was impressive.) He had served long enough, it was deemed, to be linked with many of the positive changes in the Bay City. Moreover, a solid portion of the voters were liberal and had little problem with Marks' pro-environment, pro–civil rights, and pro–civil liberties record. His opponent, former San Francisco District Attorney Joe Freitas, on the other hand, had high negatives; he had, among other things, bungled a high-profile murder case some years earlier.

It was agreed that Marks' theme should be that he represented the compassionate, progressive side of government. San Francisco residents should be proud of their city, and Marks represented many of the reasons why. He was a San Franciscan to the core!

As to who should receive this message, polling data, demographics, and prior electoral information highlighted several key Democratic areas. Solid Republican neighborhoods were cut from the pile. With regard to resources, because of his numerous contacts in state and city government, Marks could count on a large war chest (overall he raised $650,000). He could expect strong support from the state and city Democratic organizations and some assistance from local organizations —particularly gay rights groups. The candidate, however, because of his age (seventy-one), was unable to do much campaigning.

The first full wave of communications was sent over the television airways eight weeks before the election. The first sixty-second spot was termed "Nostalgia." The goal was to link Marks to Bay Area pride and to appeal to the city's strong Democratic roots. The spot incorporated news footage of local residents, home movies of Marks playing with his children when they were young, Bobby Kennedy in 1968, the 49ers, Willie Mays, Chinatown, and a gay pride parade. The piece concluded with Marks saying: "A lot has happened in the Bay Area over the last thirty years. And our future might be pretty interesting too." This "feel-good" ad was in sharp contrast to Freitas' theme that the city was falling apart (Clarence Johnson 1992; Sheingold 1993, 41).

The second wave was more targeted. An aggressive telemarketing and direct-mail campaign was put together, and the most liberal sections of the city were selected as bull's-eyes. In one mailer a map was drawn and voters were asked to "take a look at the `Marks of achievement.'" Dozens of specific accomplishments, tailored to each community the mailing was sent, were highlighted by an "X." (The caption read: "X Marks the Spot.") According to consultant Larry Sheingold, the literature was a perfect follow-up to the "Nostalgia" spot (1993, 41). Other mailers touted his strong environmental and civil liberties records.

In the end, the election was a blowout. Marks received 83,144 votes; Freitas, 33,024. The key to his success, notes Sheingold, was that "the Marks campaign had a communications plan and made it work" (1993, 41). They had bucked a powerful anti-incumbent tide and a strong challenger by carefully calculating and implementing a strategic plan.

A BRIEF HISTORY OF CAMPAIGN STRATEGIES

In the early days of campaigning, before the rise of television, sophisticated polling, and high-priced consultants, choice of strategy was a simple matter. Candidates ran for office as part of a larger ticket, and their success depended upon voter affinity toward that party. There were significant advantages to linking one's fate in such a way, including party resources and operatives. Campaigns were often a foregone conclusion; if the candidate were a member of the favored party, he or she would generally win. The converse was also true. About the only time the outcome was uncertain was when the partisan division in the electorate was roughly equal. But even so, the strategy used during this period was party based.

Things had begun to change by the 1970s. For one, a declining number of voters used party identification as a cue or even conceptually tied themselves to a party label (Wattenberg 1990). Voters began to use issues and candidates to make up their minds (Nie, Verba, and Petrocik 1976), causing, among other things, less predictable outcomes. Much related, party organizations were providing fewer campaign services, especially in a relative sense as special-interest groups (political action committees) flooded the campaign arena. Changes in election laws allowed candidates to seek party nominations without the blessing of party leaders (Broder 1971). Polling let them know precisely what was on the minds of voters and consultants; trained in product marketing, they began using their talents in the political arena (Dinkin 1989). Added on top of this, television allowed voters to "see candidates in the flesh with no mediating influences—not through the lens of party workers" (Salmore and Salmore 1989, 43).

Not surprisingly, campaign strategies changed just as quickly. In the simplest terms, candidates began centering their races around issues (especially those that mattered to most voters), personality characteristics, and image, or the interplay of contextual elements and style. As the fortunes of candidates moved from the umbrella of the party, questions surrounding different strategies were brought to the fore. The party-based approach was occasionally used, but only in areas where partisanship appeared to be an overwhelming force, which was increasingly rare.

Unfortunately, while strategy decisions have become increasingly important and complex, there are no cookbook recipes for what works and what does not. A review of the literature on modern campaigning suggests little agreement on what strategies are and what they might provide. Perhaps because the term is vague, and can mean different things to different people, it is even common to hear a consultant provide unique views as to what "strategy" implies. For some it is the core message, for others it is the allocation of resources or an appropriate style, and for still others it centers around when campaign activities should take place. Here it is argued that strategy is the prudent consideration of several key elements. This chapter is designed to overview these elements and to provide tips on how they might be merged into a winning plan.

WHAT IS A CAMPAIGN STRATEGY?

Simply put, a campaign strategy is a blueprint for winning an election. As noted in Chapter 1, campaigns are about communicating a message to voters in an effort to persuade them. This does not mean simply putting one's finger to the wind and, when a breeze is detected, begin looking for votes. Random, unfocused approaches are rarely successful. Just as with any other aspect of modern campaigning, meticulous care must be given to strategy.

There are five components of a campaign strategy: determining which voters in the electorate to approach, creating the message to communicate, obtaining necessary resources, timing the activities, and tactics.[1] Each will be discussed below.

Which Voters to Approach

By now it should be clear that a wise campaign will not attempt to reach all the voters in the electorate. Far too many candidates head out for a day of campaigning by simply selecting a populated area, or one that is geographically close. We know from Chapter 5 that the number of voters heading to the polls will vary from community to community, and that areas less populated might indeed have more voters. We know that in some areas Democrats never stand a chance, while in others they always win; the outcome in these areas is generally "fixed." We also know that in some districts, labeled swing areas, there is considerable variance in outcome. From our prior electoral targeting, these areas can be labeled, in the broadest sense, either for us, against us, or swing. A logical query is what is the appropriate mix for a strategic plan?

The answer to this question is, "It depends." There are three possible goals of campaign communication: to *reinforce, persuade*, or *convert*. To reinforce, we simply convince voters to do what they are inclined to do anyway. Persuasion is a process of moving undecided or "leaning" voters to your side, and conversion implies an attempt to get voters to do what they are *not* inclined to do on their own. Which approach will be used depends on the standing disposition of the electorate.

It is obviously easier to reinforce or persuade voters than it is to convert them. In some instances, such as when the candidate is a member of a heavily favored party, the entire focus might be on reinforcement. We might label this a partisan-based strategy, where the objective is to get party voters to the polls. In electorally volatile areas, where neither candidate has an edge at the outset, persuading voters would be the name of the game. If we find that most voters are inclined to vote for the opponent, some conversion is necessary. In many instances, such as when a challenger takes on a popular incumbent, unless a degree of conversion takes place, the candidate stands no chance of success. Because incumbents are generally popular and conversion is so difficult, few challengers win.

If elections are a struggle to get a majority of votes, does it not make sense to approach all the electorate? In other words, do not campaigns stand a better chance of getting 50 percent plus one from a larger pool of voters than from a smaller one? If the appeal does not work, what harm can it do—they were not going to vote for us anyway? Why not think of the entire electorate as "undecided" and go about helping them make their decision?

There are two reasons why new-style campaigns rarely attempt to communicate with the entire electorate. First, there are always finite resources in a campaign, and it makes sense to use them where they might do the most good. As noted, it is much easier (cost effective) to reinforce and persuade than it is to convert. By utilizing the same resources on each group of voters, a campaign might, for example, persuade ten to every one converted. In instances where the campaign is a long shot, it may be cost effective to forgo reinforcement altogether in order to persuade and convert the required number of voters.

Second, and perhaps more to the point, campaigning in areas where there is little chance of success can do more harm than good. Optimistically, we might hope that voters in these areas pay no attention to the race and forget to vote. This may be more likely when there is little activity drumming up interest. On the other hand, if voters in these areas receive literature, greet volunteers on their doorsteps, and hear radio and television advertisements, they may be drawn into the race and be more inclined to vote. Heavy campaigning in these areas might lead voters to believe that "their candidate" (your opponent) is in trouble and therefore not only should they vote, but they should send a contribution and volunteer to help at the campaign headquarters. It is often said, and novice consultants should take it to heart, that the best approach is often to "let sleeping dogs lie."

Consultant Joel Bradshaw suggests that one of the best ways to decide what portion of the voters in each group to approach is to conceive of the electorate on a continuum, where the extreme left side represents your strongest supporters, the center area denotes swing voters, and the right side represents those solidly in the opponent's camp(1995, 31–33). Making this determination for the entire group of likely voters is somewhat of a conjecture; we do not know how each individual will vote on election day. Nevertheless, with careful research, we can know some information about each voter and a good deal about each election district, county, or neighborhood. We might, for example, use voter registration lists to note voters enrolled in our candidate's party as favorable, those in the other party as unfavorable, and independents as undecided. This is a bit simplistic, but it should be recalled that party identification is still the best single predictor of voting habits. Yet we can take several additional steps by examining prior election data (including careful attention to turnout, party performance, and electoral volatility), demographics, geography, other contextual information, and survey findings. All this information will help make a determination as to the strong, weak, and swing areas of the district.

The size of each segment is therefore different for every race and every district. The goal of the strategists is to know the extent of these groupings overall, and where each can be found throughout the district. This information is used to create an overall "target group"—the voters to be approached.

Three examples of voter predisposition and the corresponding target groups are noted below. Figure 9.1 illustrates a campaign in which the candidate is in good shape. It is perhaps a highly partisan area where the candidate is a member of the majority party. It could be that our candidate is the incumbent or is exceedingly popular from another public office. In any event, the odds appear to be in his or her favor. The goal in this race should be to reinforce those already in the candidate's camp and to persuade a portion—perhaps 30 to 40 percent—of the undecided. It is not necessary to convert a single voter in order to win.

There was little question as to which portion of the electorate Jesse Jackson, Jr.(D) should target in his 1995 special election to fill Illinois' 2nd Congressional District. African Americans make up more than two-thirds of the district, which extends from Chicago's South Side, to the suburbs in the southern part of Cook County (Benenson 1995, 3836). On top of this, party enrollment roughly paralleled demographics, with the inner-city areas overwhelmingly Democratic and the suburbs solidly Republican. The campaign targeted only those voters in the city. On election day, Jackson won a whopping 98 percent in the inner-city precincts, and 51 percent of the suburban vote. This was enough to give him a 3 to 1 plurality overall (Dick Johnson 1995, B17).

Figure 9.2 presents a less certain outcome. This race, at least at the beginning, appears to be a toss-up. An appropriate strategy might be to reinforce all of the voters we already have, persuade the undecided group, and convert some in the "against" camp. The campaign does not need any of the against group to win, but if some criteria can be used to discern who in this group is more likely to be converted than others, we might extol some effort here and feel a bit more secure. It should be assumed that the opponent has an excellent campaign staff—one that has devised a strategy based upon the same view of the electorate. They will fight hard for the undecided as well. If we approach only our voters and the undecided, and the opponent is slightly better at winning votes from the latter, the race will be lost. Although it may be difficult to do, winning some voters from the against group may offset any deficit with the undecided. This does not mean *all* the voters in the against group should be targeted, rather only the "best of the worst."

Figure 9.3 presents a discouraging scenario. Here the chips are stacked against victory, as more than 50 percent of the voters are projected to vote for the opponent. We have little choice but to attempt to convert a large portion. Things appear so bleak that we must shift resources from reinforcement to persuasion and conversion. In other words, because the election is a long shot, it is necessary to take it for granted that most of "our" voters will stick with us, and no time or resources will be spent in these areas—save for a last minute get-out-the-vote drive. Unless a significant number of voters can be converted, the race is lost. If possible, an attempt should be made to sort out those in the against camp, excluding areas where we have a near zero chance of conversion.

The target group, therefore, is the voters to be approached during the campaign. This is based upon the electorate's predisposition and where your candidate stacks up given this information. Deciding which voters should be included and which should be left out is a difficult task, and great care should be given to it. But once this determination is made, it is imperative that the campaign not engage in midcourse second-guessing. Moreover, everyone in the campaign, including the candidate, must adhere to this decision. It is common during the heat of the campaign to have "concerned" volunteers and party activists call the headquarters to complain that their community has not seen any campaign activity. "Gosh," one might say, "we haven't seen any sign of the campaign whatsoever." No one wishes to have their community left out of a campaign, so care should be taken when answering these inquiries. The best approach is to explain the constraints of time and money and assure the concerned citizen that his or her community is important and that the campaign will do the best to "get down there for a visit."

Figure 9.1
A Favorable Electoral Predisposition

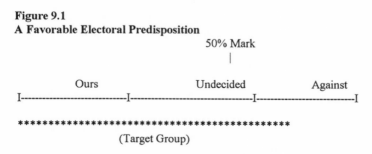

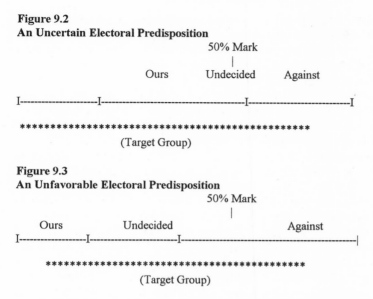

Figure 9.2
An Uncertain Electoral Predisposition

Figure 9.3
An Unfavorable Electoral Predisposition

Unfortunately, candidates who wish to meet all the voters in the district are often the worst offenders. In one especially close state house race in upstate New York, a candidate disappeared for an entire day. Neither the candidate's spouse nor members of the team could find him until late in the afternoon when he arrived at the headquarters, worn-out from a long day on the campaign trail. When asked why he had not appeared at predetermined areas and events, he commented that it had occurred to him that morning that the voters in a small town, in a far-off corner of the district, had not had a chance to meet him during the race. So he had spent the day walking door to door, visiting in diners, and "waving to folks on the corner." What the candidate failed to understand was that the town was a "shoe-in" for the opponent and that he had probably kicked up the turnout in the area. On election day, he lost by 186 votes, out of nearly 40,000 cast.

Finally, as noted in several chapters below, certain types of campaign activities are much easier to target than others. For example, direct mail is one of the most controlled; radio and television, on the other hand, are less tight. When precise adherence to the target group is needed, activities should be selected accordingly. The important point is that the target group is the intended audience for all campaign activities.

What Message to Communicate?

The selection of the message is just as important as deciding who should receive it. There are two possibilities when considering a message. The first is the overall theme, discussed in Chapter 8. As noted, the theme is carefully crafted from what the voters want, what your candidate has to offer, and what the opponent brings to the table. It is imperative that the voters in the target group be repetitiously exposed to the theme. "If you stick to it, and say it often enough, you will define the criteria for the voters that they should use to make their choice" (Bradshaw 1995, 44). Or, as Denise Baer writes, "A campaign strategy...is designed to bring the campaign theme to life in the persona of the candidate" (1995, 51).

An important element of the overall theme is the communication style. There are three broad possibilities. An incumbent-based style is one in which the symbolic trappings of the office are used to denote the candidate's strength, competence, and integrity. A challenger-based style is nearly always centered around change. Here a comparative element must be incorporated. A third possibility is a mix of the two, in which the advantages of each are used whenever appropriate (Trent and Friedenberg 1991).

Political novice Peter Hoekstra stunned the Washington establishment by knocking off the chair of the National Republican Congressional Committee, Guy Vander Jagt (R-Mich.), in a 1992 primary contest. On a shoestring budget, Hoekstra pounded home the theme that it was time for a change and that Vander Jagt was a career politician, more interested in national affairs than in the voters back home. Even when Hoekstra appeared in a parade this message was echoed: his mode of transportation was a 1966 Nash Rambler, made the year Vander Jagt was first elected. The sign on the car read, "Isn't it time for a change?" (Morris and Gamache 1994, 116).

Many pundents were also surprised in 1995 when Jesse Jackson, Jr. turned his youth (thirty years) and inexperience into a powerful message. Throughout the campaign, he cast his age as an advantage, arguing that he was "young enough to stay long enough" in Congress to reap some of the fruits of Washington for his constituents (Dick Johnson 1995). This message, along with careful audience considerations, seemed to work with the voters.

The second possibility is a message designed to reach a specific subgroup of the target audience. The goal of a campaign is to find and push the right button for the right voter. Demographic research and polling data may tell us, for instance, that college-educated women are particularly concerned about environmental issues and that blue-collar men under the age of twenty-five are concerned about job opportunities. Targeted messages, highlighting the candidate's stand on these topics, should be communicated to these subgroups of voters. Treating all voters in the target group as one and the same is a grave mistake. Astute care should be given to finding the concerns of each voter, if possible, and pushing his or her button.

A strategic blueprint, therefore, should incorporate the repetitive use of the theme, as well as the particularized communication of specific messages to subgroups of voters.

In 1994 Bob Barr ousted a ten-year incumbent in Georgia's 10th Congressional District. His successful strategy was a clear example of theme repetition, while at the same time highlighting the specific concerns of subgroups. Barr's opponent, Buddy Darden, was painted as out of step with average voters in the district because of his support for several Clinton initiatives. The voters were told again and again that Darden was "too liberal." To reinforce this theme, specific illustrations were pulled from Darden's record and conveyed to various groups of voters. For instance, Darden had voted for the 1993 Crime Bill, which, among other things, restricted the sale of certain assault rifles. Mailings were sent to gun owners throughout the district stating that Darden was unconcerned about protecting their rights to bear arms—just another symptom of his disdain for the wishes of the voters back home. In the end, voters sensed that Darden had gone adrift in Washington, and most had a concrete example with which to back it up.

A Resource Assessment

Although the campaign may have taken great care to select a target audience and hone a message, reaching voters is often easier said than done. A complete strategy blueprint must pay careful attention to resources because, without them, there can be no communication with voters. When conducting a resource assessment, there are three items to weigh: resources needed to reach the target group, expected available resources, and the projected resources available to the opponent.

It is perhaps *not* an oversimplification to say "the more the better" when considering necessary resources. Repetition is the name of the game, and the more assets on tap, the more often the voters will hear the message. At the same time, however, not all races or districts are created equally. There are several criteria to keep in mind. One factor is the level of the race and, much related, the size of the electorate. U.S. Senate and gubernatorial elections confront statewide electorates, and even in smaller states (population), there are simply a great number of voters to reach. Congressional seats contain roughly 300,000 registered voters, and many state senate seats boast over 100,000. There is tremendous variability in state house electorates, ranging from a few thousand voters to over 100,000. Municipal races are, of course, generally smaller, but even countywide districts can contain millions of voters. Accordingly, the first factor to consider when estimating the resources needed is the size of the electorate.

The geographical size of the district is also important. In some ways it costs more to run an election in spread-out districts, than it does in condensed ones. In the latter, one or two carefully placed billboards might reach 60 to 70 percent of the voters; in rural areas, this is not possible. It is also easier to canvas in urban and suburban areas, than it is in farm country. Just driving through a large district can chew up valuable time and resources. On the other hand, urban districts may be only a part of a much larger media market, thereby making it exceedingly expensive to use electronic media. It is simply too expensive for a state house candidate in New York City to buy radio or television time.

Another item to bear in mind is that political norms and traditions vary from district to district. In some areas, voters expect a certain type of campaigning, such as the candidate's walking from door to door or erecting massive yard-sign displays, and in others they might be accustomed to billboards or frequent radio commercials. In still others it might be deemed "showy" or "too much" to use television commercials for a particular office. In brief, it is a mistake to assume that all electorates expect the same thing during campaigns; knowledge of these differences is helpful when assessing resource requirements.

As to what resources will be available, money should be the foremost consideration. Hoekstra was able to unseat Vander Jagt with less than $50,000, but such instances are exceedingly rare. There is little debate that money is the mother's milk of politics. In most congressional races, for example, incumbents generally raise and spend over $1.5 million, and competitive challengers spend nearly $1 million (Morris and Gamache 1994). State legislative posts are becoming similarly expensive (Shea 1995a). While much of the importance of money and how it might be raised will be discussed in Chapter 10, it is enough to note that there is a strong, albeit imperfect, relationship between a candidate's war chest and his chances on election day. It simply takes money to communicate a message. This correlation is stronger for high-level offices, such as U.S. Senate, gubernatorial, and U.S. House campaigns, but this is also true in state and local races.

Estimating precisely how much money a campaign will collect is a somewhat tenuous chore, but some parameters can be gauged. For example, the sum raised by the candidate or his predecessor in prior campaigns is often a good indicator of future fund-raising success. Whether or not the candidate (or his family) will be able to contribute a large sum of cash will help, as will the extent of interest groups and party organization attention to the race. Another simple indicator is whether the district is affluent. In some areas, $1,000 per plate fund-raisers are common; in others, $100 per plate is more the norm. In short, numerous indicators suggest the parameters of the campaign war chest.

With that said, there are several other potential resources to consider. Whether the candidate will have time to campaign is significant. In some instances, the candidate will campaign full-time throughout the summer and fall; in others, they will do so only in the evenings or on the weekends. The candidate's knowledge, energy, and communication styles can also be important resources. If he or she is willing to "walk door to door from dawn to dusk," this can be a tremendous boost. On the other hand, candidates unwilling or unable to pound the pavement can present a hurdle. If great time and care are necessary to sharpen a candidate's knowledge of the issues, as opposed to one that is "ready to go," this too can be an important consideration. Will the candidate's spouse and family lend a hand?

If the candidate has solid name recognition throughout the district at the outset, good relations with the media, and a record of achievement, then he or she has a stockpile of important resources. On the other hand, a shortage in any of these areas should be considered, generally speaking, an impediment. A campaign that can bypass the cognition stage and move directly to the affect stage is surely at an advantage. This, in part, explains the tremendous boost incumbents get—and consequently their high rate of reelection.

Volunteer and in-kind assistance can constitute an important resource. Candidates strapped for cash can sometimes make up for it with hoards of volunteers. Possibly the campaign cannot afford to mail literature, but it can harness dozens of volunteers to drop it off on doorsteps. They may not have enough money to run radio or television spots, but a volunteer telephone operation could get the message out just as effectively. In many instances, a helpful business or law firm will contribute office resources, such as photocopying or the use of telephones at night.

The expected level of party and interest group assistance is an important consideration. In some areas viable party organizations can carry much of the campaign banner, but in others there is only a skeleton committee. Interest groups and associations, such as labor unions and business organizations, can be quite supportive in some districts. Once again, a good way of predicting the level of auxiliary organization involvement is by looking at what has been done in the past.

Carefully assessing the potential resources available to your campaign is only half of the story. It is imperative to consider the resources the opponent might be able to garner. It is not necessary to go "dollar for dollar" with the opponent, but at the same time the prospects of being outspent four to one should be considered daunting. If the opponent is an incumbent, he or she brings to the race significant resources unrelated to his or her war chest, as noted above. Will, for instance, the opponent have to spend resources on cognition, or is it well known that he is running for the office? Will he or she get a hand from party organizations, labor unions, business groups, or any other interest? Will the opponent be able to bring in prominent public officials and celebrities? An exact estimate is not needed, nor should the campaign be geared solely by the fortunes of the opponent. Rather, knowledge of what cards the opponent has in his or her hand will help a campaign strategy. It will also aid in the development of a plan, well in advance, for overcoming any resource deficit.

Patty Murray's (D-Wash.) successful bid to the U.S. Senate in 1992 is a superb illustration of how a campaign can overcome a resource deficit through planning and a carefully executed strategy. Murray surprised the political establishment when she declared her candidacy; she was considered far too green for such a job, having served only one term in the state senate and a few years on her local school board. She was virtually unknown, and her opponents, in both the primary and general elections, were better known, much better financed, and certainly more experienced. Murray's strategy team, the Campaign Design Group, paid close attention to what she had to offer and what the voters wanted (Fairbank 1993).

Their strategy was to portray Murray as a "symbol of a citizen legislator—fighting for a change on behalf of average working families" (Fairbank 1993, 44). They were able to turn her lack of resources into a positive. A particularly powerful television spot satirized the image of a state legislator who told Murray earlier in her career, "You can't make a difference, you're just a mom in tennis shoes." During the final stretch, when Murray was gaining in the polls, her opponent chose to attack by arguing that she was too inexperienced and that electing her would be too risky. This, of course, only helped reinforce the average-citizen, middle-class background image Murray sought to represent. "The contest between outsider and insider favored her because it matched the voters' mood" (Bradshaw 1995, 39). She was outspent two to one, but defeated her general election opponent by nearly ten percentage points.

Timing

Few topics dominate strategy sessions more than issues related to timing. When should the candidate announce? When should the benchmark proceed? Do we attack early or late in the campaign? When should the radio ads be aired, and what about the direct mail? When should he or she begin walking door to door? These and untold other decisions await the strategy team. Added to this maze of choices, there is little consensus among consultants regarding the timing choices; much of it is up to the knowledge and intuition of the strategy team.

There is, at the very least, agreement among consultants that, during any election, voter attitudes go through three distinct phases: *cognition, affect,* and *evaluation* (Salmore and Salmore 1989, 13–14). Cognition is the level at which voters become aware that a candidate is running. We might term this "simple name identification" or raw recognition. The affect phase occurs when voters develop opinions about the candidates. Often this is a simple calculation, based on party affiliation, gender, incumbency, or a host of other cues. For some voters, it is a complex process that requires a good bit of examination. Evaluation occurs when voters make their final decision. For some voters, each of the phases may merge within a split second; for others, it may take some time, perhaps completed only when in the voting booth. Either way, each phase must take place—one cannot be skipped.

Campaign strategists must understand the phase their candidate is in at the outset and plan accordingly (Guzzetta 1987; Salmore and Salmore 1989). For example, a candidate cannot offer the reasons why he or she is better than the opponent before the voters know he or she is running. Raw name recognition must precede thematic and issue messages. Because he understood the importance of first achieving name recognition, Oregon U.S. Senate candidate Gordon Smith (R) flooded the television airways with ads early in his 1996 special election campaign, even though it temporarily depleted his treasury (Gruenwald 1995). In some campaigns, particularly those for lower level posts, the first phase is not well achieved until late in the campaign—if at all. Consultants Ron Brown and Nello Giorgetti go so far as to suggest that

for nine out of ten campaigns for local professional offices, the message is the candidate's name—repeated endlessly as election day draws near. It's more important to place the candidate's name before the voter, than a discussion of the office itself. (Brown and Giorgetti 1992, 51)

In high-profile races, the shift from cognition to affect can begin early on, thereby allowing for the discussion of issues and other thematic messages.

Beyond these broad considerations, scores of other timing decisions should be studied, including when money should be raised. Incumbents make it well known that they are running for reelection and thus have little difficulty raising funds throughout their term. Challengers face a more difficult dilemma. Early money is critically important; it not only allows the campaign to get a jump start on the incumbent, and therefore minimize a name-recognition deficit, but it also attracts more money. It is a truism in politics that successful politicians are popular politicians. The same is true for fund-raising efforts; successful ones lead to other successful ones. However, early fund-raisers run the risk of lackluster success because the race is too distant and few would-be contributors are thinking one or two years in advance. They can be a waste of resources and can suggest the campaign is in trouble—just the opposite of the bandwagon effect.

Careful consideration should be made to the timing of resource distribution. Few dispute that many campaigns are often won and lost during the final week. There is even some scholarly evidence to suggest that as much as 15 percent of the voters make up their minds during the final few days (Shea 1995b). Notwithstanding, this is also the period when scores of other candidates are vying for voter attention, and the airways are filled with candidate appeals. It is also possible that a large number of voters simply "zone-out" campaigns during this period as a reaction to an overload. Would it not be wiser to spend resources and communicate the message when others are not doing so—perhaps months before the election? After all, 85 percent of the voters make up their minds well ahead of election day. The fear of running out of resources during the final stretch, however, sends shudders up the spines of most strategists.

Another topic that occupies considerable time at the strategy roundtable is candidate definition. To many, it is deemed essential to "define" your candidate to the voters, and not allow the opponent to do so. Put a bit differently, when voters have no information about the candidate, they are believed to be susceptible to the first information they hear—not unlike an empty sponge. And there does appear to be some research to suggest that communications are most likely to be effective when there is an absence of "a nexus of mediating factors" (Whillock 1991, 9, citing Klapper 1960, 8) and that voters pay more attention to messages that reflect their preexisting views (Diamond and Bates 1992). If the sponge is to be filled, why not with information provided by the campaign? Conversely, would it not be advantageous to define the opponent before he or she defines himself or herself? Discussion regarding candidate definition leads to speculation about when the opponent will open fire and when a preemptive strike should occur. Campaigns should not peak too early, but neither should they be tardy in defining their candidate.

One of the hottest recent debates relates to the timing of attack ads. Most challengers, for example, attack from the beginning in order to unseat an incumbent. Should incumbents sit idly by, knowing the attack is coming? Campaign communications scholar Marilyn Roberts suggests, "Incumbents can no longer ignore attacks. What we may see in the years ahead is a growing number of incumbents attacking challengers right from the get-go" (Shea and Brooks 1995, 23). Consultant Gary Nordlinger sees little choice for challengers: "Challengers only have one-fourth the money that incumbents have, so they need to concentrate on the sleeping giants." This, of course, means attacking early and attacking often (Shea and Brooks 1995, 23). Yet still other professionals suggest that a candidate's creditability must be established before attacks are effective (Whillock 1991). Without the weight of a valid source behind it, charges may not stick—especially in today's political environment where charges and countercharges are thrown around like confetti during a parade.

Clearly, this is only the tip of the iceberg when it comes to timing decisions. The strategy blueprint should incorporate only the larger concerns, leaving second-tier decisions for when issues arise. The goal is to know when the campaign will move from one stage to another.

Tactics

The final piece of the strategy puzzle is the appropriate mix of voter contact techniques. How a campaign goes about conveying its message is often undervalued. In the early days, rallies and interpersonal communications were the mainstay. Party activists simply pounded on doors and twisted arms. By the turn of the century, print became the dominate mode of communicating with voters, and, of course, of late it is the electronic media. But there are scores of possibilities and no campaign relies upon just one. Many will seem suitable at first glance but, on careful inspection, be deemed unfit for one reason or another.

A majority of the remainder of this book speaks to the use and misuse of numerous voter contact tactics. For purposes at hand, it may be enough to note that political communication falls into two broad categories: *direct* and *indirect*. Direct voter contact methods are those in which the candidate or another member of the campaign personally contacts the voter. Some possibilities are door-to-door canvas, events, rallies, and greetings outside the voter's place of work, such as a factory gate. We might even place telemarketing in this category if the calling is being done by local volunteers, instead of out-of-town professionals.

The foremost advantage of direct voter contact is that it is effective. The best way to win a vote is to have the candidate ask for it (Whillock 1991, 78). Closely behind are personal appeals from the candidate's spouse, family, and friends, followed by local volunteers. It is interesting that, with all the changes and mind-boggling technology that now defines new-style campaigning, the best way to win a person's vote is the old-fashioned way—to ask for it personally. This type of campaigning is inexpensive and highly targeted; you can send the candidate and volunteers into a very specific part of the district and even regulate which houses to approach. Resources do include the candidate's time, but, at the very least, direct contact techniques cost few dollars. In addition, when a candidate walks door to door or stands at a factory gate at 6:00 a.m., a theme centered around "caring," "one of us," or "a voice for the people" is reinforced. If a candidate never gets out to meet average folks, it's hard to say that he or she is "just like all of us."

A drawback of direct voter contact is that, although it is effective, reaching a large number of voters is difficult, relatively speaking. It simply takes time to talk to people and ask for their votes. Even the most aggressive direct contact program can be surpassed, in terms of people contacted, with just one television commercial. Interpersonal campaigning is especially difficult where the electorate is large, such as in statewide races. It also ties up the candidate's time when other activities, such as fund-raising or meeting the press, may be pressing.

Indirect tactics convey a message impersonally or through someone detached from the campaign. It can be divided into paid and earned media. As for *paid media*, the list includes television commercials and radio spots; billboards, posters, bumper stickers, and other outdoor advertisements; paid newspaper advertisements; direct mail; video cassettes; literature drops; and professional telemarketing. *Earned media* means the coverage of a campaign issue, event, or development by the news media. It can be conveyed over the airways (radio and television news) or in print (newspaper and magazine news).

The advantages of paid media are that they are timely, extensive, controlled, and targeted. That is to say, the right message is carried to the right person quickly and on a massive scale. Direct mail, for instance, is perhaps the most narrowly targeted indirect communications medium. It can deliver a precise message to a precise list of voters in a brief period. By paying close attention to the time of day and format, even radio and television spots can be targeted to a particular group of voters. More important, they can transmit the campaign's message to thousands of households instantly. Outdoor advertising is a bit less targeted, but it too can be restricted to certain routes and neighborhoods.

As for the type of message, paid media can fall into four categories: positive themes, negative messages, comparisons, and responses. "The kind of message a candidate sends is affected by the stage of the campaign, the status of the candidate, and the competitiveness of the race" (Salmore and Salmore 1989, 145). Paid media, as such, afford the campaign considerable leeway, and it is no surprise that most rely heavily on it.

It is not without its drawbacks. For one, it is expensive. The cost of radio and television commercials alone can place a massive strain on the campaign treasury—drawing resources from all other activities. In turn, it places a premium on fund-raising. We might say that campaigns that rely solely on paid media are slaves to fund-raising and live or die based upon their success. Second, although a far greater number of voters are contacted, paid media tactics are less effective per voter. In fact, paid advertisements are rarely productive unless they are repeated several times. If the campaign was interested in converting, persuading, or even reinforcing a voter, direct contact would be deemed far more effective than indirect techniques.

Media consultants would argue, nevertheless, that campaigns are generally not interested in reaching one or even one hundred voters. Instead, tens of thousands of voters must be contacted in a short period. Although indirect tactics are less effective per voter, it is the only way to reach a vast number of voters. It may be expensive and somewhat ineffectual, they argue, but one television spot can reach more voters than a team of volunteers in a year of canvasing.

There are tremendous benefits to earned media. For starters, it is inexpensive and far reaching. A press conference or news release costs the campaign nominal resources, but if it is picked up, thousands of voters throughout the district are exposed to it. Getting the candidate on the 6:00 p.m. local news is very useful. Earned media is also seen as more creditable. That is, voters seem to place more stock in messages received through the media, than they do if the message comes directly from the campaign. A newspaper article or headline is simply believed more quickly than a piece of direct mail or a radio advertisement.

The principal negative of earned media is that it is uncontrollable. As will be seen in Chapter 12, luring the media to an event or sending off a release does not, in any way, imply they will cover the topic as the campaign would like. In his 1992 reelection race, George Bush invited the press along on a trip to the supermarket. The Bush team envisioned coverage of the president shopping, suggesting a "down-home," "average-guy" persona. But when the president marveled over the technology that allows cashiers to move an item over the counter, without punching the price into a cash register, things backfired. The headlines the next day revealed that George Bush had never before seen a supermarket scanner, which supported Clinton's claim that he was out of touch with average Americans. Earned media can backfire.

Second, it is never a sure thing that the media will cover an event or story at all. For numerous reasons, the press may shun all campaign stories or your candidate. Finally, it is difficult to target earned media. Other than media market considerations and subscriptions patterns, there is no way to put one message in the eyes of some voters and keep it out of the eyes of others.

This brief overview of voter contact techniques only scratches the surface of decisions the strategy team must face. As noted above, most campaigns use a mix of each. With that said, the strategic blueprint should provide, in modest detail, the ways in which the campaign will reach voters. Financial considerations are certainly a big part of this calculation, but other issues, such as the message (can it be stated well in a thirty-second spot?), media market, your place in the polls, norms and traditions of the area, your candidate's status, the office sought, and many other contextual concerns, must be included.

Pulling the Pieces Together

Even the most seasoned consultant can find the job of pulling together the five aforementioned pieces into a coherent, comprehensive strategy daunting. There are no tricks or shortcuts. It is a difficult and time-consuming task, and as Napolitan suggests, it should be undertaken by "the best political minds in the campaign" (1986, 21).

In the end, the campaign strategy should be able to answer the following questions:

- Who is the target audience?
- What is the message?
- What resources are needed to reach the target audience?
- When will the target audience be reached?
- How will the audience be reached?

Once each of these questions can be answered, a strategy statement should be put in writing. This serves two purposes. First, it helps the strategy team see how all the pieces of the puzzle fit together. It helps bring *both* the forest and the trees into clear focus. Second, a strategy statement provides for easy reference during the heat of the campaign. This may help to bring the campaign back on line or to reassure members of the team, including the candidate, that certain steps are necessary and have been carefully planned.

SOME PARTING TIPS

To conclude the chapter, some tips on implementing strategy are given below. These suggestions, as well as the entire chapter, should not be considered a recipe for success, but rather ingredients to consider.

A sound strategy, suggests Napolitan (1986), must be compatible with the candidate. Unless the candidate is comfortable with the blueprint for reaching voters, the end result can be disastrous. Strategic plans often imply difficult choices, including where, when, and how the campaign will take place. If the candidate is not enthusiastic about these decisions, hostility and second-guessing can occur later. Much related, everyone else in the campaign must strictly adhere to the strategy as well. "One of the worst things that can happen is to have a campaign go off in several different directions simultaneously" (Napolitan 1986, 27). New-style campaigns consist of a set of well-coordinated maneuvers. When activities occur when and where they are not supposed to, and when the wrong message is being conveyed, the machine falls apart. It may even be a good idea to consult the candidate's spouse as to why certain decisions were made.

Careful attention should be paid to message consistency. Throughout the campaign different messages, all related to the core theme, will be conveyed. It is imperative that messages overlap as little as possible. If, for instance, the campaign is interested in pursuing a pro-environment track during a given week, all communications during this period should reinforce an environmental theme. When the radio spots concern consumer protection, the mail should discuss consumer protection, just as the earned media should be talking about consumer protection. Overlap, to a degree, is inevitable. Yet the strategy team should bear in mind that with overlap comes message diffusion and often outright confusion.

While paid and earned media often serve different purposes, they can also complement each another. Earned media coverage is rare, but extensive and creditable. Accordingly, one possibility is to use it to commence a message period, then paid media to reinforce it. This is particularly effective when a press event draws focus to an attack on the opponent. Paid media, in essence, bolster notions planted in the minds of voters through the press. It is also quite common to use paid media to highlight an unforseen development in the press, such as an opponent mishap or an endorsement.

It is also important, suggests consultant Mark Weaver, "to predict the counter-attack and be ready—because it will come" (Shea and Brooks 1995, 29). Sound strategies not only contemplate what the campaign will do and when, but make informed forecasts of what the opponent will do. For example, if the candidate has a glitch in his record—one that could cause serious damage—perhaps it is wise to preempt the attack by addressing the issue early. It is conceivable that the voters and the media will tire of the issue well before the heat of the campaign.

Once the strategy has been agreed upon by the management team and the candidate, it should be considered permanent. These blueprints are not written in stone, but neither are they transient givings. The only reason to alter strategy significantly is when at least one of the aforementioned elements changes drastically. For instance, if fund-raising is vastly more or less successful than anticipated, some strategy revision might be in order. If the opponent moves in an entirely unanticipated direction, some elements of the game plan could be revised. If the strategy is well thought out, there is no reason not to have faith; it should be given time to work. Unless the strategy is considered permanent, players in the management team, including the candidate, are far too likely to become anxious and second-guess the plan as the campaign progresses. Identical to putting together a campaign strategy, only the best minds of the team should alter it.

It was indeed a surprise to most observers when Jerry Estruth's (D) strategy to pin opponent Tom Campbell (R) with House Speaker Newt Gingrich backfired in his attempt to capture California's 15th Congressional District in a 1995 special election. The charge put Campbell on the defensive, but it also drew national media attention to the race, which, in turn, greatly aided Campbell's fund-raising efforts. In all, Campbell raised $1.5 million—four times the expected budget. This was enough to alter their strategy and allow the campaign, after careful deliberation, to move aggressively into the Bay Area media market (Greenblatt 1995).

If the candidate is running for reelection, or has run for other offices, it is wise not to follow the same strategy year after year. Because it has worked in the past, there is no reason to think it will work in the future. It should also be assumed that the opposition has carefully studied how the past campaigns were conducted and will begin to anticipate similarities. According to GOP bigwig Ed Brookover, "There's nothing more pleasing, from the point of view of a strategist, than to work against an incumbent who runs the same campaign again and again" (Shea and Brooks 1995, 43).

Finally, strategy teams should not be afraid to go out on a limb and take a chance. Unless the odds are overwhelmingly in your favor, defensive strategies are often losing strategies. Voters are bombarded with candidate appeals, and new ways of reaching them are outdated quickly. A wise strategist never rests on past glories but is always looking ahead to new and improved game plans.

NOTE

1. This list parallels Whillock's discussion of "Available Means of Persuasion" (1991, Part 2).

Part Three

VOTER CONTACT TECHNIQUES

Chapter Ten

Fund-raising Strategy, Tactics, and Tips

Many were shocked by the outcome of Ohio's 1994 gubernatorial election. George Voinovich, the incumbent, was popular, well regarded by the media, and had a massive war chest—leading most to speculate that he would win. He not only won, but produced one of the biggest landslides in Buckeye State history. His opponent, State Senator Robert Burch, garnered just 28 percent of the vote. For students of modern campaigning, there are lessons to learn from the blowout, and several relate to fund-raising.

Voinovich benefited from one of the strongest axioms in American politics: popular candidates are well funded, and the more resources they have, the more popular they are—thus more likely they are to win. Voinovich certainly fit the bill and when no prominent Democrat was willing to forge a challenge, the odds of his victory seemed even brighter. His fund-raising machine when into high gear.

In April before the election a dinner was held at the New Albany Country Club—part of the 4,000-acre luxury housing development of billionaire clothier Leslie H. Wexner. The price of admission was $25,000 per couple, which netted hundreds of thousands (Lane, 1994b). Voinovich's war chest mushroomed to nearly $2 million. A "birthday party" was then implemented in July. The cost was only $57 per person in honor of the governor's fifty-seventh birthday, but for those wishing to contribute more, a $1,000 per couple gathering was held before the event (Lane, 1994a). The money kept rolling in, and by the fall the incumbent had on tap $7 million. Three individuals—Leslie H. Wexner, the owner of The Limited; Richard Jacobs, the Cleveland Indians owner; and Wayne Boich, a Steubenville coal mine operator—each gave six times the opponent's entire budget (Marrison, 1994).

The story of the Burch campaign was different, to say the least. Perhaps because few pundits gave him any chance of beating the popular incumbent, Burch's fund-raising never got off the ground. To start the ball rolling, the Burch team planned a large fund-raising event—an outdoor country music festival—for the third Sunday in May. Planning for the event appeared to be going fine; use of the amphitheater was donated and so was the entertainment (lead billing was Bobby Cyrus, brother of Billy Ray Cyrus). To sell tickets, they had secured the services of a direct mail house and sent tens of thousands of invitations. The mailings were expensive but to be worth the investment since only a small percentage was needed to show up in order for the event to make money. The weather also seemed to be cooperating, with the weekend before the event reaching unseasonably mild temperatures.

As the day approached, however, things fell apart. For one, feedback from the mailing was slow, at best. According to Gail Grewell, the campaign's finance director, very few supporters had indicated a willingness to attend. Two days before the event, a cold front descended on the state, locking in drizzle and record low temperatures. In fact, it was so cold that nearly all of the entertainment backed out. Finally, the location of the event—some twenty miles into the hinterlands from the nearest interstate—proved difficult to find.

In the end, the campaign team frantically sought "bodies." Only 100 people attended. Some were die-hard supporters and others were given their tickets for free. Rather than brave the cold and rain, cars were pulled up to the edge of the stage. The event was, in the words of Grewell, "an utter embarrassment." Far more was spent on the mailing than was collected at the gates. The only good thing was that the media never got wind of the flop.[1]

Things never really improved for the Burch campaign. In all, the candidate raised only $63,000—a mere pittance compared to Voinovich's war chest. In fund-raising, as in much of life, when it rains, it pours!

THE PUSH FOR CAMPAIGN RESOURCES

Resources are required to convey a message. While it is true that volunteers, knowledge, reputation, access, and time are forms of campaign resources, they are also supplements to finances. Indeed, much of what volunteers or candidates might contribute to the race costs money, such as handing out leaflets or making telephone calls. The foremost resource in any campaign is money, and races without it face a long, uphill battle. As fund-raising expert David Himes notes, no matter how resources of a campaign are defined, money is always critical (1995, 62).

There are examples of candidates who overcame a massive financial disadvantage—such as Michael Patrick Flanagan's (R-IL) defeat of longtime incumbent congressmen Dan Rostenkowski in 1994. Flanagan spent less than $100,000—an extremely modest sum in any congressional district, much less in a high-priced media market like Chicago. Notwithstanding, such upsets are rare, and usually when they do occur something else was going on to pull voters away from the better financed candidate. Rostenkowski was, for example, in the midst of fighting off several indictments. Better funded candidates are not always the most successful ones, but many of the most effective strategies and tactics in new-style campaigning require resources—and that means money. "No campaign ever lost because the candidate spent too much time raising money" (Himes 1995, 62).

Money is also a valuable resource because it can purchase most other political resources. It is much more difficult to convert person power into an effective mass media campaign or to transform access to the media into person power, than it is to convert money into either media exposure or campaign workers (Adamany 1969, 8–9). Money cannot convert all resources; for example, a candidate's knowledge of the issues or reputation cannot be purchased. But a deficiency in most areas can be more easily overcome with money than with any other resource.

This chapter is designed to acquaint the reader with several issues related to money in elections. It provides a brief look at the history of campaign finance, including the general cost of elections and some issues dealing with the incumbent advantage and finance reform. It then proceeds to outline various techniques to raise money and ends with a discussion of finance operation staffing.

A BRIEF LOOK AT MONEY IN CAMPAIGNS

Campaigns have never been cheap. In Colonial times, candidates were expected to treat the voters with food and drink. George Washington purchased 160 gallons of various beverages, an average of a quart-and-a-half per voter, in his first bid for the Virginia Assembly (Dinkin 1989, 3). During most of the last century, campaigns were conducted in the partisan press and through party organizations. Rallies and events were held, party workers "hit the streets," and handbills were printed and distributed. Parties, rather than candidates, raised the necessary campaign funds. In turn, candidates were expected to contribute to the party — frequently, it was a condition of receiving the party's nomination.

By the turn of the century, several changes began to alter the flow of money in campaigns. First, a host of new technologies were available, including quicker and more efficient printing presses, railroads, photography, radio, and motion pictures. Party workers were still important, but they were not the only avenue for reaching voters. Second, the reforms of the Progressive movement, such as direct primaries, the Australian ballot, civil service, and nonpartisan municipal elections, weakened the role of party machines. As a result, organized business, farm, and labor groups began to break the monopoly that parties had on the loyalties of Americans — leading to greater competition and less predictable, more costly elections. Third, during this period, the electorate became more educated and there was a modest slowdown of immigration, which led to less straight-ticket voting. Fourth, charismatic candidates, such as Teddy Roosevelt, and even unsuccessful ones, such as William Jennings Bryan, highlighted the import of candidate image (Sorauf 1988, 16–17).

It should be noted that, although parties were less critical, they continued to play a lead role in elections until around the 1960s. In most areas they still controlled party workers and thus elements of the nomination process. It is also true that the campaign "experts" of the day were seasoned campaigners of the party organization. Most important, parties were still able to amass large war chests.

Throughout most of this period, government was unified—that is, one party held the reigns of power, at both the federal and state levels. To influence the outcome of government activity, one would contribute to the party closest to his or her concerns, or to the one in power at the time. Providing funds to any candidate, save perhaps a presidential one, was deemed a waste since they were just one member of a larger organization. The result was a massive influx of party funds from business organizations, labor unions, and "fat cats" (wealthy individuals). In 1928, for example, roughly 70 percent of the funds raised by both the national parties came in contributions of $1,000 or greater. Whereas this may not, at first glance, appear to be a hefty sum, it should be recalled that in the 1920s two of Henry Ford's Model T's could be purchased with a thousand-dollar bill (Sorauf 1988, 3).

The weight of big contributors helped party organizations maintain a degree of control. By 1960 even this began to change. The principal culprit was the proliferation of television and, to some extent, radio.

Television shattered the old pattern of campaign finance. For one, television is expensive—not only the airing of spots, but the production and placement as well. Between 1972 and 1986, the sum of all money spent in congressional campaigns jumped from roughly $77 million to over $450 million—a 482 percent increase (Sorauf 1988, 25). The same thing has occurred at the state level (Jones 1984). According to the Congressional Research Service, 51 percent of the cost of modern U.S. Senate campaigns can be linked to television (with another 20 percent tied to radio). This figure represents twice the size of any other expenditure and ten times the disbursement for print advertising (Cohn 1992, 15–17). The percentage spent on television is a bit lower in congressional and state legislative races, yet there is no doubt that it is a big part of the mushrooming cost of elections at these levels as well.

Television allows candidates to circumvent traditional intermediaries—namely the party—to reach voters. Potential candidates need not kiss the ring of party leaders in order to run for public office. In the days of old, the only way to reach a large number of voters was to have party minions carry your banner to every doorstep. Today this can be accomplished with a thirty-second television advertisement. Candidate-centered campaigns have replaced party-centered campaigns.

It is now necessary for candidates to solicit money on their own behalf—and to do so vigorously. The cost of running a state legislative race in California increased 4,000 percent between 1958 and 1986. Prior to 1980, no California state legislative race cost more than $1 million. In 1986 twelve cost more than that amount and five exceeded $2 million (Jones 1993, 47). Again, a majority of this increase can be directly tied to the use of television and radio.

It is interesting to note that, although many elected officials owe their jobs to television advertising, the strain of raising enough money to acquire spots keeps many would-be candidates from running for office, and it is driving others out. A record number of U.S. Senators are slated to retire in 1996. Asked why they are leaving, nearly all suggest that the pressure of raising massive sums for reelection is simply too much. Senator Paul Simon of Illinois notes; "You begin the first day you're elected and it never stops. It takes all the fun out of it."[2] Susan Manes speculates that, in order for a U.S. Senator to have won reelection in 1990, an average of $12,500 must have been raised every week for the Senator's entire six-year term (1990, 19).

Several other changes occurred during the 1960s and 1970s, unrelated to television, which played a role in the skyrocketing cost of elections. The baby boom of the 1940s and 1950s, the Voting Rights Act of 1965, and the Twenty-Sixth Amendment (which gave eighteen-year-olds the right to vote) all expanded the size of electorates (Adamany and Agree 1975, 21). A host of other new technologies, including sophisticated survey research, direct mail, telemarketing, computerized targeting, and video production pushed up the cost of getting elected. The rise of the campaign consulting profession has added a new burden as well. With these new technologies comes the need to hire people who understand how to use them. Fifty of the U.S. House candidates in 1992 *each* spent over $500,000 on consultants alone. One of them, Michael Huffington (R-California), spent over $3 million on professional help. Senator Alfonse D'Amato spent nearly $7 million on consultants alone in his 1992 reelection bid. One media consulting firm collected over $11 million in 1992, *just for their services in congressional races* (Morris and Gamache 1994).

In an effort to limit the impact of corporate influence and fat cats in campaigns, the federal government passed a series of reform measures in the early 1970s. The 1972 Federal Elections Campaign Act (FECA), and its several amendments, mandated a number of restrictions, including a $1,000 limit on individual contributions at each stage of the election—primary, general, and runoff election (if necessary)—and a $5,000 limit on donations from political parties.[3] Most important, while labor unions, corporations, and incorporated trade and membership organizations are prohibited from using general treasury funds to make contributions to candidates, the FECA did allow for their financial participation through separate segregated funds. These funds, along with the political committees of other organizations (such as ideological and issue groups), are known as political action committees (PACs) (Cohn 1992, 9). Whereas a few PACs had been around since the 1940s, the official "green light" given by the FECA led to their proliferation. In 1974 there were just over 600, and in 1992 there were nearly 5,000 (Herrnson 1995, 106). They are also limited to $5,000 direct contributions to each candidate at each stage of the election process.

It is difficult to overstate the import of PACs in the financing of elections. They contributed just over $12 million to congressional candidates in 1974, and in 1992 it was $178.3 million (Herrnson 1995, 107). They provide roughly 40 percent of incumbent congressional and senatorial campaign coffers. As each is limited in what they can give, a premium is placed on soliciting funds from a broad range of PACs. Some candidates hire full-time PAC fund-raising experts.

The growth of special-interest involvement in state- and local-level elections parallels the national trend. Government at this level has become much more involved in various forms of regulation in the last two decades. Business, labor, and consumer groups have become quite interested in the outcome of these elections. In some states, such as Michigan, roughly one-half of candidate war chests come from special interests, while in others, such as North Carolina, about two-thirds come from individuals. Surprisingly, seventeen states do not restrict the flow of corporate money in state elections, and twenty-two are hands-off when it comes to labor union contributions (Jones 1993, 51–59).

Arguably, PACs have not *caused* the massive increase in campaign spending over the last two decades. Rather, they are simply responding to candidate needs. Candidates need more money to run their races, and PACs fill this demand. However, as one candidate accepts PAC funds, some argue, other candidates must respond accordingly. By flooding the campaign arena with money, PACs have greatly contributed to the upward spiral of campaign costs.

In sum, campaigns have become very expensive. This has led to a host of new issues, including where to get sufficient funds and how to spend them. One might ask whether all this spending is really necessary. Could candidates spend less and still win? Perhaps costs have increased dramatically because candidates mistakenly believe that to win they must spend as much as possible on television, radio, and direct mail. How much of the increase can be attributed to this perception? Is there a relationship between money and the likelihood of success? Unfortunately, a second lesson to be garnered from this review is that money does seem to matter. In the 1990 state legislative races in California, for example, 96 percent of the candidates who had the most money won. At higher level races, the same is true. Successful open- seat congressional candidates had a two-to-one fund-raising advantage over unsuccessful candidates in 1992. Even when factors such as incumbency and prior office experience are factored in, the better financed candidate generally wins (Herrnson 1995, 219).[4] There may not be a perfect fit between fund-raising success and the outcome at the polls, but candidates and consultants are not likely to gamble on being the exception to the rule.

The Incumbency Advantage

The premier controversy in the campaign finance literature concerns the disparity between incumbents and challengers. When party organizations carried the banner and voter preferences were fixed by a partisan badge, candidate status had only a marginal impact. Even the most casual observer of American politics knows that incumbent reelection rates are now staggering. Congressional and state legislative incumbents face little serious opposition; over 90 percent are returned to office. A whopping 98 percent of the members of Congress who ran for reelection were returned to office in 1986 and 1988. In 1990 this percentage dipped to 95 percent, yet even in the "throw-the-bums-out" elections of 1992 and 1994, nine out of ten incumbents were returned (Shea and Brooks 1995). Whereas higher profile campaigns, such as gubernatorial and U.S. Senate races, yield a somewhat lower rate of reelection, incumbents are much more likely to be returned to office than in years hence (Krasno 1994).

If it is true that there is a tight fit between money raised and candidate reelection, a logical query would then be whether campaign finances are at the root of high reelection rates. Put a bit differently, do incumbents win because it is easier for them to raise money? The answer is that easy access to funds is at the center of the incumbent edge controversy, putting challengers at a serious disadvantage. Scholar L. Sandy Maisel reports that, between 1978 and 1986, U.S. House incumbents raised and spent nearly three times the amount of challengers (1990, 124), and Frank Sorauf notes roughly the same pattern in Senate races (1988, 156). More recently, Paul Herrnson finds this disparity to be growing (1995, 128–153), and Sorauf suggests that in 1992, 75 percent of PAC money went to incumbents; 9 percent to challengers (1995, 80). At the state legislative level, Ruth Jones (1984) and Sorauf (1988) found the same pattern. In the 1984 California state legislative contests, for example, incumbents had a 14-to-1 fund-raising edge (Sorauf 1988, 265).

Why do incumbents find it so much easier to garner funds? For one, PACs give disproportionately to them. Herrnson reports that while U.S. House incumbents raised an average of $261,952 from PACs in 1992, challengers received on average just $26,179 (1995, 133 and 140, respectively). This 10-to-1 advantage is the same at other levels. This occurs because organizations wishing to promote their view of government policy are anxious to get the biggest bang for their buck. This implies giving to projected winners; there is no payoff in losing candidates. Because incumbents are usually expected to prevail, they receive the lion's share of contributions. As noted by Keith Abbott, former director of the Democratic Senatorial Campaign Committee; "Washington money is, by and large, smart money. Most PACs are not a bit interested in supporting people they don't think will win" (Luntz 1988, 178).

On top of this, incumbents generally have leftover cash from their last campaign and tend to get a good deal of "early money" PACs and individuals. This further discourages "good" challengers, leaving the field to less qualified ones (Maisel 1990, 125). Incumbents also have an edge in experience; they have run successful campaigns (fund-raisers) in the past and already have a reliable list of contributors.

For some, the fund-raising edge incumbents possess is disquieting. A number of reform measures have been suggested, including more stringent reporting requirements which would at least bring the inequities to light. The enormous disparity might be reduced by such measures, yet, short of public financing of elections, it seems overly optimistic to expect any real change in the years ahead.

State and Federal Reporting Requirements

Budding campaign professionals should be keenly aware of the contribution and expenditure limits and the disclosure requirements applicable to each state and race. This is a complex topic, and it is not possible here to provide more than a cursory look.

The Federal Election Commission (FEC) now regulates election laws applicable to House, Senate, and presidential candidates. House and Senate candidates are required to disclose, at four predetermined dates during the election cycle, all sources of contributions greater than $100, along with the contributor's address. Expenditure information must also appear on these forms, detailing precisely where and when campaign funds were spent.

There are no limits on the amount of money a federal office candidate can spend in an election, but there are limits to how much certain individuals or organizations can give. Candidates and their spouses can contribute as much money as they like, individuals can give $1,000, and PACs can donate $5,000 per election (primary, general, and runoff elections count separately). As for political parties, the regulations are more complicated. They can give assistance in two ways: through direct contributions and by making payments to service vendors, called "coordinated expenditures." The national party committees, which include the national party and the House and Senate campaign organizations, are each allowed to contribute directly $5,000 per candidate per election. "That amounts to a total of $20,000 in party money for the candidate's primary and general election races for the House, but there is a $17,000 limit for Senate candidates" (Cohn 1992, 13). State and local party committees are allowed to give a combined total of $5,000 per candidate per election. Regarding coordinated expenditures, the amount is fixed by a formula based the population of the state and the inflation rate. For House races in 1996, this amount ranges from about $35,000 to $65,000. In the Senate, this figure ranges from about $70,000 in less populated states, to approximately $1.3 million in California.[5]

As we might expect, financial regulations at the state level vary. All fifty states require financial reporting, but only forty-five mandate expenditure itemization. Similar to federal races, there is no overall limit on spending, except in those states that provide public money to help finance campaigns. To date, four states do so—Iowa, Minnesota, Utah, and Rhode Island. However, as mandated in the Supreme Court decision *Buckley v. Valeo*[6], these limits can be discarded if the candidate chooses to decline public financing. Regarding contribution limits, twenty-nine states restrict contributions from individuals, twenty-two from family members, thirty-three from businesses, twenty-eight from labor unions, and thirty from PACs. Only thirteen states limit the amount of money political parties can give to state and local candidates. Surprisingly, twenty-six states restrict loans to campaigns (Jones 1993, 53).

Generally speaking, state laws are used to regulate election finances for local-level offices. There are, nevertheless, scores of municipalities that provide their own restrictions and limitations as well. Several cities have initiated programs in which public agencies or tax dollars provide some funds for local candidates.

This brief review represents just the tip of the iceberg. Campaign finance regulations are exceedingly complex. The first step in the fund-raising efforts for any campaign is to read and understand the laws. Far too many campaigns get tripped up by a weak understanding of these restrictions. In 1992 alone 110 candidates violated FEC laws (Morris and Gamache 1994, 30–31). Countless others did so in state and local races. The penalty for breaking finance regulations can range from a small fine to imprisonment. Either way, the media and the opponent love to remind voters of these infractions.

WHY INDIVIDUALS AND GROUPS GIVE TO CAMPAIGNS

In every election year the number of unsuccessful fund-raisers greatly exceeds the number of successful ones. Many operatives and candidates blame tactics—believing a direct-mail drive would have worked better than an event, or that a series of small events might have worked better than a telemarketing approach. In order to raise money, it is important first to understand *why* individuals and groups give to campaigns. "The process is bilateral," writes Sorauf, "both contributors and candidates pursue political goals" (1995, 78). Knowledge of these motivations will help create an effective fund-raising strategy leading to the appropriate choice of tactics. This section looks at some of the reasons why individuals and organizations contribute to campaigns, and why they might not.

Why Individuals Give

Roughly 40 percent of campaign funds come from individual contributions.[7] These people give to campaigns because they are asked. As simple as this might sound, it often gets lost in the hysteria to raise money. Without being asked, it may never occur even to the most attentive citizen (recall that most are not) to support a candidate financially. Or they may think the campaign already has enough money—after all, no one came looking for it. Another possibility is that people simply like to be asked; it makes them feel that they are needed and appreciated. Perhaps, as Sorauf suggests, "the request for money activates some generalized, even vague, feeling of loyalty or sympathy, whether for the cause or the solicitor" (1988, 49). In any event, it is rare to find unsolicited money in a campaign.

Individuals give to a campaign because they are personally connected to the candidate—either as friends or family. There are few topics that transcend partisan or ideological differences more quickly than an intimate relationship.

Another possibility is an interest in certain government actions or policies. Many individuals are interested in what government does, and by helping one candidate win office they believe the preferred outcome will be more likely. Sometimes this is related to a specific policy, such as the candidate's stand on abortion, gun control, or industrial deregulation; other times, it is part of a larger set of beliefs, partisanship, or ideology.

Party activists and those keenly interested in the outcome of government are more likely to give; or loyalty to a group or membership organization may compel them to send a check. If, for example, the potential contributor is a member of a public employees' union, and that union has expressed a strong desire to elect a candidate, that person may give to the candidate out of loyalty to the union. Racial or gender group loyalty can sometimes spur contributions.

Some individuals give to candidates as an expression of reward for his or her past behavior. Conceivably the candidate voted to lower property taxes or curb the crime rate, and the contributor simply wishes to demonstrate an appreciation for these efforts. Mere habit can be a compelling reason for why people give (Yeutter et al. 1992). About 10 percent of Americans contribute to political candidates in a given election (Sorauf 1988, 47). On close inspection, we find there is a good deal of consistency from one election to the next; that is, the same 10 percent contribute year after year.

It is an interesting paradox that politicians as a class are disdained, but at the same time individual pols are held in high esteem. Everyone would like to be close to their member of Congress or state legislature. One's desire to have an ongoing relationship with the successful candidate, as such, can be a strong motivation for contributing.

Many times this simply means having the elected official answer telephone calls, and other times it implies a much closer relationship—perhaps sharing some leisure time. Candidates and contributors alike rarely examine the "chicken or the egg" matter—whether contributors were friends first, or became friends after contributing.

Another reason why individuals give to campaigns is because they are requested to do so by someone outside the campaign. It is common in state legislative politics, for example, for the leader of the party caucus to "request" safe members (one's whose reelection is secure) to contribute to their colleagues who are marginal or to targeted challengers and open-seat candidates (Shea 1995a). Often these contributors will know little about the candidate; they are giving out of deference to the requestor.

Finally, some individuals can be compelled to support a candidate because they fear what will happen if the opponent wins. They may have little affinity for the candidate but dread the prospect of the opponent's ascendance to office. Apprehension, scorn, and a host of other ill feelings should never be discounted when it comes to fund-raising—they are strong motivations. As suggested by one prominent GOP fund-raiser; "Ask yourself, who hates the opponent—who wants to beat him as bad as I do. This starts the donor list process" (Shea and Brooks 1995, 44).

Why Groups Contribute

Many of the reasons for individual campaign contributions apply to group contributions. The main difference is that groups are most likely to give because they are interested in the outcome of public policy. They desire to elect officials sympathetic to their concerns—to have access to the elected official. This is precisely why incumbents receive the vast majority of group contributions; again, there is no payoff in funding losers. It is also the reason why close races are highly funded, and it is common to find groups giving to both candidates—termed the "CYA" strategy.

It is a mistake to assume that groups are "buying" candidates when they provide funds. There is a high correlation between the concerns of groups supporting a candidate and that official's voting record once in office, but the payoff connection is never clear. Instead, groups contribute heavily to candidates with the expectation that after the election they will have access—be allowed to present their position to the elected official. Groups seek "a chance to persuade, an opportunity to make a case or argue a point" (Sorauf 1988, 314). At the same time, however, the appearance of a conflict of interest can be powerful in electoral politics. Groups give to one candidate over another because they see their chances as better with that person. Precisely why they are better can be a matter of great speculation.

Why Individuals and Groups Do *Not* Give

As a final note, it is worthwhile to suggest why people and groups might *not* contribute to a given campaign (Yeutter et al. 1992). First, many would-be contributors are not asked. As noted above, campaigns receive few unsolicited checks. Second, an amount has not been specified in the appeal. Not knowing how much to give or how much is needed, a potential contributor may simply pass up the opportunity. As will be seen below, not specifying an amount is a "cardinal sin" in fund-raising. Third, the potential contributor has not provided a clear way of giving. In other words, the appeal is vague. Should it be mailed, and if so, to whom? Should it be cash, check, or money order? How much can I give? If these and other questions are not clearly answered, the would-be contributor may simply pass.

Another reason why someone might not give is that the appeal is offensive. Instead of feeling that their money would be appreciated, perhaps they felt they were being used, taken advantage of, or patronized. Along similar lines, the appeal may be unconvincing. Potential contributors need to feel as though their money will make a difference. If they feel as though the money is unneeded or will be wasted, they have no compelling reason to write the check. Finally, the appeal may come from the wrong person or in the wrong format.

Summary

Many other tips and strategies will be provided below. The aim of this section was to underscore the motivations behind individual and group contributors, and what might lead them to refrain from lending a hand. This insight helps lay the foundation of a fund-raising strategy and tactics. Knowing why people give helps a great deal in getting them to do so.

FUND-RAISING STRATEGY AND TACTICS

According to expert Mary Sabin, there are three keys to successful fund-raising, "and they are work, work, work. This isn't rocket science or brain surgery. What it is working hard, staying at it, and concentrating on raising the money while feeling completely obsessed about it" (Shea and Brooks 1995, 44). Notwithstanding, most would also agree that in order to raise money, careful attention must be paid to the appropriate strategy and tactics. As with nearly all new-style campaign techniques, a thoughtful, written plan must be devised.

There are four principal elements to a fund-raising plan: the amount of money needed, when it is needed, potential sources, and fund-raising tactics. It is a familiar mistake to discern how much money is needed by assessing how much can be raised (Himes 1995, 63). The correct approach is to acknowledge the goals laid out in the campaign plan, and further illustrated in the strategic blueprint (see Chapter 9). By setting specific goals, the fund-raising team has a clear motivation. Also detailed in the strategy scheme will be the timing of activities and thus some indication as to when fund-raising activities should take place. Deadlines are strong motivators. If, for example, the strategy calls for a massive television campaign in early spring, fund-raising efforts must be planned well in advance—that is, unless you already have the money.

One of the greatest financial obstacles a campaign faces is "seed money." This money pays for the numerous activities that must be undertaken before the campaign can move into full gear, including hiring consultants, undertaking a benchmark poll, and writing a plan. The difficulty is that many would-be contributors are hesitant to give to hapless campaigns—ones without a sizable war chest. The situation is little different from a recent college graduate's being unable to find work because he or she lacks experience. The fund-raising plan must pay special heed to, and somehow overcome, this dilemma.

Many of the potential sources, as noted above, include the candidate's family, friends, colleagues, and associates; partisans; political action committees; habitual givers; enemies of the opponent; and political parties. It is wise to group potential givers, or "prospects," into three general categories: small donors, medium-size contributors, and large donors. Precisely how these categories are defined will depend each race; a large contributor in a city council campaign might be a small donor in a congressional race. It should be kept in mind that the tactic used will often vary depending the category of prospect, and the broader the fund-raising plan the better (Beaudry and Schaeffer 1986, 164).

Choosing the appropriate set of tactics is a bit more complicated; there are numerous possibilities. No technique is a surefire one for every race, and often the mix depends as much on the preferences of the candidate and the consultant, as it does on the audience or anything else. Some candidates, for example, are simply better at asking for money than others, and some consultants are more seasoned in direct - mail than they are in PAC solicitation. There are also risks to consider with each technique; many yield a high rate of return in some instances, but can be disastrous in others. There are "safer" choices, but many times the return is modest. The norms and traditions of the area are important to consider as well. Not all techniques work equally well in every district. Below is a discussion of several of the most commonly used fund-raising techniques.

Personal Solicitation

When Representative Rod Chandler (R-Washington) decided to leave Congress in 1992, Jennifer Dunn saw her chance. What she lacked in campaign experience, she made up for in fund-raising savvy. Having been head of the Washington State Republican party for eleven years, Dunn understood that the best way to raise money is to ask for it personally. "With help from friends and volunteers, Dunn worked her way through the 5,000 names in her personal files, raising $492,44 from individuals and $168,373 from PACs" (Morris and Gamache 1994, 152). She out raised the opponent by a two-to-one margin the "old-fashioned way"—she asked for it!

One-on-one solicitation is the most cost-effective way to raise money. Simply put, this technique requires the candidate or someone in the campaign to ask for money personally. For many, this is not an especially appealing way to spend an afternoon. Nevertheless, it has proven to be extremely productive; particularly with large donors, over a short period of time, and for up-front money. On top of this, it is an inexpensive undertaking.

Before one starts to solicit funds, a master list of prospects should be drawn. The list, which may include leaders of an organization, labor union, business firm, or a professional group, should be segregated by interest—political, business, professional, or personal contact (Allen 1990a, 49). Personal solicitation can work with small-scale donors, but it takes the same amount of time and effort to ask for $1,000 as it does to ask for $10—with about the same percentage rate of return. So it is best to spend time on people or groups likely to give more. Besides, personal requests are often the only way to set fat cat contributors to give.

The fund-raising team must do their homework before the "the big ask." In other words, the solicitor should know the personal and professional interests of the prospect and be ready to detail precisely where the campaign is going and why the money is needed. They should provide the contributor with polling information, campaign brochures, a summary of the candidate's policy stands, and a list of specific items to be paid for with the money. In some instances, it may be worthwhile to bring a modified copy of the campaign plan in order to demonstrate the professionalization of the campaign. The prospect should feel as though they are being asked to join a tightly run, highly organized campaign team.

The people doing the asking should be optimistic, aggressive, and sincere. They should be convincing, but at the same time flexible. It is always wise to ask for a specific amount, never letting the contributor choose a figure out of thin air. According to fund-raising pro Robert Kaplan, "Choose a number that is 10 to 25 percent in excess of what your research shows contributors should donate" (1991, 54).

Another tip is to look at the situation from the potential contributor's point of view: Why should he or she donate money to your race? Part of the approach must be to demonstrate the impact the contribution will have. For instance, suggest that a $1,000 check will allow the campaign to reach voters in a different media market, thereby narrowing the gap between your candidate and the opponent. Most important, the solicitor should, if at all possible, never leave without a check or, at the very least, a firm commitment. If the contributor hedges, Kaplan suggests saying; "Let me give you my Federal Express number. I need your check tomorrow" (1991, 55). It is also a fine idea to ask that person for a list of names of additional people to meet.

A number of campaigns have profited from the development of a "pledge system," where the contributor is asked to donate at periodic intervals. This approach can often increase the amount of the overall contribution (Beaudry and Schaeffer 1986, 168). Some, nevertheless, see this approach as a bit risky and would rather get as much as possible all at once—fearing future donations will taper off. Also, as noted above, seed money is critical: not only does it allow early activities to take place, but it leads to better fund-raising.

Once the person has contributed, he or she should be formally thanked by the candidate. If the candidate was not the one to ask for the money, a good idea is to have the candidate call the contributor personally, as well as send a personalized follow-up note. Keeping in mind that this person may be tapped for another contribution, or in another race down the road, periodic updates should be mailed.

One of the hardest things a fund-raiser will confront is a candidate reluctant to ask for money. To many, it is demeaning or beneath them to "beg for dollars." They must be made to understand that people do not give without being asked, and large donors seldom contribute without being asked by the candidate. It is an inexpensive way to raise money, it can be done quickly, and it can take place early in the race. Personal solicitation is the oldest and most common way to raise money precisely because it works.

PAC and Interest Group Solicitation

As noted above, national and state political action committees have become first-string players in the funding of modern campaigns. It is a common miscalculation to presume that these organizations will flood your race with donations simply because the candidate holds the right policy stand. A careful strategy must be devised.

The first task is to analyze all potential PACs. At the federal level, they are registered with the FEC, and at the state and local level most are required to register with the elections commission or the secretary of state. After getting the list, the amount given, the policy concerns, and the types of candidates contributors gave to in the past are assessed. The amount of contributions can be found on financial disclosure reports. If your candidate is utterly on the wrong side of the policy fence, or it would be an embarrassment to receive a donation from a certain PAC (perhaps creating a perception of a conflict of interest), the PAC should be scratched from the list. If they have consistently given to the opponent (or only candidates of that party), they should be eliminated as well. All others should be included on a "PAC master list."

The next step is to create a database for each PAC. The name, address, and telephone number of the PAC are included, along with its director or treasurer, the contact person, groups represented by it, the foremost issues of concern, names of affiliated organizations, their average contribution, and the names of supporters who are affiliated with that PAC. Careful attention should be paid to any "hooks"—things that could draw the attention of the PAC to your race. Some possibilities include a high density of members in the district, any personal or professional connection the candidate might have to the group, issues in the district that may be of interest to the PAC, and any aspect of the candidate's or the opponent's record that may be of interest to that organization—such as bill sponsorship or voting record data (Yeutter et al. 1992). Developing this database, will be a time-consuming chore, but the more detailed the base the better.

From this list, personalized "PAC kits" are developed. These packets contain every bit of information the PAC official will need to make a decision to support your candidate—indeed, why they "must" support him. Each kit should contain:[8]

- A cover letter, signed by the candidate, detailing precisely why that PAC should support him or her and loathe the opponent. Many of the hooks should be incorporated here as well.
- A narrative biography, clearly stating what the candidate has accomplished overall, particularly items relevant to the PAC. A picture of the candidate should be included.
- A profile of the district, including a discussion of demographics and the media market.
- A campaign outline, including a brief discussion of how the race is being run and who is on the campaign team.

- A list of the consultants working on the race. One way PACs assess a candidate's chance is by the caliber of the consultants on board. If your candidate is a Democrat and, for instance, Bob Squier is doing your media (arguably one of the top pros in the field), the PAC might take a hard look. (Ironically, it is often difficult to get top-name consultants without first getting PAC money.)
- A summary of the candidate's positions, particularly those related to the PAC. The candidate's voting record can be included.
- Opposition research highlights, especially anything remotely connected to the PAC.
- Press clippings indicating that the campaign is rolling.
- Endorsements.
- A sample of campaign material, such as brochures and radio and television scripts.
- Perhaps most important, an overview of favorable polling results. PACs rarely fund long shots and the best way to show that your race is not one is to provide survey data. It also helps if the polling was done by a consultant they recognize and respect.

If the list of potential PACs is large, as it should be, most PAC kits will be mailed. A follow-up telephone call, by either the candidate or someone high up in the campaign, must be made about two weeks later. For the "hot prospects," it is wise to have the candidate hand deliver the packet to the PAC official. This personal appearance might make a strong impact (hopefully a positive one) and tip the scales in your direction. When visiting a PAC, it is especially important to do your homework and be ready to "make the case" (Hesla 1992).

As to when they should be sent or delivered, a few rounds can be made, the first roughly one year out; the second, to those who have not contributed or reached their legal limit, about eight months before the election; and a final one during the summer. There is no harm to ask more than once, but obviously, the kits should be updated each time.

Sending or delivering PAC kits is by no means the only way to get special-interest money. If your candidate is an incumbent, or at the very least well connected, a reception might be held. Here scores of PAC officials are invited to meet the candidate in a social setting. Of course, the cost per ticket covers a bit more than dinner and drinks. Receptions in Washington and in some state capitals costing $1,000 or even $2,500 per ticket are common. The more prestigious the incumbent, the higher the price.

The process is a bit more difficult for challengers and open-seat candidates. Here party organizations, such as the "Hill committees" in Washington and the legislative campaign committees in state capitals, can be a big help. They can provide, for selected candidates, strategic advice about which PACs to approach and how to do so. Most PACs will send candidates questionnaires where even the slightest slip can bar a candidate from funding. Parties tutor candidates on how to fill out these forms. It is illegal for parties to earmark checks they receive from individuals or PACs for specific candidates, but they can make "suggestions" as to where the PACs might best spend their money (Herrnson 1995, 93). Often party organizations will hold a "meet and greet" reception, where PAC decision makers and selected candidates are invited to the same gathering, allowing the candidate direct access—often a difficult hurdle in the PAC fund-raising process. Little different than a dating service, the party's goal is to bring the two parties together, leading to the consummation of the marriage by the writing of a big check! Party leaders also badger PAC leaders to give to their candidates and prod members of the media to see certain races as competitive—leading to more PAC money. Overall, party committees can be a big help with PAC fund-raising, but there is an obstacle: In order to get this assistance, they must believe that the candidate stands a good chance of victory. More than one candidate has puzzled despairingly at the irony of this logic.

A PAC fund-raising plan, and all of the necessary components, represents an arduous task. One should bear in mind that these organizations can make or break a campaign war chest. The average congressional incumbent received over $250,000, and the average open-seat candidate over $100,000 in PAC funds in 1994 (Herrnson 1995, 133 and 146, respectively). With such big money at stake, few deem it not worth the trouble.

Direct Mail

Direct-mail solicitation, one of the newer kids on the block, can be a powerful fund-raising tool. There are myriad success stories, beginning with the rapid growth of Republican National Committee coffers in the late 1970s. This process, it might be argued, epitomizes new-style campaigning, and there has been an explosion in the number of professionals who specialize in it. At the same time, it is a complex, confusing process, and the number of failed direct-mail efforts probably outweighs the number of successful ones.

The traditional direct-mail approach is based upon the notion that a marginal rate of return can surmount production costs and lead to big gains if it is multiplied by enough contributors and these contributors give repeatedly. It is a step-by-step process in which initial losses are absorbed in the hopes of future gains.

The process begins with a "prospecting list." This is an extensive catalog of potential contributors, broadly defined. By "potential," it is assumed that those on the list have some characteristics or qualities that make them susceptible to the candidate's appeal (Sabato 1989, 88). Often, lists may be available through a government agency (such as the voter registration catalog), the party organization, or prior candidates of the same party, or they can be pulled together from several lists. They can be purchased from list vendors, including magazine subscribers, people who buy products through the mail, owners of certain types of automobiles and boats, and those in a certain profession within the district, such as attorneys (see Chapter 4).

From this group, a "contributor" or "house list" is created. These are the people who responded to the prospect solicitation by sending a check. They are proven donors, and the chances of them sending again are higher. Throughout the campaign this group will be cultivated and harvested repeatedly.

Direct mail is generally a long-range program, and many are surprised by the losses that are incurred at the beginning.[9] For instance, let us assume that the prospecting list contains 40,000 names. The production costs and postage for letters to this large group will run (roughly speaking) $.50 per letter, or a total of $20,000. (Bear in mind that fund-raising letters must be on quality stock and include both a response card and a return envelope.) It is customary to receive roughly a 2 or 3 percent response rate from a prospecting list, meaning only about 1,000 people will send something back. The average contribution from this group will generally be rather small, for example, about $19. The total income from the mailing will be $19,000 (1,000 x $19), but we will have laid out $20,000 for postage and production. The campaign will have incurred a $1,000 loss!

The good news is that, once a contributor list has been established, the cost of mailing to these folks again is smaller (the list is 97 percent reduced), and the rate of return is much higher. Our next appeal should be a bit more refined, being the second time around, and we might pay as much as $.65 per letter for production and postage, for example. It is mailed to all the contributors, requiring a $650 outlay. Our rate of return might be as high as 20 percent, with an average contribution of $18. We laid out $650 and received $3,600 in return making a $2,950 profit.

Mailings to the house list can be repeated several times. The rate of return will probably become smaller with each mailing—as people grow tired of sending more money—but it can be assumed that the contributors will rotate: a different 20 percent or so each time. The average contribution will also decrease somewhat. With ingenuity and thoughtful appeals, nonetheless, this process can lead to vast proceeds. Consultant Nessa Hart suggests that by using a different approach each time, the campaign should send the house list a new mailing every week (1992).

It should be obvious that the traditional direct-mail process will not work for every campaign. It works best—is worth the risk—when the prospecting list is massive. Larry Sabato neatly demonstrates how a $200,000 investment can lead to a $2 million profit, but his prospecting list is nearly 1 million people (1989). Such numbers are rare in congressional, state, and local campaigns, and for many at these levels it is not worth shelling out $20,000 in the hopes of eventually raising from $10,000 to $15,000.

One way to enhance a direct-mail program for lower level races is to begin with a "suspect" rather than a prospecting list. Here the number of potential contributors is smaller, but the likelihood that they will give is greater. For example, it may be a list of habitual givers to candidates of your party, or the candidate's personal or business contacts. Often criteria can be combined, such as partisanship and geography. If your candidate is a Democrat, why not ask all the Democrats in his hometown to lend a hand? The idea behind the suspect list is to improve the rate of return—to perhaps as high as 15 or 20 percent—from the initial mailing. Hart suggests a number of other refinements (weeding out unlikely donors from any list and combining households into one mailing) to improve the response rate (1992). In addition, smaller lists can be created, personalized, and mailed in-house, saving a good deal of expense.

Whether the campaign proceeds along traditional lines or with more refined lists, several elements of a direct-mail appeal must be kept in mind. The letter must convey an urgent message to the reader. "Dull is dull," writes Ron Kanfer, and "the most successful direct-mail programs are built around [a] compelling story" (1991, 22). Appeals must be personal and hit upon a hot issue. Other suggestions are always to give the reader the impression that the campaign is catching up, but still behind in the polls. (Nothing kills a small-donor program faster than the perception that the race is in the bag.) The letter should provide an easy mechanism to respond and always include a response card and a self-addressed envelope.

One technique that seems to work well is to ask the prospect to purchase something. For instance, you might call upon them to buy a thirty-second radio commercial, at a cost of $55. At a minimum, specific dollar amounts must always be requested. Contrary to popular wisdom, longer letters, with hand-written notes in the margin, seem to work better than short notes. It seems that, in order for people to send their hard-earned money, the case must be laid out in detail—even if they do not read beyond the first page. Finally, every contribution must be followed with a personal thank-you note from the candidate. Remember, the heart of the direct-mail process is the notion that people will give more than once.

Obviously, organizing a direct-mail program is a complex process and is full of risks. For many candidates and consultants, it is the best way to go, and for others it is a secondary technique. It is advisable for the budding consultant to rely on a fund-raising expert until he or she is well seasoned in this area. These firms are often one-stop units, which provide copy, layout, printing, list rental, and postage know-how. Billing is generally handled in two ways: a retainer or a fee per piece mailed. There are pluses and minuses to each method (Kanfer 1991). The important point to remember is that no agency can deliver quickly. Start early; direct mail is a long-term investment.

Events: Big and Small

When San Mateo County Supervisor Anne Eshoo (D-California) decided to take her chances in a run for Congress in 1992, one of the first issues she faced was raising enough money to get the job done in an expensive media market. Among other tracks, she turned to Gloria Steinem, a longtime friend, for help. At one event, billed as a "Tea for Two Terrific Women," 200 supporters paid $100 per ticket to witness an informal conversation between Eshoo and Steinem. A few months later, Steinem was invited back for a sit-down luncheon. Nearly twenty supporters paid $500 apiece to dine with the longtime champion of women's rights (Morris and Gamache 1994, 154).

A fund-raising event is an activity in which an admission fee is charged. They can be large affairs, such as dinners, cocktail parties, concerts, or boat tours, or they can be small events, such as coffees, ice-cream socials, and chicken barbecues. These activities can produce large sums of money, demonstrate to the media and general public that the campaign has momentum, reward past donors, and build a list of contributors (Yeutter et al. 1992). They can also serve an important social function. Campaigns that do not provide a social outlet are not only boring, but they are also usually losers. Many voters and contributors are drawn to candidates because of the excitement they create.

Like direct mail, nevertheless, fund-raising events can also pose a gamble, as noted in the introduction of this chapter. The logistics of pulling off an event, particularly a large one, can be overwhelming and tie up numerous members of the campaign team for weeks. Ticket sales may falter, and uncontrollable events may cause disaster. An event that flops causes financial problems and, more important, suggests to the media, voters, and potential contributors that the campaign is going nowhere fast. Botched fund-raising events can kill a campaign.

The idea behind large events is either to charge a hefty fee per participant, or to get a large number of participants to attend at a smaller charge. This is done by providing the right "show" for the right audience. Ironically enough, the best show for large contributors is often the least complicated. Black-tie dinners are quite common, where upward of $500 per plate is charged, depending on contextual elements (type of race, demographics of the district, candidate status, and so on). One way to help ensure the success of such an event is to use a prominent figure, a VIP, as "top billing." In 1994 Ohio congressmen Tom Sawyer (D) raised over $100,000 in one dinner event. His guest speaker was the president.

Large events that target small contributors—such as concerts—are more precarious. The best approach is to limit the overhead so that, if ticket sales do falter, there is less to lose. For example, the campaign must ask the entertainment to "contribute" their time. Many Democrats have benefited from the generosity of such musicians as Jackson Brown, Carly Simon, Barbra Streisand, and more recently, Natalie Merchant. It may even be possible to hold the event in a hall contributed by a supporter. So long as the overhead is low, the campaign is safe—that is, unless the media get wind of a flop. Far too many candidates invest heavily in enormous, low-ticket-price events, only to get burned.

Occasionally, celebrities can be harnessed for big-ticket events as well. In 1986 Barbra Streisand held a fund-raiser at her ranch for six Democratic candidates for the U.S. Senate. The tickets were $5,000 per couple, and the event netted more than $1 million (Sorauf 1988, 174).

Imagination is the only limit on the type of small-scale fund-raising event a campaign might hold. A few examples are auctions (where the merchandise is contributed); wine and cheese receptions; folk dances; walking, jogging, or swimming marathons; ice-cream socials; coffee receptions; birthday parties; and so on. These can be wonderful to reward the faithful, raise some money, and develop lists for additional solicitation. The campaign should try to expand the donor list with every event, rather than simply to the same well each time, knowing the target audience and not overcharging them (Wachob 1991). The campaign should understand that no one event will make a lot of money, but dozens of them can add up quickly. The candidate can often attend several small events in the same evening, such as a chain of $10 neighborhood cocktail parties in one town.

Not surprisingly, there are scores of fund-raising event consultants available for hire. In 1992 Dick Gephardt (D-Missouri) paid three planners a total of $27,792 for organizing events in three different cities. One consulting firm alone netted nearly $500,000 from congressional candidates in 1992 (Morris and Gamache 1994, 210–222). The foremost benefit of these outfits is the expertise and experience they bring, and the chance to turn over the headaches of logistics to someone else. They generally charge a flat fee per event or are obliged to take a percentage of the net receipts for each event. The latter may be preferable, as it provides a clear incentive to make the event a success.

Telemarketing

One of the newer devices in the fund-raising arena is telemarketing. The process is similar to direct mail, but suspect donors are given a pitch over the telephone. Also, like mail, telemarketing is an investment and is normally only as good as the list. Very often it is done in tandem with direct mail; roughly two or three days after the prospect receives the letter, a campaign worker calls to "make sure they got a note from the candidate asking for help." Other possible objectives in a telemarketing fund-raising operation are to reactivate donors who have not contributed in some time, to prompt one-time contributors to give a second time, and to enhance the outcome of events (Himes 1995, 76).

Kaplan suggests that telemarketing can be improved with a "peer-to-peer" program. Instead of having callers contact people they have never met before or have no connection to, this process encourages business, industry, and professional organization leaders to call others in their field to solicit a gift. This process is made more efficient by providing the volunteer with an assistant to help with dialing. Kaplan suggests that twice as many calls can be made this way, with much higher returns per call (1993, 41–42).

Telemarketing can be conducted by professional firms or with volunteers. Professional operations are more efficient; most now use computer-assisted calling systems, termed Automated Telemarketing Work-station (ATW). The rate of return can be stunted if prospects detect that the callers are paid and are located hundreds, if not thousands, of miles away. Careful attention should be paid to the inflection and dialect of the callers. There is also the cost to consider. Most telemarketing firms charge a flat rate per contact, which adds up quickly. Volunteers give a local flare to the telemarketing effort, but they tend to be less efficient (few campaign activities are more tedious than calling voters for money). Volunteers can also waver when it comes to pushing the prospect to contribute. Aggressive telemarket fund-raising is not for the weak of heart.

Overall, telemarketing can be a tremendous boon for a campaign treasury, especially if it is done in conjunction with direct mail. Response rates can be significantly higher. Conceivably this is a result of the one-two punch, but it may also be that telephoning bridges the gap between personal solicitation and the remoteness of direct mail. Unfortunately, telemarketing is getting a bad name these days as it has become the tool of choice of many marketing rip-off artists and get-rich quick schemes. Automated or computer-controlled marketing over the phone has not helped matters (Himes 1995, 75).

Recent Innovations

Lately, a number of fund-raising innovations and candidates have been collecting money in ways never before envisioned. As a final piece of this section, a few of the more interesting approaches are highlighted below.

Campaigns might bridge the gap between personal contact and prospecting with a paid canvas. Here workers are assigned sections of the district, ones targeted in advance as possibly the most productive, and asked to walk door to door in search of funds. As compensation for their efforts, they receive a percentage of the collection. This process is similar to the tactics used by many environmental and public interest research groups (PIRGs) across the nation. It can serve several goals, obviously making money being the first. It also secures a list of contributors to be approached again, perhaps through the mail, and at the very least puts a piece of campaign literature in the voter's hand.

The drawbacks of paid canvas are that the workers are motivated by money, not by the needs of the campaign or the candidate, and can cause problems. More important, for some campaigns, this may appear a bit too desperate; the idea of workers scouring the district searching for funds may be too much for some candidates and campaign professionals to swallow.

Former pol and current campaign consultant Bill Wachob suggests that one-page fliers, asking for donations of from $5 to $25, and a return envelope should be passed out at every campaign event. The idea is to hook people with small donations and put them on a monthly newsletter list. These reports, filled with "confidential campaign information" are designed to link the donor emotionally into the race and, of course to ask for more money. He suggests that such small-scale strategies can yield big bucks and can be completely volunteer driven (1991, 51–52). About the only thing that seemed to work in the 1994 Burch gubernatorial campaign in Ohio was their "Give Me $5 for the Future" program, where envelopes were distributed at events such as labor union and Democratic committee meetings.

Another small-scale approach is to conduct a "friends of friends" campaign. Each recipient is asked to contribute $5 or $10 and to request five friends do the same. The process can quickly lead to hefty profits and also to a large number of contributors to add to the house list.

Another recent innovation is the pledge system, which the contributor allows the campaign to make small monthly withdrawals from hie or her checking account or credit card automatically. For the contributor, this eliminates the hassle of being asked repeatedly and, as with all direct deposit systems, gives a "no pain" illusion. For the campaign, it is a secured source of revenue and it eliminates many costly fund-raising activities.

Finally, in 1992, presidential candidate Jerry Brown aggressively summoned his supporters to call his 800 number, where each time they did, $10 would be added to his treasury—and to their telephone bill. This mass-based approach was particularly appealing to Brown, as his campaign theme was "an insurgent campaign against an entrenched leadership." Over 280,000 callers made the effort (Hart 1994, 1). This might work well for most campaigns. Like telemarketing, however, there is an explosion of 900 numbers and there may soon be a consumer backlash.

STAFFING

As noted above, it is imperative that the finance program proceed from a written plan. This sets goals and deadlines, organizes the effort, and measures progress. It can also be used as a fund-raising tool. Potential contributors are anxious to use their money wisely. A finance plan demonstrates precisely how and when their money will be used. It adds credibility to the appeal, leading people to believe that they are making a good investment (Yeutter et al. 1992, 11–12).

A key piece of a finance plan is the clear delineation of staffing, duties, and responsibilities. The first step is to appoint a fund-raising chair. This position is mostly ceremonial. It should be given to a well-connected individual who can aggressively tap wealthy friends and associates. Some campaigns even go so far as to create a "finance board," composed of a large, diverse group of well-connected individuals. Often a minimum donation, such as $1,000, is a requisite. The larger the board, the greater the campaign's financial base.

The most important figure in a fund-raising operation, other than the candidate, is the campaign finance director. This person has the burdensome, straightforward task of raising the necessary funds. The director is defined by an immense commitment, including the ability to work long hours each day. He or she should be extremely aggressive and the type of person who refuses to take "no" for an answer. Credibility and maturity are vital and the knack of managing and motivating others is vital (Bennett 1987). Because this job is so difficult, good finance directors are worth their weight in gold—quite literally.

A finance treasurer will obviously be needed. This person will be responsible for the accounting of receipts and expenditures, as well as keeping up with paying the bills and state/federal election reporting requirements. This person should be well versed in accounting. In most higher level races, the treasurer is a full-time, paid position.

Depending on the size of the campaign, a fund-raising activities coordinator is generally needed. It will be his or her responsibility to implement many of the fund-raising activities. For instance, the coordinator would be charged with overseeing the small-scale events, the volunteer-centered telemarketing program, or the benefit concert. This person must be skilled in the art of "logistics management," a knack for details and follow-up, and can use the telephone like a weapon. This is the person you never see during the campaign without a telephone attached to his or her ear!

Geographic finance leaders, such as town or county chairs, are beneficial. These folks will be responsible for many of the volunteer fund-raising activities undertaken in their areas. By spreading the base of responsibility outward, and by assigning goals to each unit, war chests can quickly fill up.

Finally, specific individuals should be assigned to different fund-raising programs. Many of these folks, like events planners and direct-mail experts, will be paid and from outside. It is their job to make sure that their activity succeeds.

Fund-raising is a difficult, and in some ways distinguished, component of new-style campaigns. Good staffing, with clearly defined roles and responsibilities, helps get the process moving in the right direction.

PARTING TIPS

Precisely how campaigns should go about raising money has been a topic of much speculation—perhaps more than any other area of new-style campaigning. Scores of articles and volumes have been written to give new and improved advice—each with a slightly different spin. Because of space constraints, this chapter has been able to offer only a brief review. The following list provides a few additional miscellaneous tips.[10]

- Fund-raising efforts should never proceed with the candidate in the dark. Quite the contrary, prospects generally do not give to campaigns, but rather to candidates. If the candidate is missing from the activity, it generally falls short.
- No matter what activity is being undertaken, a specific amount must be requested. Letting the prospect decide the amount will lead to smaller donations, if any.
- As with voter persuasion, fund-raising efforts should be coordinated and repetitive. The effort should entail a broad set of ongoing, integrated activities, rather than a series of isolated drills.
- Knowing as much as possible about the interests and financial capabilities of potential donors will net greater profits.
- Although innovation is wonderful, proven methods are often the most productive. One way to know what has or has not worked in the past is to ask other candidates and party leaders, or to check the financial reports of prior candidates.
- Always tie the request with specific expenditures — how will their money be used. It may even be helpful to send a follow-up note detailing how their money was spent. Telling the contributor precisely when "their spot" will be aired on television or radio is a good example.
- Deadlines should be attached to any appeal; the prospect must feel urgency.
- The laws and requirements of the applicable election law (local, state, or federal) must be clearly understood before the fund-raising process begins.
- Donors must see the requestors contribution before they will give. If the candidate has not sacrificed for the race, why should the prospect? Likewise the finance chair should be the first to throw a check into the pot!
- All contributions should be followed with a thank-you. New-style campaigns are fast paced and aggressive. A good consultant knows, nevertheless, that they are made of individuals, not machines. If nothing else, it is the polite thing to do.

NOTES

1. This information was collected from Gail Grewell, Burch finance director, in an interview conducted over the telephone with this author on January 26, 1996.

2. This comment was made during a *60 Minutes* television interview, which aired on December 16, 1995, and was echoed by each of the eleven other retiring Senators interviewed during the program.

3. Political parties can also provide assistance through payments to vendors in a candidate's

behalf. Such payments are called "coordinated expenditures." See Cohen (1992, 13–14).

4. The only exception would be, as Herrnson notes, that unsuccessful incumbents tend to spend more than their successful challengers. See Herrnson 1995, 219–220.

5. Cohen (1992) provides figures for 1990. The amounts noted for 1996 are estimates based on a modest inflation rate between 1990 and 1996.

6. 424 U.S. 1 (1976).

7. This figure is an estimate based on data compiled by Herrnson (1995, 133–46), Cohen (1992, 11), and Sorauf (1988, 53–65).

8. Much of the following list was extracted from Yeutter et al. (1992), 24–26, Himes (1995), 66, and Herrnson (1995), 94.

9. For an excellent review of the step-by-step direct mailing process, see Sabato (1989).

10. Elements of the following list were pulled from several sources including, Yeutter et al. (1992), Beaudry and Schaeffer (1986), and Hart (1992).

Chapter Eleven

Paid Media

Mark R. Weaver

When examining the term political media, many modern-day students of political campaigns think of flashy gimmicks and catchy slogans aimed at fooling voters into putting yet another selfish politician in power. Most people assume that this is a recent trend, but as far back as 1836, political media were being crafted to affect voter attitudes in strikingly similar ways in a race for president of the United States. Candidate William Henry Harrison employed campaign posters that featured an image of himself in full military uniform astride a dapper white horse. The message was clear: Harrison's exploits as a major general in the War of 1812, and his valor in the Battle of Tippecanoe, gave him leadership qualities that his opponent, Martin Van Buren, lacked.

Despite the unprecedented political media used in that race, Harrison, a member of the Whig party, was defeated by Democrat Van Buren. However, four years later, Harrison added the popular politician John Tyler to his ticket; and the duo beat President Van Buren with the now-famous slogan, "Tippecanoe and Tyler, too." Each side elevated political media to never-before-seen levels, including dozens of campaign songs, elaborate ribbons, and miniature log cabins touting Harrison's humble roots. Harrison supporters even mass-created a cardboard pull-tab device which pictured President Van Buren first smiling while holding a goblet of expensive champagne, then grimacing when he is forced to drink a mug of hard cider, a common man's drink. This crude yet ingenious bit of political media foreshadowed a political media technique that would become infamous a century and a half later—the morph. Nowadays, candidates use this high-tech video maneuver to take an image of their opponent and animate it into a different, unflattering image.

Curiously, many historians criticized this race as being too heavy on gimmicks and too light on issues. Political historian Keith Melder called it "all form and no substance, contrived to disguise the true Whig purposes of capturing the government away from the people to enhance [big business] interests. Yet the hurrah devices of 1840 created extraordinary interest among the electorate" (Melder 1992, 89).

Tune in to ABC's *Nightline* or any other political talk show and you will likely hear some modern-day pundit making the same point about the political media employed by presidential candidates running campaigns over 150 years later. Therefore, in order to truly appreciate the current state of political media, one must first recognize that it is not a new phenomenon. The technology may change with time, but the essential purpose of political media—to change attitudes and elect a particular candidate—remains unchanged.

TELEVISION BEGINS ITS ASCENT

The first true political television campaign can be traced to the 1952 campaign of Dwight Eisenhower and Adlai Stevenson. Historian Melder writes, "By 1952, television's power to project a candidate's personality had proven politically significant—and had sealed the fate of political Americana" (Melder 1992, 161). Eisenhower employed successful New York advertising executives and even a noted documentary film maker to produce advertisements that took advantage of America's growing curiosity about television. One memorable Eisenhower spot featured everyday people asking the former general questions about his position on a variety of issues. Harnessing television's compelling format proved successful for Eisenhower. The technique, which was repeated four years later, propelled him into two terms in the White House.

But it was the presidential campaign of 1964 that introduced the kind of political media to which modern-day observers have become accustomed. In that race, President Lyndon Johnson marshaled the raw power and force of television literally to overwhelm Republican Barry Goldwater. Although Johnson's campaign ran several hard-hitting television attacks against Goldwater, the most famous was the "daisy girl" spot.

As the Cold War with the Soviet Union was reaching its lowest temperatures, the Johnson campaign attempted to paint the conservative, anticommunist Goldwater as a man who would put America at risk of nuclear war. The "daisy" spot showed a little girl in a field counting the petals off a daisy in an innocent, singsong fashion. As her countdown continued, the camera quickly zoomed into her eye and her voice changed into that of a male missile countdown announcer. The screen then filled with the flash of a nuclear explosion followed by a mushroom cloud. The spot ended with the audio portion of a passionate Lyndon Johnson speech which concluded "We must love each other or we must die." The screen went black and the final words read, "Vote for President Johnson."

Although the political folklore concerning the daisy spot states that the commercial was a turning point for the subsequent Johnson landslide, the point is overstated. The ad ran only once, and it was just one of many provocative spots aired by the Johnson campaign. The commercial's true legacy is the opening salvo in the still-running intellectual skirmish over negative political advertising.

UNDERSTANDING POLITICAL MEDIA

In order to understand modern political campaigns, one must certainly have a strong grasp of political media. Political media are the various prisms through which most voters gain access to the information they use to make voting decisions. Although the news media are one source of information about political campaigns, research has proven that the majority of information voters rely on is obtained through political media paid for and produced by a campaign.

In order to create effective political media, one must first be familiar with how voters think and how they act. For example, one well-known tenet of political behavior states that most voters do not actively seek out political information. Accordingly, campaigns must design media strategies that will reach voters who have a wide variety of other matters on their minds.

Once a connection has been made with a voter, the challenge becomes how best to communicate the campaign's chosen message. One of the best methods to do that is to provide the voter with a cue. As described in previous chapters, a cue is a shorthand method of directing a voter toward a desired result. Because most voters do not devote a lot of time or energy to analyzing candidate positions on issues, cues help them make up their minds.

When Republican George Bush was running for president in 1988, his campaign ran a television commercial showing a line of prisoners walking out of prison through a revolving door. The point of the spot was that Democrat Michael Dukakis had approved a controversial prison release program that allowed murderers to roam free on weekend passes. The commercial was a cue to voters that Dukakis had the wrong attitude about crime and that, as president, he would likely allow similar soft-on-crime initiatives to be implemented at the federal level.

Cues can take many different forms. In a mid-1980s campaign, a photograph of Texas Senator John Tower refusing to shake his opponent's hand was featured prominently in the opponent's media. The photo gave Texas voters a cue toward thinking that Tower was not a man of honor—an important trait in that proud state. When a candidate points out that his or her opponent has taken two different positions on the same issue, that is a cue indicating that the opponent cannot be trusted to be consistent. In 1968 Democrat Hubert Humphrey aired a television spot depicting a weather vane caricatured as opponent Richard Nixon. As Nixon's issue positions were recited, the weather vane spun in different directions—a cue that Nixon's ideology would shift with political pressure.

Because the very nature of political media requires brevity, effective use of political cues is a necessity. Because voters are barraged with constant advertising pitches from every possible marketer, political campaigns must make their message easy to comprehend.

Another important political cue media consultants often utilize is the metaphor, which uses one easily understood situation or description to explain a more complex situation or description. Particularly in television commercials, metaphors can communicate a great deal of political information in a short period of time. For example, in 1984, President Ronald Reagan's reelection campaign featured a commercial that showed a dangerous bear walking through the forest. The announcer said, "There's a bear in the woods." The announcer then pointed out that some people think the bear is dangerous, while others do not even believe there is a bear. The spot ended with a visual of the bear backing away from an armed hunter as the announcer reminded people that, if there is a bear, it is best to be ready to deal with it.

This metaphor, although somewhat obtuse, was aimed at explaining President Reagan's attitude toward the former Soviet Union. Reagan believed the Communist superpower to be a consistent threat to world freedom and human rights. He believed the best way to avoid a military confrontation with the Soviets was for America to be always stronger than their Cold War rival. This advertisement used the bear and the hunter as a metaphor to make the more complicated point.

One very striking point about the effectiveness of political metaphors involves cognitive retention. Simply put, people retain metaphors. They may also use the campaign-placed metaphor to process further political information—even many months later! At some point, the voter forgets where the placed metaphor came from but continues to use it as a framework for evaluating new political information and making political decisions.

In the 1992 race for governor in North Dakota, businessman Ed Schafer was the Republican nominee. Schafer's strategists crafted a plan to remind voters that the state's failing economic base was the foremost issue on the gubernatorial race. By telling voters about Schafer's knack for turning long-shot businesses into thriving enterprises, the campaign hoped to provide a metaphor for how the businessman would help the troubled state.

A Schafer campaign ad showed an abandoned barn, torn into nothing but boards. The announcer pointed out that, although many people see the wood as unwanted junk, Ed Schafer sees opportunity. The spot then showed a small, North Dakota–based carpentry firm which Schafer had helped build into a growing export business. The carpenters built trendy furniture from old barn wood. The metaphor was very helpful. Once North Dakotans realized that Schafer had a knack for seeing opportunity in efforts abandoned by others, they transferred that knowledge to a conclusion that Schafer would be able to help turn around the state's economic situation.

Political Media Message

By far the most important aspect of political media is the message. All else being equal in a typical campaign setting, the best message usually wins. That is not to say that the best candidate or the best credentials will win; it is the best message. In order to create an environment in which a political campaign's message can dominate the race, the media consultant must first prepare an effective media strategy.

The first step to choosing the right message is to change the candidate's perspective. This requires the campaign team to analyze their own strengths and weaknesses the way a news reporter or even the opponent might do. The next step involves committing these points to writing. Only by changing your own perspective can you properly evaluate the problems and potential of your own campaign. Once that is done, the campaign should identify the political context. As noted above, this includes looking at campaign messages from past local races (and how they worked), election results, polling results, demographics, and the basic facts about your candidate's record as well your opponent's record.

The next step is to select a message or theme, and it must be creditable (outlined in Chapter 8). Voters—particularly those with weak partisan ties—tend to screen out any messages that do not seem believable. It must be demonstrable from the facts established in the first two steps; and the chosen message must be the logical thread that connects the strengths, weaknesses, political history, and all other data.

Once the theme of the campaign has been established, the media strategist should design a metaphor or an image that will communicate the message in a very simple, direct manner. Think visually. This means finding a way to show the voter what you mean—particularly if television is within reach of your campaign budget.

Starting in 1984, the Ohio Republican party set its sights on retaking the majority in the Ohio State Senate. Polling data indicated great voter discontent with a 90 percent income tax increase put into effect by the Democratic legislature and Democrat Governor Dick Celeste. The Republican State Senate candidates that year all used roughly the same message—Republicans will fight future tax increases. The selected metaphor was an animated wallet being locked with a sturdy padlock. This trusty image was used to regain control of the Senate and was featured in television commercials though the 1988 cycle.

Another important point in message selection is to avoid extremes. If a metaphor or image is at the edge of mainstream voter thinking, it may not be well received. Campaigns should try instead to relate the message to a common experience of the voter. It may be necessary to test the metaphor or image with a group of average voters. But campaign workers should remember that they are not necessarily creating a slogan—they are setting up a thought that votes can soon call their own.

Once a message is created, the campaign must decide how best to deliver it. The medium for delivery is actually a creative choice that affects the message itself. Strategists should evaluate budget considerations as well as voter habits. The inclination should be toward a medium that allows repetition of the message to as many likely voters as possible. Once the message is finally implemented, the campaign must monitor it constantly. Is it internally consistent? Is it consistent with changing events of the campaign and changing attitudes of voters? Candidates should listen to real people to gauge this rather than evaluating it from inside the campaign inner circle.

When necessary, the political message should be refined to keep it consistent. Although it is rarely a good idea to change horses midstream, it is preferable to drowning! One must understand the rhythm of the attack; it will likely come, or you may even start it. But be prepared in every way. How can the message be used in your own attack? Or, if you are attacked, how can the message be used in the response? Every decision in the media plan must be compared against the message. And crafting the right message takes a great deal of time. But once selected, the right message will win nearly every time.

PAID MEDIA OPTIONS

For the purposes of this chapter, political media tactics include newspaper advertisements, radio, broadcast television, cable television, direct mail, and campaign collateral.

Newspapers

In general, newspaper advertising is the least persuasive of the media commonly used for political campaigning. However, campaign managers and consultants often defer to the tradition—and in some cases, the expectation—in some areas that candidates will utilize ads in local newspapers. In recognition of that tradition, newspaper ads must sometimes be included in the overall media mix.

One of the main drawbacks of utilizing newspapers as an advertising medium for political campaigns is their inherently passive nature. Readers choose where they want to look—both inside the newspaper and on the actual page. Therefore, to catch the reader's attention, the ad must stand out. Even if the reader notices the ad, the reader must then actively choose to read it. Despite the difficulty of making an effective political communication in this manner, there are ways to take advantage of newspaper advertisements.

In 1990 Minnesota Senator Rudy Boschwitz was ousted by newcomer Paul Wellstone. Although Wellstone's creative television ads clinched the race, his media consultant used eye-grabbing newspaper ads to reinforce the other media. In one notable newspaper ad, Wellstone showed a short list, "What Rudy Boschwitz Did for You" (followed by a few frivolous bills sponsored by Boschwitz), next to a long list of "What Rudy Boschwitz Did to You" (followed by several anti-Boschwitz points). The design won a "Pollie Award" from the American Association of Political Consultants.

The best bet for an effective newspaper advertisement is usually a professionally designed layout similar in style and content to other print pieces utilized by the campaign. Another effective approach is to use a cartoon as a newspaper ad—particularly if the newspaper does not have a comics section. The more creative the layout, the more likely it is that the ad will be noticed and read. Another option is to include as much white space as possible. Advertisements that are cluttered get "lost" in the rest of the paper.

Radio

Radio is a time-honored method of political communication. In political districts outside of major television markets (as is the case in many rural areas), radio may even be the foremost medium of communication.

Radio is used best as a tool to reach certain targeted segments of the voting population. If one thinks about it, there are many more radio stations than television stations. Each station has a format that attracts certain types of listeners. For example,

Big Band music is appreciated mostly by older voters. A candidate with a strong senior citizen message might choose that type of station to broadcast his or her advertisements. An urban contemporary format is more likely to reach Black voters; farm reports certainly reach farmers. The examples are endless.

Creatively, radio can be a very flexible medium. Radio is a theater of the mind. With a careful mix of voice, music, sounds, and even silence, a very effective political message can be sent. Many candidates also prefer radio because it is much cheaper than broadcast television. Experienced campaign managers can often relate war stories that recount stubborn candidates who push for campaign decisions based solely on the ultimate cost. Although a savvy media buyer knows that less cost usually means fewer voters reached, overall budget concerns often favor radio. A radio spot can cost just from 15 to 20 percent of what a television ad in the same market might cost. Many campaigns also choose radio because the television market where their district is located covers so many different political districts that much of the media buy would be "wasted" on people who cannot vote for the advertised candidate.

Some reports indicate that nearly a half billion radios are used in America. This common link among voters makes it very attractive for political candidates. When the low cost is added into the equation, it is no wonder many local campaigns include this medium in their overall plan.

Finally, radio is a better medium in which to bring a negative attack. Because it lacks the visual power of television, radio is a favorite medium for the attack ad. Voters seem to be less offended by harsh radio commercials than they do by similarly harsh television commercials. In 1990 Missouri Congressman Jack Buechner was running for reelection. His opponent was a Democratic political consultant turned politician named Joan Kelly Horn. Although Horn's campaign was extremely negative in tone, the turning point came about as a result of a harsh radio commercial. As romantic music played, the radio spot play acted a fictional conversation between the unmarried congressman and his girlfriend, who had accompanied him on a trip to France. The young woman gushingly thanked the congressman for using tax dollars to take her on the trip, but she worried that the trip might be keeping him from pressing business back in D.C. The congressman calmed the woman, saying that all he was missing was "a few votes on the Savings and Loan crisis."

The ad was devastating and was the beginning of the end for Buechner's congressional career. However, had Horn run the same ad on television, it likely would have backfired. The subject matter was simply too explosive to be communicated in an already powerful medium like television. All in all, radio is an extremely versatile political tool.

Broadcast Television

Most media consultants believe that there is no more persuasive tool than television advertising. Nothing—mail, radio, or press—can match the effectiveness of television in a statewide race. Simply put, broadcast television is the Tyrannosaurus rex of political media. That is why the bulk of most statewide campaign budgets is spent on television advertising.

Most voters get their news from broadcast television, a trend that is getting stronger all the time. As a result, the television set is on in the average home for more than four hours every day. That is why political messages sent through broadcast television are received by more people than any other combination of political media. In addition to the sheer number of people reached by television, its visual nature makes the political messages sent through it more powerful than anything short of a personal encounter with the candidate or a campaign volunteer.   People understand television—they welcome local television news anchors into their homes everyday. They actually feel as though they know the people on television.

Visual images are retained by viewers for many years after they are seen. For example, you can probably now visualize the set from the television show *Cheers* even if you have not seen an episode for quite some time. Because voters remember these images for such a long period of time, paid political ads often are retained as independent news accounts—which is just another reason why television is so powerful.

Cable Television

Cable television is viewed by most political consultants as a medium separate and apart that of broadcast television. Although the compelling visual nature of cable television are virtually the same as for broadcast television, the kind and amount of voters reached is very different.

In the early days of cable television, very few American households were wired to receive cable. In addition, there was a very limited selection of cable television. As any one who has ever spent a few minutes channel surfing through today's cable channels already knows, the wide variety of choices is increasing all the time.

These specialty cable stations are watched by many, more so than people watch traditional broadcast stations. The narrow interest classification of cable channels provides a radio-like opportunity to reach certain kinds of voters. A candidate wishing to reach upscale African Americans might choose to advertise on Black Entertainment Television. A female candidate might want to use Lifetime or the E! Network to speak to young women voters.

In order to utilize these cable choices effectively, the local cable system must provide local advertising opportunities. Campaign staff should investigate those possibilities before designing a media plan that includes cable advertising in the overall mix.

A word of caution may be useful: Many candidates (and, it seems, candidate spouses) will want to eschew broadcast outlets in favor of cable television. This decision will be urged because cable is cheaper and because whoever is urging the choice watches cable television. This line of thinking presents two extremely common amateur missteps. The first mistake involves choosing political media based on price. Candidates want to save money, but to use a handy metaphor, buying a Chihuahua as an attack dog might save money but it will not give the protection a Doberman can. It is a point that cannot be emphasized enough—in almost every case, fewer dollars spent will result in fewer voters reached. If there were a cheap shortcut to reaching voters, it would already have been discovered.

The other key mistake involves candidates or supporters who assume that their own personal habits and outlook mirror those of the electorate. Insightful politicos understand that the fact that they are involved in politics at any level, by definition, means that they think about politics in a completely different way than the average voter. This is most true for the candidate and the candidate's family. These people are so wrapped up in the campaign that they are quick to forget that their life revolves around politics. To make media selection decisions based on this warped perspective would result in a dubious strategy.

Direct Mail

One of the most effective ways of targeting a specific group of voters is to use direct mail. Over the last two decades, political direct mail has become a specialty unto itself and it now boasts an entire array of consultants who practice this craft. Raising money through the mail is a separate and distinct task from persuading voters with mail. Fund-raising mail is addressed in chapter ten.

Direct-mail persuasion in political campaigns is as old as the U.S. postal system. Friend and family would often discuss political choices in their written correspondence. It was not until campaigns became big business that mail was created in mass quantities to influence voter attitudes. In 1952, after vice presidential candidate Richard Nixon gave his famous "Checkers" speech defending his ethics, thousands of Americans wrote to him to express their support. Nixon's campaign mailed each of those voters a mass-produced postcard featuring a photo of the Nixon family and what appeared to be a hand-written note from Nixon himself (Melder 1992, 168). This may have been one of the most effective pieces of voter persuasion mail ever utilized in political campaigns. The design—a mass-produced mailing that appears to be personalized—has become a classic form of persuasion mail.

Direct-mail experts start their work by ascertaining who needs to be convinced to vote for their candidate. Strong supporters need no persuading, and strong opponents should not be communicated with at all, as discussed in Chapter 5. The likely voters who have not made up their minds are most often targeted with mail.

By using voter lists organized with demographic information, direct-mail consultants can pinpoint voters and push their political buttons. For example, in a 1991 referendum campaign for a library tax in Louisville, Kentucky, the proponents targeted voters in zip codes near library branches. When those lists were cross-referenced with census tract information indicating households with children, the optimal target voters were selected. Those homes then received direct-mail brochures that detailed the run-down condition of the library branches and the top-quality books and improvements that would be available if the referendum passed.

While television and radio can reach millions of voters at once, direct mail can break the campaign's message down into just a few dozen people. By personalizing the message for each subset of the target group, a very intimate political connection can be made with the voter.

More than any other political technology, direct mail has changed dramatically in the past two decades. The ability of personal computers to produce high-quality print jobs that appear to be individually prepared, combined with the mind-boggling ability of computers to compare available lists, has created a direct-mail environment in which individual preferences of voters can be addressed specifically in a mass mailing. This creates the great advantage of being able to communicate different political themes and messages to different political subgroups. However, should a candidate be caught saying two different things about the same issue, there could be trouble ahead.

Direct mail is often used to reinforce messages put out by other media. This coordination actually improves the overall message recall of voters. Direct mail can also be conducted inexpensively, since the voters sought out by the campaign are the only ones who receive the message.

Campaign Collateral

Yard Signs. Yard signs have a place in many political campaigns; but if the effort the typical local campaign spends talking and arguing about the design, color, typeface, content, and placement were channeled into a more important area such as fund-raising, the candidate's cause would be much better served. The first and most important thing to remember about yard signs is that their purpose is very narrow—to create and reinforce name identification. The secondary effect of yard signs is to show increasing support, but many campaigns carry that relatively minor task to monumental proportions.

In Pennsylvania's top-targeted state house race in 1984, the Republican candidate (now congressman) Jon Fox posted in excess of 500 yard signs in a district of less than 60,000 people. Signs were seen on side streets and even at the end of cul-de-sacs. It took two or three staffers from 40 to 50 hours a week just to post and re-post the yard signs. An effective yard sign campaign will be limited to placement on busy roads. First-time candidates often fret that supporters on side streets and less-traveled avenues will feel slighted, but the resources saved by bypassing those sites greatly outweighs any miffed supporters. An effectively designed yard sign will simply state the name and office sought. Any other information (such as party identification, slogan, photo, or the date of the election) will only clutter the sign.

When designing the sign, campaign staffers should remember that it will be typically viewed by moving cars from great distances. A good test to determine whether a sign is readable is for someone to take the mock-up of the sign (the design before printing), walk thirty big steps away, and flash the sign at you for two seconds. If you can read all of it during that time, it is probably an effective yard sign.

Outdoor/Transit. Billboards, train station signs, bus signs, cab signs, and other such political media can be addressed effectively as one category. These are good ways to increase a candidate's name identification, but they work much better in an urban district than a suburban or rural district. They also tend to be rather expensive.

For campaigns that choose to employ outdoor or transit advertising, the roles as stated for yard signs apply. Name and office sought are typically the only information needed on the sign. Candidates and their staffs should remember that most voters see this type of advertising as part of the everyday jumbled scenery of their environment. Even the most-well designed outdoor ad is likely to be overlooked by many—if not most—of the people who pass by it. Used purely to increase name identification, outdoor or transit advertising can be effective. However, before entering into a legal agreement to place such advertising, campaigns should attempt to determine just who will see the signs and whether those people are likely voters in the district where the candidate is running.

If billboards are used, the designer should remember that the latest trend is to create an eye-catching advertisement that seems to break free of the traditional rectangular billboard shape. Some advertisers have items (for a political campaign, perhaps a capitol dome) jutting out from the billboard, creating a bursting-out effect. Other techniques are to have components of the design hanging off the edge of the sign or even to alter the overall shape of the billboard. But, as with any political media, the message is much more important than the delivery.

Buttons and Bumper Strips. Campaign buttons and bumper strips (also called bumper stickers) are traditional political items, but long ago they lost their appeal as effective forms of political communications. Most people shun wearing campaign buttons or displaying a bumper strip. In fact, over the last thirty-five years, the percentage of people who were willing to do either of these political activities has been cut in half. In 1960, 21 percent of voters wore a campaign button or displayed a bumper strip. More recently that figure has dipped to less than 9 percent (Conway 1985).

Buttons in general have lost their novelty value, and as more people treat their cars like prized possessions, fewer people are willing to affix bumper strips. In addition, most bumper strips are difficult to read from a safe following distance. The average voter does not look for political bumper strips and certainly is not likely to risk a collision just to read one. Although candidates and campaign managers will be deluged by catalogs from button manufacturers and bumper strip printers, the best approach is to ignore these outdated items.

Campaign Junk. Most experienced campaign consultants can tell interesting and humorous stories about the collateral that candidates purchase to publicize their names. The aforementioned button and bumper strip catalogs are likely also to include emery boards, balloons, unbreakable combs, pens, key chains, bottle openers, pot holders, tie clips, mugs, t-shirts, and a large selection of hats. No matter what the gimmick is, when questioned about why it is a necessary campaign expenditure, the candidate is likely to respond; "People around here just love those (insert type of campaign gimmick)! I keep running out of them." When you point out to the candidate that the same could be said about silver dollars or free cans of beer, they are not likely to be amused. These collateral campaign advertising specialties are impulse purchases—that is all.

The point to remember about campaign junk is that it has only one purpose: to boost name identification. One must carefully analyze how the intended object will do that. Here are a few examples. Most yardsticks wind up in closets, so they tend to be a poor choice to increase name identification. Refrigerator magnets are popular despite the fact most Americans have dozens of magnets on their refrigerator and few people even notice them after a day or so. Baseball caps with messages printed on them have become so commonplace that few people even bother to look at the inscription anymore.

Consultants who have fought this battle with candidates time and time again typically dismiss all such gimmicks as ineffective. At many county fairs, it is customary for candidates to hand out some sort of gimmick. If your campaign needs to conform with such a custom, buy something cheap and do not fool yourself into thinking you are creating much name identification.

Although it does little to win votes, campaign collateral items are minimally necessary to show some basic grassroots presence. They also provide something to be given to those who call or write to ask about the candidate. Nevertheless, new-style consultants strongly advise against spending money for these items.

Emerging Technologies

Internet. Currently, thousands of businesses are rushing to establish home page sites on the World Wide Web or create other Internet-related connections. Political campaigns of the future will no doubt rely on this technology heavily. However, the vast majority of Americans currently do not have access to the Internet because they lack either the interest or the necessary computer hardware.

Campaigns can, however, generate a certain amount of earned media by creating some sort of Internet connection and showing it to the press. It can also be an effective way to transfer data to the handful of people who want more information about a candidate. Some consultants use e-mail and other computer file transfer abilities to hasten the data exchange with far-flung campaigns. The Internet can also be an effective research tool. This should be seriously addressed when undertaking opposition research or issue research, as noted in Chapter 5.

For the purposes of selecting among paid media, the Internet has not really reached a level of effectiveness for political campaigns to consider it seriously. Staying on top of technology in this area is important, but until more voters are linked to the Internet, this is mostly a future trend.

Videotape Mail. Many candidates are now creating short campaign videos from ten to fifteen minutes in length, to describe their backgrounds and discuss their political philosophies. This most typically occurs in the early stages of a campaign when opinion leaders are "shopping" for a candidate to support. A video tape showing the candidate speaking and being seen in a variety of settings can be a very effective way of introducing the campaign to an opinion leader (or, in some cases, a party delegate preparing to endorse someone).

The trend is to use video or film footage, which is shot for political commercial use, then edit the scenes into a long-form piece. After an announcer's portion, graphics, and music are added, the program is dubbed to VHS videotapes, a label and box sleeve are created, and the entire package is mailed to opinion leaders or delegates with a written appeal to watch it. Done properly and in large quantities, videotapes can be produced for as little as from $5 to $7 each.

SELECTING AMONG POLITICAL MEDIA

This chapter has addressed most of the major political media available to modern-day political candidates. The campaign manager or media strategist must examine the available options and somehow craft an effective media mix. An important first step in achieving this goal is to design a media plan. Some consultants include a media section in the overall campaign plan; others design a separate media plan. Either way, media strategy must be planned and agreed to by all advisors in advance. Campaigns that make most media strategy decisions as the campaign progresses typically fail.

Media tasks will be the most important political programs conducted by a campaign. Although many different activities will occur, it is important to remember that most voters will make their decisions based on television ads, radio spots, newspaper ads, and direct mail produced by the respective campaigns in the race. Therefore, while every aspect of a campaign budget is important, special attention must be paid to the content, timing, and mix of the paid media. Toward that end, the purpose of the media plan must be to discuss and plan each aspect of television, radio, and newspaper exposure. Once agreed to by campaign officials, the media plan should be the central guide to all the media strategy for the candidate. After that, strategy should be altered only if circumstances significantly change.

Media Production and Placement

Newspapers. Newspaper ads can be produced by a professional designer or by the consultant or campaign staff. Many newspapers will include the cost of ad design with the advertising space cost. If that is the case, a newspaper's in-house designer can create the final product from a sketch, design, or mock-up created by the campaign.

Newspaper advertisements are placed through newspaper cooperative associations (for a multipaper purchase) or through the display advertising sales staff of a single paper. Ads are measured and purchased in column inches, which helps a media buyer compare layouts and prices.

Campaigns should pay close attention to circulation figures of various newspapers and should familiarize themselves with the reading patterns of voters in the area. In most American communities, the Sunday edition of a newspaper is the most well read. An ad in a Sunday paper will cost much more than an ad in a Saturday paper, which tends to be the least read paper of the week. A certain amount of targeting can be created by choosing the proper section for the ad. Political campaign ads do well in the local news section of the paper, but campaigns targeting women voters may want to consider the family or entertainment sections; male voters can be targeted in the automotive or sports sections. While these delineations may sound like stereotypes to the uninitiated, political campaigns must often make these kinds of assumptions.

Radio. Placement of radio requires an innate understanding of the listening habits of likely voters. For example, radio is an important way to reach voters in rural areas. Farmers bringing in the harvest often listen all day, and people who drive to work listen in the morning and the afternoon. Stay-at-home Moms often listen throughout the day, and blue-collar workers listen during their lunch hour. Further more, since the advent of such hosts as Don Imus and Rush Limbaugh, talk radio has picked up many listeners, which provides conservative candidates with a particularly effective medium for reaching voters.

Because radio allows campaigns to target voters more narrowly, campaigns should tailor their radio message accordingly. For example, in those areas in which a candidate is well known, the radio spots could reflect local issues, local personalities (endorsements), or local conventions.

Radio placement costs more during popular time segments (such as the morning "drive time") and costs less during times when fewer people are listening (such as the middle of the night). It also costs more to put a radio ad in an exact time position; campaigns can save money by floating the spots over a longer period of time.

Radio spots are much simpler to produce than their counterparts in television, and less time is required to do it. When it is necessary for a campaign to get a message or response message out quickly, radio is the natural choice.

Television. Because political candidates should communicate with people who are most likely to vote, television placement strategy should consist first of, buying commercials in and around news broadcasts and on the early morning talk shows. The next step is to purchase spots within the "access" period, which falls between the evening national news and the prime time schedules. If there is still money left to spend, campaigns should purchase prime time spots, where the candidate can be assured of a large audience, but have less of an ability to target the message to people who vote.

Gross rating points (GRPs) are a measure of frequency and reach—advertising terms that describe the number of viewers who see a spot and how often. The cost per point varies depending on the size of the media market. A moderately effective political television buy for a week typically consists of from 500 to 600 GRPs, while a saturation political buy would consist of from 1100 to 1200 GRPs.

Filming of television spots usually takes place in the district, and the final editing process usually occurs later. Savvy consultants film certain "defense lines" which show the candidate's responding to potential attacks. Those filmed lines are held back—to be used only in the event of an attack.

NATIONAL MEDIA QUALITY ON A LOCAL CAMPAIGN BUDGET

In America, there are perhaps two dozen nationally respected political media consultants. This elite group of men and women understand how images, metaphors, wordplay, and other such thematic concepts influence voting behavior. These consultants command princely sums to offer advice, create strategies, and ultimately, produce election-winning media.

Many of the techniques used by these consultants are easily obtained through careful reading and researching. The overall mystique of these national experts clouds the simplicity of many of their methods. This section will help you learn those techniques and point out ways to use them without spending a fortune.

Print Media

The first thing to learn when designing a palm card, brochure, yard sign, or any other form of political print media is to use a professional. By asking a local graphic artist to volunteer his or her services, you will greatly improve the look of your materials without adding to the cost. This tip sounds very logical, but you will find it very difficult to actually carry it out because so many people in the campaign will want to design the print piece themselves. Loud and long discussions will go on about color choice, typeface selection, whether to use this photo or that—in other words, a bunch of amateurs will want to inject their own opinions into a matter best left to a professional artist.

A good graphic artist (hopefully someone who has designed political pieces before) will be able to use a modern computer layout program, like PageMaker or Quark Express, to design an attractive, easy to read print piece. A good artist will also be able to offer advice on ways to save money with a printer and how to link the visual look of all the campaign media.

Direct Mail

Find ways to make your direct-mail piece look personalized. Voters have become wary of computer-generated mailings. They get them every day. People know how to look for the signs that indicate whether the mail is "junk mail."

Use your volunteers to hand address all envelopes. Even if you are using a bulk rate permit, affix an actual stamp (called a "live" stamp) to each envelope. Have the candidate hand write a note that can be mass produced and included with a brochure. Some campaigns are even applying hand-written Post-it notes to brochures to give the personal touch. Others design large cardboard envelopes that appear to be overnight mail packages to entice the voter to open the letter immediately.

Be careful not to be too tricky. In 1990 a state senate campaign in Ohio featured a mailing designed very much like a legal summons. Sent to a rural area where voters tend to take things more seriously, the piece created quite a controversy for the candidate.

Radio

Media consultants understand that radio is a specialized medium that requires a special approach. A rather common local campaign mistake is to take the audio portion of a television ad and record it for radio. Another amateur error is to let the candidate write out several thoughts and then have the candidate read them on to a tape.

Professional and effective radio commercials have a sound unto themselves. If you want to hear the difference, try this experiment. Tune into the lowest rated religious or ethnic format radio station late at night. What you will typically hear is poorly produced, monotone commercials and public service announcements. Then tune into a national news report from National Public Radio. The difference is striking. NPR news reports from the field use an interesting blend of ambient sound, different voices, music, and conversational speaking.

It does not cost much extra to give radio commercials that NPR sound. Instead of recording the candidate portion of the spot in a studio, have him or her speak about the economy from a grocery store, about crime from a police station, or about education from a school playground. Although you can passably fake these sounds with sound effects if you have a good radio technician, going into the field will give your spot a very unique sound.

Outdoor

Billboards are rather expensive political campaign vehicles. However, they can be an effective way to reinforce name identification. Yard signs are more affordable but present similar creative challenges. The biggest amateur mistake made with billboards and yard signs is to cram too much information into too small a space. Consultants know that the most a driver will see while passing a sign by the road is the name of the candidate and perhaps the office being sought.

IMPORTANT MEDIA TERMS

Because paid media is such an important and quickly expanding part of new-style campaigning, the final section of this chapter quickly defines several of the most important terms.

Agency Commission. The money paid to the media placement firm for buying the media space or time. The standard commission is typically 15 percent of the gross amount of advertising purchased.

Arbitron. The name for the system used by the American Research Bureau which gathers data to rate television and radio. The higher the rating, the more the television or radio station can charge for the time.

Audit Bureaus. These organizations verify the circulation figures of newspapers and magazines. The higher the circulation, the more the newspaper or magazine can charge for the space.

Boards. This means outdoor advertising, such as billboards. Boards have long been a fixture in political campaigns. In this industry, a "75 showing" denotes the fact that 75 percent of the people in that area will see the board's message over a month.

Buying the Market. This strategy, used by media buyers, allows a candidate to saturate almost every television and radio spot available. This is the best way to raise name identification quickly.

Copy. The actual words used in a political ad. Copy is a written or spoken script designed to run in spots or print ads. The media consultant is the master of what an ad's copy should say.

Cost per Thousand (CPM). An industry-wide measure of how efficient a particular medium is in reaching audiences. It stands for cost per thousand people reached by the message. CPM allows media placement firms to compare different media by effectiveness. Typically, television produces the lowest CPM.

Disclaimer. The legally required authorization notice on almost all forms of political media. Depending on the state, it should indicate who paid for the ad. Disclaimers are also required by the Federal Election Committee.

Equal Time Rule. A federal rule based in Section 315 of the Federal Communications Act, it allows political candidates access to the broadcast media. Television and radio broadcasters must provide the same air time to all candidates as they give to any one candidate. Broadcasters may choose not to sell time to nonfederal candidates, but they must do so for all candidates in a given nonfederal race.

Flat Buy. A strategy used in media buying which distributes campaign media dollars evenly over the last few weeks of a campaign. This is also called a media blitz, except that a blitz implies a large amount of money bought flat over just a few days.

Full Position. In newspaper advertising, this is a carefully selected placement area for a political ad. Often, campaigns will want their ad near a news article on a certain topic. Other areas can be specified such as near the front of the paper (which costs more) or "run of the paper" which is wherever space permits (which costs less).

Gross Rating Points (GRPs). This is the most important measure used to evaluate the impact of commercial television. GRPs represent the overall number of people in a target audience exposed to a message. It is calculated by multiplying reach and frequency. Reach means the number of people who receive the message; frequency is the number of times these people are exposed to the message.

Lift. The portion of a television or radio commercial taken out and used in another ad. A short commercial might be made from a longer one. The short spot would be called "the lift". For reinforcement purposes (and because it saves money), lifts are one smart way to produce media.

Lowest Unit Rule (LUR). This federal rule guarantees that candidates can purchase television or radio advertising at the lowest possible rate. Whatever rate the station best advertiser is entitled to becomes the LUR. However, this rule is only in effect during the political "window" forty-five days before a primary election and 60 days prior to a general election. Some campaigns will pay more than the LUR to bargain with another campaign for a particularly coveted spot of air time.

Make Goods. Commercials are run again at no charge due to some mistake in the original broadcast. If the spot was played in the wrong time slot, or was partially cut off, a make good can be requested.

Media Market. The geographic region reached by local television and radio broadcasts or newspaper circulations. Also known as ADIs (or areas of dominant influence), a media markets pool a certain amount of viewers into one ratings area.

Political media buying strategy is based almost exclusively on media market considerations.

Political Window. The political period forty-five days before a primary election or sixty days before a general election. During this time, broadcasters may charge only the lowest unit rate (LUR), a special low political rate for campaigns.

Rate Card. The standard price list for media space within any medium. Newspaper rate cards show the rates and the specifications for the actual ad.

Rating and Share. A measure of television viewership. Ratings represent the number of households in an audience of a program as a percentage of the total number of households with television sets. Share is the number of households in the audience of a program, as a percentage of the total number of households that actually have television sets on at that time. A television program with a 10 rating means that 10 percent of all homes with a television were tuned to the show in question. A share of 20 would mean that 20 percent of all homes with a television on were tuned in to that show.

Storyboard. This drawing describes each scene of a proposed television commercial using a series of hand-drawn panels and dialogue. Storyboards are usually created by a media consultant hired to produce the campaign's advertising and, once approved, help the director of the television ad film the necessary sequences.

Time Buying. The very important task of placing political media in the appropriate time slots in either television or radio. Media time buyers use polling data and demographic information and compare them with viewing trends as established by rating services. Time buying requires great political skill because media dollars must be targeted at certain voter groups.

Chapter Twelve

The Advantages and Perils
of Earned Media

One of the foremost scholars of Congress, Richard Fenno, believes that former Vice President Dan Quayle got a bad rap from the press (1989).[1] During the months he spent in Quayle's office, while Quayle was a U.S. Senator, Fenno was impressed with his hard work, aggressiveness, and, yes, even his intelligence. He was a rising star. This behind-the-scenes view would be a revelation to most Americans—this is *not* the picture most of us hold. The paradox between the insider view and public perception of J. Danforth Quayle underscores the risks of earned media in campaigns.

Many examples of Quayle media blunders could be noted. Perhaps the most damaging came during the heat of the Bush/Quayle reelection effort. In June 1992, Quayle was sent on a mission to promote the administration's "Weed and Seed" after-school tutoring program. The press was invited to tag along when the vice president visited a grade school in Trenton, New Jersey. Sticking to the script, Quayle sat next to a twelve-year-old student, William Figueroa, and began to help him with his studies. When Figueroa went to the board during a spelling bee, calamity struck. After correctly spelling the word "p-o-t-a-t-o," the vice president, relying upon a cue card, instructed the boy to add an "e" to the end. The room suddenly grew silent, and the press knew they had their story.

The damage control offered by Quayle's staff was that, although the current spelling of "potato" did not boast an "e," the old English version did. But it was of little use; the vice president was shown to be a worse speller than the twelve-year-old. Nearly every newspaper, radio, and television station in the nation carried the slip in glaring detail, and of course late-night talk show hosts were given a new arsenal of farcical ammunition. Adding insult to injury, Figueroa held a news conference the next day, where he told reporters the vice president was a nice guy but "needed to study more" (Nieves, 1992). The administration's effort to highlight their ingenuity in after-school programs was lost; while most Americans know of the "potato" gaff, few have ever heard of the Weed and Seed Program. The event was yet another hint that Quayle was incompetent and the GOP ticket was out of touch.

If press events can backfire like the "potato" affair, why do candidates take the risk? Is it really worth exposing candidates to the press—often quite hostile to all politicians—in an unstructured format? The answer, of course, is that candidates can successfully garner media attention, providing a tremendous boost to their overall efforts. About the same time Quayle was learning the correct spelling of certain vegetables, Bill Clinton and Al Gore were traveling around the nation on their postconvention "bus tour." Day after day newspapers and television news programs were filled with these two men jogging, throwing the football, meeting average folks, and generally having a good time (Ifill, 1992). Accompanied by their young wives and families, the candidates portrayed the message of the Democratic ticket's youth and vigor, a new generation—precisely the theme the campaign had in mind. Moreover, the bus trip successfully snatched the media limelight prior to the GOP convention. There are many reasons why the Clinton team was successful; surely at the top of the list is their careful use of the press.

This chapter looks at the advantages and perils of earned media. The activity entails attempting to persuade media outlets (newspaper, radio, or television news stations) to run a story favorable to your campaign. Once termed "free media," few now see it as cost free. But all agree now that earned media is one of the most important areas of new-style campaigning. Stories generated from press releases, press conferences, events, editorials, actualities, and other activities add creditability to the campaign message, and do so at a modest cost. The discussion begins with an overview of the history of news coverage in campaigns. Why candidates regard such coverage as so attractive is considered, and what reporters and editors see as "newsworthy" is reviewed. Several approaches to attracting earned media are also delineated.

A QUICK LOOK AT THE HISTORY OF CAMPAIGN NEWS COVERAGE

During the colonial period, candidates used newspapers in several ways, including announcing their interest in running for a particular office and carrying anonymous essays on important issues. By the late 1700s, newspapers began to take on a more assertive role. Many would print lists of candidates worthy of support, and others would openly extol their virtues—while brutally attacking their opponents. Beyond helping or hurting particular candidates, most papers aligned themselves with one side of the political debate of the day, giving rise to the partisan press, which lasted throughout the 1800s (Dinkin 1989, 7–9). Candidates during this period had unlimited access to the newspaper controlled by their party and received consistently hostile coverage from the paper on the other side. A candidate's success or failure in the press depended more on the number of readers each side could boast than on their ability to control the type of story they received.

As the American population increased throughout the nineteenth century, so did the number of newspapers. Media did not become big business, however, until the rise of "yellow journalism" in the 1890s. In an effort to expand readership, papers began highlighting sensational, dramatic stories and downplaying partisan appeals. It was deemed more profitable to attract readers from both sides of the political fence than from just one. Additionally, as a backlash against yellow journalism a few decades later, there was a growing view that the press should present information in an accurate, impartial way. This was helped along by the introduction of wire services, which tended to balance national news (Dinkin 1989, 99). "Objectivity" had become the mainstay of journalism by the 1920s. Politicians were treated fairly, yet with kid gloves; journalists accepted what they were told and rarely scrutinized the private lives of candidates—leading a foremost scholar of the press aptly to label this period "lapdog" journalism (Sabato 1991, 25).

During the 1960s and 1970s, the news industry entered a period of "investigative journalism." Shocked by the revelations of misinformation provided by the Johnson and Nixon administrations, reporters no longer took it for granted that politicians were trustworthy or sincere. They scrutinized and checked each policy statement and, more important the behavior of candidates. The race in the media was to dig beneath the surface and find the dirt, leading some to tag this period "watchdog journalism."

At precisely the same time investigative journalism took hold, the import of television news was brought to the fore. Whereas only 34 percent of American households had televisions in 1952, two decades later nearly all contained at least one, and most had two (Sorauf 1988, 25). Doris Graber reports that the amount of time Americans spent with the news media jumped 40 percent with the advent of television (1987, 152). Not only was it critical for candidates to get on the local or national news, but the image they portrayed in these stories was now equally, if not more, important.

A decade later, during the 1980s, the press took yet another turn to "junkyard-dog" journalism (Sabato 1991, 26). Rather than objectively reporting campaign news, reporters attempted to "make news." Political reporting during this period was harsh, aggressive, and intrusive, and as much about gossip and innuendo as about fact. When 1988 presidential candidate Gary Hart was rumored to be having an extramarital affair, reporters took it upon themselves to hide in the bushes to find out if it were true. When they discovered his close relationship with Donna Rice and reported it, Hart removed himself from the race. The bitter animosity between pols and the media, common in today's political world, has its roots in this period.

Recently there seems to be a modest step back from overly aggressive attack journalism; the "feeding frenzy" may have subsided. The personal lives of candidates are still fair game, but overly aggressive, intrusive reports are increasingly scorned by the public. What is picking up the slack in campaign news reports are horse-race stories (who's ahead in the polls) and extensive coverage of strategy, tactics, and candidate personalities. Few campaign stories center on the policy stands. There is even a growing interest in internal campaign activities, such as expenditures, fund-raising successes or failures, the hiring of new consultants, and the production of the latest commercial. We might say that "the mechanics of campaigning have become a better story than the campaign itself" (Luntz 1988, 33).

WHY PRESS COVERAGE IS VALUED

Candidates with a large enough war chest can, in some ways, bypass the media. Instead of relying upon reporters to cover an event or story, they can bring it to the voters through paid advertisements. Paid media offers complete control over the timing, audience, and message. Nevertheless, few campaigns have unlimited funds and, as will be seen below, while earned media is never free, it can be significantly less expensive than paid advertisements. But the foremost benefit of news coverage over paid advertisements is that the message is deemed more creditable (Salmore and Salmore 1989; Herrnson 1995). Voters believe that because the message is coming from a neutral observer, it must be true—or at least it is more believable than the commercials sponsored by candidates. It also comes to voters when they are apt to be thinking about politics—when they sit down to watch the news or read the morning paper.

It is a mistake to assume that if a campaign relies only paid advertisements and does little to solicit press coverage that the media will stay out of the race. The opponent will, in all probability, seek media attention in various ways. If the press is courted by only one side, it makes sense that they will provide that candidate with the lion's share of reporting. They may even think that the first candidate has something to hide. Thus another reason to seek earned media is to minimize the coverage garnered by the opponent. Newspapers and some local television and radio stations will also become involved in the race through editorial endorsements and press conferences, releases, and events that may help the candidate win favor with the editorial board. Finally, favorable press coverage complements paid media efforts. As noted above, effective message articulation comes from numerous sources.

Earned media is not without its drawbacks, of course, paramount of which is the loss of control. Even the best-laid media plans can misfire—leading to unintended coverage, as with the case of Dan Quayle's spelling bee. Sometimes these stories are not altogether harmful, just different than what was intended. Other times they can be quite damaging. As noted by Gerald Phillips; "If you are brilliant, wise, competent, and a leader of nations, the media will make you appear even better. If you are foolish, incompetent, indecisive, or wimpy, the media can cripple you" (1984, 77).

Press coverage of any kind is generally difficult to receive, particularly if the candidate is less well known, is the challenger, or is running for a lower level office (all three suggest a long, uphill battle with the press). Even state legislative candidates, many of them incumbents, find it hard to get members of the media to pay attention. Often other news events, unrelated to your race or even to politics, will keep reporters away. When Bob Graham (D-Florida) decided to run for the U.S. Senate, he planned a large press extravaganza to kick off the race. Slated was a multi-city rally, using expensive satellite hookups to carry the candidate's message live in each of the media markets at the same time. Since Graham was the sitting Governor, the campaign press team anticipated front-page/lead-story coverage. On the same day of the event, however, the *Challenger* crashed. Needless to say, there was nothing about Graham's event in Florida papers the next day.

What Appeals to Reporters and News Outlets?

In order to understand why some candidates find it easier than others to obtain favorable press coverage, it is important to understand what reporters and editors perceive as news and what variables lead them to select one news story over another. Even if they would like to, the press cannot cover everything; they lack the time and the staff to monitor all that happens and the space and time to report it. Understanding why, in a general sense, some stories make it into print or on the six- o'clock news helps campaigns target their earned media efforts, reducing wasted time and effort.

To reporters and editors, news is something that happens. Put a bit differently, media gatekeepers (those who decide what should be reported and what should not) value event-centered stories because they perceive that their mission is to update the public, and provide accounts about what has existed for some time. News, in their view, is a dynamic rather than a static process. It occurs when something takes place—such as the release of new polling numbers, fund-raising successes or failures, candidate appearances, guest appearances, and new strategies and tactics. Policy stands, on the other hand, remain static; once they are reported or become known, they become inconsequential. If a candidate changes his or her position on an issue, or gets tripped up with an inconsistency, this becomes an event; otherwise, it is not generally considered news. Added to this, adherence, to the cannon of objectivity leads to event-centered news; reporting on policy stands implies a bias, and the news media wish to steer clear of value judgements (Salmore and Salmore 1989, 149–50).

Simply being an event does not guarantee its coverage. A second criterion is that it must be different—out of the ordinary or unexpected. Media outlets wish to inform their audiences, but they also wish to make money. This means that their stories must be entertaining as well as educational. It is common for campaigns to send press releases when they receive a new endorsement; these are, after all, events. Yet most are never reported because they are expected to occur. It is only when an unanticipated endorsement occurs that the media may take notice, such as when a prominent Republican backs a Democrat, or vice versa. Mistakes often make the news because they are out of the ordinary. As GOP media bigwig Roger Ailes notes:

It's my orchestra pit theory of politics. If you have two guys on stage and one guy says, "I have a solution to the Middle East problem," and the other guy falls in the orchestra pit, who do you think is going to be on the evening news? (As reported in Dunn 1995, 121–122)

Another criterion of newsworthiness is whether the story excites the audience. This suggests painting events in a way ordinary citizens can understand and putting the worst or best possible light on the subject. A jump in the local unemployment rate from 6 to 7 percent is less stirring than the layoff of 2,000 workers, even though they may both represent the same development. It is more newsworthy to report that the opponent had "skipped dozens of important votes," than it is to say he had a 5 percent absentee rate.

Gatekeepers seem to value conflict in stories. A campaign would do well to paint all releases/events as a clash or struggle between the candidate and the opponent, or the candidate and some greater force—such as the "Washington Establishment." Many women candidates have made hay out of running against the "old boy's network." Along similar lines, attacks often draw media attention. As noted in Chapter 3, most local reporters do not have the time or inclination to sort out the validity of these claims, yet they will report them because they are exciting and different.

Scandals always seems to catch the eye of reporters and editors. They often contain all of the aforementioned elements; they are out-of-the-ordinary events that push a button with the audience. Many Washington "insiders" were surprised in 1993 when local media outlets seemed fixated on the number of checks bounced by various members of Congress. After all, no public money was used and all the checks were eventually covered. Yet it became a "scandal" because most people could identify with it—nearly everyone has bounced a check at some time and paid the penalty. Although the fervor of attack journalism may have slowed, gatekeepers still value stories about moral and ethical shortcomings.

There are even greater constraints on television "news." For one, reports must be exceedingly short. Most local news broadcasts contain just twenty-three minutes of information. After sports, the weather, and national stories, it is possible that only six or so minutes remain for all local stories including crimes, fires, business closings, and politics. Wise consultants understand media events must be collapsible, either by the news editors or the campaign itself, into an eight-to-ten-second bite. In other words, there must be a few second's clip that is appealing to editors and conveys the right message to the voters. A second criterion is that it must contain strong visuals—something out of the ordinary that catches the eye of viewers. In fact, it is likely that more stories are selected on the basis of the visuals they offer than on the information provided. It is much more profitable to charge the opponent with disregard for the environment by standing in front of a toxic waste dump than it is to make the same charge in a drab campaign headquarters. More will be said on the importance of visuals below.

Finally, campaigns have better luck with stories that are easy for reporters to cover. Reporters are overworked and under-paid, and anything that makes it easier for them to cover the story is worth the effort. This means furnishing all relevant information, meeting deadlines, providing adequate lighting, holding events at accessible locations, and so forth. Believing a unique backdrop will bring media attention, many candidates head out to distant locations: work sites, farms, and schools. When the media fail to attend, candidates are puzzled. What they did not appreciate was that reporters have deadlines and busy schedules, and they may not have had the time to travel to the event. Given a choice, reporters stick to the most accessible way to gather news (Salmore and Salmore 1989, 151). The trick is to merge strong visuals with handy locations.

The Incumbency Advantage Revisited

As with campaign finances (Chapter 10), the disparity between incumbent and challenger earned media access is profound. Democratic consultant Anita Dunn suggests that the media have become unintended coconspirators in the alleged "permanent incumbency" (1995, 113). Incumbents simply find it much easier to get favorable "ink" than challengers (and open-seat candidates as well). There are several reasons for this.

Incumbents have early money, vast resources, early name recognition, and much else going for them. Accordingly, they are expected to win; their campaign is everywhere, and it makes sense that reporters and editors will take stock in the race. What is more, their positions and pledges during the campaign are expected to become their official stands once in office. Challengers, on the other hand, are often given little chance of success and so are believed to be a waste of time. This, of course, creates a self-fulfilling prophesy: the more media attention incumbents receive, the greater the likelihood of their victory; conversely, the less attention the challengers garner, the weaker their chances of victory.

Incumbents also have stronger, ongoing relations with news reporters and editors. After all, they have served in office for several years and have, in all probability, been contacted by the same reporter scores of times on policy matters. Reporters may return to the "incumbent well" again and again out of habit. Most incumbents are on a first-name basis with the reporters in the district. Challengers often struggle to develop any kind of connection. Also, reporters might look to incumbent-generated stories because they are less risky; the source is already established.

Failing to receive media attention is one thing; getting only negative coverage is another. Paul Herrnson notes that Democratic challenger Ed Heffernan (D-Maryland) was able to get his name in the *Washington Post* (the major newspaper serving the district) only ten times during his 1992 bid. In each instance, he was described with terms such as "chafe," "an embarrassment to the party," "facing long odds," and "an underdog" (1995, 193). Such is the fate of most challengers.

With the odds stacked in favor of incumbents, do challengers stand any chance of getting favorable coverage? The answer is a qualified *maybe*. Competitive races receive more media attention than blowouts. According to Dunn, "A challenger who is 'hot' suddenly becomes the beneficiary of celebrity coverage that I call 'pet rock' coverage—the challenger is treated like a new fad" (1995, 119). This implies that the challenger can break the cycle and lead gatekeepers to view his or her chance as, at the very least, possible. This needs to be done at the beginning of the race, or the cycle will set in.

If the incumbent is caught up in a scandal, the media appear quite willing to jump ship. With significant help from the media, challenger Peter Torkildsen (R-Massachusetts) was able to defeat seven-term congressional incumbent Nicholas Mavroules in 1992. Mavroules was, after all, indicted on federal charges of bribery, extortion, and tax evasion during the summer of the election (Herrnson 1995, 193).

Successful challengers, according to consultant Cathy Allen, are not afraid of the media: "They must be willing to stand in front of the camera and refuse to be ignored"

(Shea and Brooks 1995). She suggests highlighting issues the press feels passionately about, such as campaign finance reform, greater access to government decision making, ethics in government, and disclosure of all special-interest dollars in campaigns. She holds that there is a close correlation between candidates who expose these types of issues and those who enjoy favorable media attention. On top of this, challengers should add reporters and editors to their direct mail lists, stop by the outlet frequently to preview print and broadcast material, familiarize themselves with the names of each reporter, and even target the reporter's or editor's neighborhood for a door-to-door canvas (1990b, 62–64).

Finally, providing a media insider's view, Edward Lifson, of National Public Radio, suggests that challengers can be successful with reporters:

Candidates think reporters are looking for a sound bite that will make my job easier, so they give us 30-second answers and don't open up. I toss this stuff out. Challengers, like all candidates, need to have good relations with the media, reporters in particular. This means you have to be open, honest, and accessible. (Shea and Brooks 1995, 44)

Summary

Attracting positive coverage, whether a challenger, incumbent, or open-seat candidate, is a difficult chore. It requires skill, aggressiveness, and luck. For local races the payoffs will be minimal, and even for most congressional races only a handful of stories can be expected. One might ask whether all the effort is really worth it. Today, perhaps more than ever, the answer should be *yes*. The electorate has become increasingly weary of slick campaign appeals. As they are bombarded with direct mail, radio advertisements, billboards, and television spots, it makes sense that they would seek "objective" assessments. This might be especially important as more voters move away from partisan cues. Media coverage may well be filling a new void. The more often a campaign makes it in the morning paper or on the six-o'clock news, the more competitive the race will appear. This leads to easier fund-raising, more volunteers, and even more media coverage.

HOW TO ATTRACT NEWS COVERAGE

Earned Media Plan

As with any aspect of modern campaigning, written plans must precede efforts to acquire earned media. These plans are drawn from the overall campaign plan (see Chapter 2) and, at a minimum, should specify the following: (1) the creation and distribution of a press kit, (2) the timing of earned media ventures, (3) the outlets pursued, (4) the intended message, and (5) the most appropriate tactic.

Press kits provide reporters and editors with background material on the candidate and the race. The kits should include a biographical sketch on the candidate, a list of the campaign staff and their corresponding telephone numbers, a brief list of the foremost issues in the campaign, samples of campaign material, favorable news clippings, and several black-and-white photographs of the candidate in different settings. There is some leeway here, but the basic idea is to help the outlet start a "file" on the candidate. Each item must be consistent with the overall campaign theme (Beaudry and Schaeffer 1986, 125–28).

Press kits are assembled and distributed to each outlet immediately before the candidate's announcement. They can be mailed to smaller outlets but should be hand delivered by the candidate to the most prominent ones. This also allows the reporters and editors to meet the candidate personally; it begins the important interpersonal aspect of candidate-media relations.

A note of caution: It is unwise to present the candidate to the press unless they are ready to answer tough questions—even if it is just an introductory gathering. State assembly candidate Tom Sheldon (D-New York) was surprised—as was his aspiring press secretary—when he "stopped by" to introduce himself to the editor of the largest paper in the district. The editor was so pleased to see the candidate that he invited him into his office and, with the aid of two seasoned political reporters, began asking questions about his background, policy stands, and views of government. Sheldon, thinking the visit would be relaxed and unofficial, was unprepared for the grilling. The visit backfired and the remainder of the campaign was spent trying to convince the paper that he was qualified for the job. Not only were these attempts unsuccessful, but Sheldon was assailed in an editorial for being opportunistic and lacking substance, which was particularly hard to swallow since Sheldon was a former college president!

A fundamental to bear in mind is that earned media should never be conducted independently of other voter contact activities. Earned media does not stand alone, rather it complements other approaches. It is imperative, then, to schedule the timing and message to coincide with paid media efforts. If the campaign plan calls for an attack during the last week in August on the opponent's poor anticrime record, both paid and earned media efforts should stress this topic. Obviously, unforeseen events arise and the timing and message of earned media appeals may change. Yet the most effective voter contact programs are the most integrated ones.

As for media outlets, an initial step is to conduct a media outlet survey for the district. This inventory, stored on a computer database system, should contain a host of information: name, address, and telephone number of the outlet; type of medium; names and titles of political reporters, editors, and publishers (their business and home numbers, if possible); number of subscribers and size of audience; geographic spread; photo, actuality, and video requirements; deadlines; affiliations; endorsement policies; and so on. A special section should be devoted to their past campaign practices including; extent of coverage, endorsements, political leanings overall, the candidate's prior exposure in that particular outlet, the opponent's exposure; and any special policies related to campaign coverage. The goal is to have ready access to all available information on each outlet. Be sure to include every radio station, television station, newspaper (both daily and weekly), and news bulletin/magazine in the district, as well as those located outside the district's boundaries but within the district's media markets.

A number of techniques are available for receiving earned media; the most significant are press releases, conferences, events, actualities, video news releases, and debates. Other possibilities include call-in shows, letters to the editor, and notes in community bulletins. An overview of each is provided below.

The Press Release

The press release is the most basic earned media tool, and it is used to provide outlets with campaign updates, to issue statements, to tell stories before or after an event, to announce an upcoming activity, to highlight an endorsement, to respond to attacks, and to provide background facts. These are important tools in acquiring both print and electronic coverage. Releases are the "utility players" in the earned media arsenal.

Press releases provide the campaign with an easy, rapid means of soliciting press coverage. Because this is by far the most commonly used technique, releases form the core of most of the candidate's favorable coverage. As former newspaper reporter and current consultant Sallie Randolph notes, press releases swing voters to your side, influence editors on the strength of your candidacy, reward volunteers and contributors, motivate staff, and confound opponents (1989).

This is not to say that all releases are created equally. It is safe to assume that hundreds of news releases, from various businesses, organizations, and individuals, not to mention campaigns, cross an editor's desk each week. Why some are selected and others are consigned to the round file is undeniably not random. There are certain essential ingredients for any good press release.

The cardinal rule in constructing a release is to make it novel and exciting (newsworthy) to the editor and easy for the reporter. Few editors wish to have boring, unimportant articles in their papers or on their radio or television news broadcast. Puffery is the single most common flaw in news releases (Randolph 1989). To make it easy for reporters, provide everything they need to write the story. The best approach is to write the release exactly the way in which you would wish it to appear in the newspaper or on the news, given the media's cannon of objectivity. Releases should help the campaign, but overly biased ones are more difficult to clean up than those that just "lean" in a certain direction.

Press releases should contain a headline, a strong lead sentence, and relevant photographs, and it should be written in the inverted pyramid format. In other words, the most important information should be at the beginning and the least pressing material noted at the end. If the reporter is going to cut the material, he or she will start from the back and move forward. Use journalism editing marks and format. All releases must include at least one quote from the candidate or some other pertinent figure (be clear about his or her name and title).

Many consultants suggest brevity in releases; the shorter they are, the more likely it is the outlet will find room. It is argued here, however, that releases should be long, containing everything the writer would wish to find in a story. It is much easier for the reporter to cut material than it is to track down additional information.

A few other tips include writing press releases in the third person, using action verbs as much as possible, relying facts instead of generalities, and keeping it simple. The writing style of the releases should, as much as possible, match the style of the targeted outlet. Everything in a release should be accurate; nothing will win the scorn of news organizations faster than to use information from releases and later find it to be untrue. It is important to establish creditability with the media so that they feel comfortable using your releases without subjecting them to extensive checking. The name and telephone number of a "contact person" must be noted at the top of each release, as well as when the story might be used. "For immediate release" indicates it can be run whenever the editor sees fit. When possible, it is also profitable to include a "zinger"—phrases or words that convey a strong, easily understood message. Often zingers are found in the lead or candidate quote.

As to how many releases should be sent, again the profession seems a bit divided. Some believe "the more the better," arguing that the campaign can never tell when an outlet will have a slow news day. Every press secretary can point to favorable news stories garnered from a release they never expected to run. Frequent releases also keep your race at the forefront of an editor's mind, and lets the editor, as well as the reporters, know what is going on in the races. More likely, however, releases should not be overused. Reporters and editors who receive bundles of releases from the same campaign quickly become turned off and assume, perhaps rightly, that because they are habitually sent, they must contain puff. The best releases get lumped with all the rest—in the round file. Media consultant Steve Snider recalls a time when an opponent was a bit overzealous with his releases, leading a columnist to write about the waste. In fact, releases were used as a scratch pad for the columnist's three-year-old (Snider 1990). The trick is to send enough releases to be part of the press's coverage of campaigns that season, but make sure each has something to say. This takes a bit of ingenuity and skill.

Actualities and Feeds

Radio and television stations should also be mailed releases. Yet it is more difficult to get "play" with the electronic media unless these statements are accompanied with material suited to that medium. In other words, it is considerably more likely to get earned media on radio news programs if it contains an audio element, and television news if it carries a clip.

Because it often requires an extra step, many candidates look to radio coverage only for conferences and events (discussed below). This is unfortunate because radio offers a massive, targeted audience. It is much easier to narrow a message to a particular geographic area or demographic group with radio than with television or newspapers. Added to this, most local stations have few reporters and crave easily available local stories, especially ones with audio segments. This can mean a real boon for local campaigns if they know how the process works.

To get radio air, each station's news reporter should be mailed or faxed a copy of a press release or press conference statement. They should then be called by the press secretary and asked to take an "actuality" (also called "beepers" or "interface") over the telephone. These are short statements from the candidate (from twenty to thirty seconds) and are used to complement the release. Actualities provide the reporter with a written account of the event—something to write the story from—and more important an audio cut to accompany it. Many radio stations cherish this process because it gives the listener the impression that the reporter went into the field to get the story, when in reality the campaign came to them.

There are several methods to provide radio stations with actualities. The most basic occurs when the press secretary calls the station to discuss the import of the release to the reporter or news editor. When they are ready, the candidate steps on the line and provides a quick statement, which is recorded on tape at the station. Although effective, this approach ties up the candidate and generally yields a poor sounding cut; telephone call-ins usually sound rough. Along similar lines, it is possible to have the candidate give one statement into a tape recorder, and then use it with each radio station, holding the recorder to the telephone microphone so that the station can capture it. The candidate does not have to be present, but the transition quality is poor.

Another means, which overcomes both the issue of time and quality, is to use what are called "couplers." Here the candidate's statement is recorded on tape in the campaign office. Again, after the press secretary primes the news editor, the statement is transmitted over the telephone line, this time with the use of an "electronic couple," which is connected directly to the telephone wiring. Because there are no background noises with these devices, the quality of the transition is high. Candidates sound as though they are sitting in the studio rather than in the midst of a storm, hundreds of miles away. Electronic couplers are relatively inexpensive.

Recently entering the market are "actuality machines." These devices, similar to couplers, transmit recordings directly over phone lines. They are a step up, however, as they rely digital technology and yield a recording of even greater quality.

A third approach, possibly the most costly both in money and in time, is to provide tapes to the stations along with every release. At the beginning of the tape, the press secretary quickly sets up the quote with a narrative, then cues the candidate's statement with a countdown: "5-4-3-2-1" (Beaudry and Schaeffer 1986, 128). This improves the likelihood of getting some coverage over the written release, but without prompting by the press secretary this approach is less effective.

A final means is to bring the candidate or dignitary to the radio station. This will require a good bit of time, and perhaps some traveling, but many radio news editors appreciate candidates coming to them and feel obliged to provide some airtime when they do. At the very least, the candidate will generally be allowed to give a quick statement. This affords a handy, high-quality cut to be used at the station's convenience.

Each of these techniques requires some planning, resources, and time. Yet radio is an untapped earned media outlet. Lower level candidates especially should look to this medium. With that said, however, radio actualities must always be newsworthy; puff is shunned by even the smallest station.

Television time is much more difficult to obtain. As will be seen below, conferences and events are the best way to get on the local news. This does not mean that they are the only ways, and much with regard to radio applies here as well. With a little hard work, and a bit of expense, news can be "brought" to the station. Two approaches are suggested. First, the technical director at each station should be contacted and asked what video tape formats are preferable. The campaign would then lease the proper equipment, and hopefully the services of someone who knows how to use it would record some of the more significant campaign events. The tape is then hand delivered to the station, along with a written copy of the story, including what the announcer might say to introduce the piece. In essence, everything is done for the station.

A second approach is to provide the stations with a "video news release" (VNR) or what is sometimes termed a "satellite feed." Here a release, outlining the topic is faxed or mailed as well as, more important, the coordinates of the satellite and the day and time when the feed will be transmitted. The stations, quite familiar with this process, simply snatch the feed off the satellite. Again, the process is made simple for the station. The story is completely edited; the only thing missing is the announcer. Often a follow-up telephone call, making sure they received the VNR, helps ensure its use.

Press Conferences

During the waning days of her 1994 unsuccessful reelection bid, Governor Ann Richards of Texas pulled out all the stops. This included actively soliciting the endorsement of billionaire and one-time presidential candidate H. Ross Perot—a native of Texas and, to many in the state, a folk hero. When Perot finally made up his mind to give Richards his blessing, three days before the election, he did so at a press conference. At the gathering he tagged Richards as "smart, tough, and disciplined." Not only was the story picked up by all the newspapers and radio and television stations in the state, it was carried by the national media as well.

If the press release is the earned media workhorse, the press conference is the show horse. Conferences provide a way to bring reporters to a controlled environment so that the candidate or another dignitary can convey a significant campaign development. They allow a personal explanation of a complex issue or dramatic new development, as well as the opportunity for the press to ask questions on that issue or any other matter. Although the odds are still not great, they are the best way to ensure a minimal level of coverage. Nearly all candidates use them to announce their candidacy, but there are numerous other reasons to hold a press conference, including leveling a robust attack against the opponent, rebuffing an attack, introducing a new round of campaign commercials, announcing unanticipated endorsements, highlighting fund-raising activities, introducing celebrities, and so on.

The greatest obstacle to overcome in planning a successful press conference is simply getting the media to attend. Chances are better than not that, if a reporter covers a conference, something will appear in their medium—hopefully the message the campaign has in mind. In deciding whether to cover a conference, assignment editors undertake a cost-benefit calculation. They weigh the benefits of getting the story firsthand, with the price of sending a reporter into the field to get it. To the campaign press team, this suggests that the issue must be exceptionally important and that it must be easy for the press to cover. When these conditions are met, most candidates for lower level offices still have a hard time getting coverage at conferences, but without them it is nearly impossible.

Considerably more damaging than dozens of puff releases, a waste-of-time conference is scorned by the media and will, in all probability, be the last one covered. The campaign may even be written off and granted no coverage whatsoever. Before a conference is called, the campaign press team should be fully certain that the topic will be found newsworthy; from an objective standpoint, it should have significant "news" potential. A notice should then be mailed to each outlet, outlining the importance of the issue, where and when the conference will be held, and the name and telephone number of the contact person. It is also a good idea to follow up with a telephone call or even visit the assignment editor or reporter. Occasionally this prodding will tip the scales in your favor; however, pushing too hard can backfire.

As to what makes a press conference less costly, location should be a foremost concern. Asking reporters to drive forty-five minutes to your gathering is a sure way of having few attend. There should be easy access to the location—the same site can be used each time. Limited parking and long trips up stairs are abhorred, particularly if television crews are invited. There should be adequate seating and sufficient space—including room for tape recorders, lights, and cameras. Many conferences have flopped because there were not enough electrical outlets.

A wise press person always has an eye out for deadlines. If, for instance, the campaign wishes to make it on the local six-o'clock news, it is a good idea to hold the event before 3:00 p.m., giving plenty of time for editing. The same logic applies to newspaper deadlines. Likewise, keen attention should always be paid to the backdrop (the area behind the candidate or dignitary) in case you are lucky enough to have a picture in the paper or a clip aired on the news. When it comes to any television opportunity, the key is to think visually. Finally, it should be made as pleasurable as possible for the reporters, including always providing top-notch refreshments. Home-baked "goodies" do little harm. The idea is to do everything possible to make it easy for the reporter to cover the conference.

Every conference should begin with a prepared statement made by the candidate or dignitary (the person presenting the endorsement), which should be handed out to the reporters as they arrive. These remarks should be rather brief, allowing time for questions. Often it is wise to provide reporters with an updated copy of the press kit. Conferences should always start and end on time.

To the surprise of many, actor Arnold Schwarzenegger appeared at a press conference in Boston in the fall of 1994 to endorse Edward Kennedy (D-Massachusetts). The high-priced actor is known for backing conservative Republican candidates, including George Bush in 1992. Perhaps his support of the liberal Democrat had something to do with his wife, Maria Shriver. After all, she is Kennedy's niece. Either way, the conference provided a rare opportunity to get a picture of the "Terminator in Bean Town" and the coverage certainly did not harm Kennedy.

Not all press conferences go smoothly. A note of caution should again be raised since press conferences are notorious for backfiring. Scores of candidates gather the press to discuss issue X, only to be bombarded with questions on topic Y. Whenever members of the media have direct access to the candidate, care and preparation should be top priorities.

Media Events

Each election, candidates seek "new and improved" ways of attracting media attention. Media events happen are when the location or activity undertaken by the candidate (or his or her agent) become a key aspect of the event's newsworthiness. Knowing that campaign activities can become "news" if they are action centered, novel, and interesting, media events attempt to add location and action to the earned media effort mix.

Candidates have made media hay out of walking or bicycling across the district, riding in a hot-air balloon, working at different jobs, sleeping with the homeless, serving food at soup kitchens, cleaning up a neighborhood, visiting toxic sites, meeting with senior citizens, greeting workers at a factory gate, and so on. On one occasion, a candidate was attacked by his opponent for putting posters on public utility polls. Conceding the error of his ways, and seeing a unique opportunity, the candidate called upon the local Boy Scouts and Girl Scouts to help him take them down, offering $1 for every poster. This seemed to the press to be a novel idea so nearly all outlets in the district covered the clean-up day. The outcome was several positive stories. There was little doubt that the few hundred dollars paid to the Scouts was well worth the coverage.

But not all press events go as planned. In an effort to demonstrate his down-home roots and support for gun owners throughout Texas, 1994 gubernatorial candidate George W. Bush (the president's son) decided to participate in an annual ritual: the opening day of dove-hunting season. Of course, he invited the press along to take a few pictures. One of the birds that fell from the sky at the behest of Bush's gun, however, was not a dove, but a protected songbird. To compound his embarrassment, the Republican candidate received a $130 fine.

For local-level candidates, events are often the only way to get the press to pay attention. This does not mean they can be approached in a haphazard way. Much of the planning and preparation necessary for releases applies to events as well, including a keen eye to what would make it easy for reporters. Prior to each, a brief notice should be sent to each outlet, indicating what the candidate has in mind, and why it is imperative that they attend. Roughly one week from the event, a more detailed packet of information on the event—including the location, travel directions, and access—should be mailed or hand delivered (Beaudry and Schaeffer 1986, 129). At the event, each member of the media should receive an "event kit," a written statement from the candidate, background information on the event, action photos, and so on.

Debates, Editorials, and Other Possibilities

There are varying accounts about to when the race began to slip away from incumbent Buddy Darden (D-Georgia) in his 1994 reelection bid. Yet few dispute the debate, held two weeks prior to election day, finally tipped the scales toward challenger Bob Barr (R). The event was covered extensively by the press, including two days before of prominent reporting by the largest paper in the district, *The Atlanta Constitution,* and a full one-half-hour program by a local television station, WGTV. It provided Bob Barr with the perfect opportunity to drive home his message that Darden was out of step with the district. Darden was put on the defensive from the beginning of the event, and he remained in that stance for the last two weeks of the campaign (Alexander, 1994).

For many local candidates, debates serve as the only opportunity to garner free press. Reporters will cover most of these events, perhaps out of desire to "inform voters," and thus feel obliged to print a few lines about each candidate. Coverage is generally balanced, meaning that each candidate will get about the same amount of ink. Unlike larger profile debates, such as presidential or gubernatorial, there are few "winners" or "losers" in local-level debates. If the coverage complements themes articulated in the paid media, the one-two punch can prove highly effective. For candidates with little paid media, debates can help a great deal in, at the very least, getting their names out. This is precisely why candidates ahead in the polls are often reluctant to debate; it provides the opponent with a minimal level of exposure.

When it comes to maximizing press coverage of debates, a few items should kept in mind. First, the remarks of the candidate should be geared to the press, not the audience per se. A vast majority of those who attend debates have already made up their minds and are there only to support their candidate. It may make a candidate feel good to receive loud applause from the audience, but unless the media pick up on it, there is little real gain. Accordingly, much of what was discussed above regarding newsworthiness also applies in debates. Candidates should strive to make clear, brief, novel, and, if at all possible, confrontational statements. It is important to reinforce the core theme, but, as noted by scholar Marjorie Randon Hershey, such repetition can become "old news" (1984, 23). New wrinkles in the speeches and off-the-cuff deviations can draw the media's attention. There should always be an eye toward the next day's headlines or the twenty second clip on the local television news.

Much related, candidates should seize any opportunity to use visuals during debates. For example, holding up a piece of the opponent's campaign literature to highlight a contradiction, or referring to a large chart, helps draw the notice of photographers and television cameras. Reporters realize nothing is more boring than a photo of two candidates sitting at a table, so anything out of the ordinary catches their eye. This does not mean one should offend local debate mores and norms or make a fool out of the candidate just to produce a "photo-op." It is only wise to always be thinking visually when it comes to attracting press.

Finally, the candidate should be well prepared for the event because the media will be there to seize upon mistakes. Any time a candidate deviates from prepared material, perhaps to attract the media, they move on to thin ice. When Ronald Reagan suggested at a debate that trees were the major cause of air pollution, and that the Vietnam War was a noble cause, the press pounced (Hershey 1984, 23). Just as important, the opponent will be ready to move on to a mistake as well. It is conceivably more likely that a slip will be exploited by the opponent, than be reported in the press. When Tom Sheldon suggested in a debate that he would rather see income taxes raised than property taxes, his opponent spent the remainder of the race telling voters that Sheldon wanted to raise taxes.

Most daily and weekly newspapers highlight their preferred candidates in editorial endorsements. Once again, a strategy should be devised to receive these plums. It is important to keep in mind that reporters play only a supporting role in the endorsement process. Although it varies from paper to paper, most decisions are made by the editors and, occasionally, by the publishers. Reporters are sometimes asked for their opinions, but the final decision is not theirs. With this in mind, special efforts should be made to win the favor of the decision makers. Periodic visits help, as do personal notes from the candidate thanking the editor for a "fair and accurate" story. It is also wise to request a meeting with the editorial board: for this, it is particularly important that the candidate be prepared.

Endorsements generally occur during the waning days of the campaign. If one is received, it is profitable to have copies printed for last-minute literature drops. New Jersey state senate candidate Gordon MacInnes (D) was given an immense boost when the leading paper in the district called his opponent, among other things, "a walking argument for term limits." Needless to say, the piece was reprinted and dropped to swing areas throughout the district (Beiler 1994c).

Other earned media possibilities are radio and television talk shows and community service programs. Dianne Feinstein's (D-California) struggle to hold on to her U.S. Senate seat in 1994 was arduous; she faced an increasingly conservative electorate and a multimillionaire opponent. When her lead began to slip, the Feinstein team decided to go on the offensive. Her opponent, Michael Huffington, had fully endorsed Proposition 187, designed to limit the flood of illegal immigrants into the state. However, it was discovered that he had employed for some time an illegal immigrant as a houseworker. The hypocrisy was sure to draw voters away from Huffington, but getting it to them quickly and inexpensively was problematic. In the end, Feinstein levied her attack on *Larry King Live*. The maneuver worked; Huffington's negatives skyrocketed and Feinstein was returned to the Senate.

Of course, candidates for local office rarely get invited to appear on national television talk shows, but there are some opportunities on local radio and television programs. Ohio gubernatorial candidate Robert Burch (D), for example, found it difficult to garner newspaper coverage in 1994, but he was able to appear on numerous talk-radio programs throughout the state, including several in large media markets. Often the station, anxious to avoid equal time issues, will invite both candidates to appear on the program. The best approach is to call the stations and find out about these possibilities. The next step is to do your homework on the host, the program's audience, and any potential pitfalls.

Occasionally newspapers will allow candidates to contribute as "guest columnists." This can prove an excellent possibility. Another option is to send "letters to the editor." Often "friends" can send letters in support of a candidate. Along with being rather easy access, the letters to the editor section is one of the most heavily read parts of the paper (Beaudry and Schaeffer 1986, 138).

The Press Secretary

To conclude this section on acquiring earned media, a few words are necessary about the campaign press secretary. In any campaign there should be two people who interact with the media: the candidate and the press secretary. One of the most frequent problems campaigns run into is that several people deal with reporters and editors, which can lead to contradictory statements, confusion, and discord within the campaign team. This situation also hampers the development of personal relationships with members of the press. By the midpoint of the race, a good press secretary will know every reporter and editor by first name, how their kids are doing in school, their favorite drinks, and even the names and eccentricities of their pets.

The press secretary handles all dealings with the media. This person understands the workings of the press, including knowing what is newsworthy and what is not, as well as the import of deadlines. The press secretary provides the race with a second public figure and thus must be knowledgeable, quick on his or her feet, trustworthy, and aggressive. He or she should be a quick writer, understand the significance of backdrops and visuals, and be able to talk a reporter out of writing a negative story through logic, skill, and perseverance. Needless to say, this person is a key player in the new-style campaign team.

CONCLUSION

Earned media is a pivotal ingredient in new-style campaigns. It provides candidates with exposure and often conveys a precise message. It is not free, but neither is it a "big-ticket" item. Because it catches voters at precisely the point when they are most likely to be thinking about politics, themes transmitted through earned media may stick in their minds. On top of all this, voters tend to see it as more trustworthy than paid advertisements. There is little debate that media coverage can make all the difference in a race, and the record books bear this out—few candidates are successful without favorable media coverage.

There are, nevertheless, risks involved with this type of campaigning. An equal, if not greater, number of campaigns have been crippled by media assaults—to many of which were brought on by the candidate. Campaigns move on thin ice whenever others control the message.

The aim of this chapter was to emphasize some topics that help minimize the uncertainty and danger of earned media. By understanding what editors look for, and what reporters prefer, campaigns can be more successful at getting good coverage. And by knowing the numerous tactics available, the campaign can further fine-tune their efforts. There are skills to be learned in the earned media process, but at its very core, the most successful earned media teams tend to be the most imaginative. With hard work and creative thinking, campaigns at every level can get the media to pay attention.

NOTE

1. Fenno's portrayal of Quayle in his 1989 work certainly suggests this. It was also echoed to the author in a personal conversation held in Akron, Ohio in March 1995.

Chapter Thirteen

Returning to the Grassroots

The Republican takeover of both the U.S. Senate and House of Representatives in 1994 surprised most observers. The fact that not a single Republican incumbent was defeated stunned the political pundits. What really shocked folks was the defeat of several long term Democrats—members who were, by all accounts, completely safe in prior elections. Representative Jack Brooks of Texas and Representative Michael Synar of Oklahoma, both rejected, were two such members. Their opponents, with different styles and accenting different themes, relied upon the same voter contact technique: they returned to the grassroots.

Brooks was first elected in 1952, making him the second most senior member of Congress in 1992. He had risen to the higher ranks of the Democratic Caucus, serving as chair of the Governmental Operations Committee for fourteen years, and was appointed in 1989 as chair of the House Judiciary Committee. He was known for his shrewdness, craggy appearance, and constant cigar smoking (Pressley, 1994). Brooks, a Texas icon, was an 800-pound gorilla on the Hill.

His opponent, Steve Stockman, was very much an outsider. He was born and raised in Michigan and eight years before the race had moved to San Antonio, where he found little work and even had to live out of his car for some time. By the time of the race, he was an accountant, living in Houston, and thirty-eight years old. Other than running against Brooks two years earlier (netting 44 percent), he had no prior political experience or even ties to community organizations. He was, according to David Terryaughty, national correspondent for the *Houston Chronicle,* "simply the other guy."[1]

Stockman had a campaign war chest to match his political experience—meager. He did, nevertheless, have the enthusiastic support of hundreds of gun owners and conservative voters throughout the district. He established a headquarters in his garage and from there planned a massive grassroots effort. Throughout the summer and fall, hundreds of volunteers scoured the district, knocking on doors, handing out leaflets, and putting up posters. As his momentum grew, Stockman was able to make a modest radio and television buy, yet for the most part his campaign was organized from his kitchen table and waged with people power. He defeated Brooks with nearly 53 percent of the vote and is now credited as being the most ardent anti-gun control voice in the House (Daley, 1995).

Mike Synar, like Brooks, was considered a powerful force in Congress. He had served only eight years, first coming to Congress when he was twenty-seven years old. But he was a rising star and was seen by his colleagues as "one of the most popular and respected middle American liberals" (Reeves, 1994). His Oklahoma district was perhaps a bit more conservative than he was, but Synar was considered secure.

His opponent in the Democratic primary was Virgil Cooper. Like Stockman, Cooper had no previous political experience. He was a seventy-one-year-old retired school principal. During the race he bought no television time: instead, he barnstormed the district himself, put up homemade posters, and handed out small leaflets. Because he was retired, Cooper was free to spend six days a week pounding the pavement.

Cooper defeated Synar in what was termed "one of the biggest political upsets in Oklahoma history" (Martindale, 1994). While Synar spent nearly $.6 million, Cooper won the election having spent just over $16,000, most of it his own money.

In every election there are examples of candidates who rely extensively on grassroots resources and prevail on election day. To be sure, personal contact is the single best means to win votes, and grassroots efforts are important in any new-style campaign. A team of dedicated volunteers can, to a large extent, compensate for weak finances and help push a well-financed race over the top. This does not mean, however, that grassroots campaigning is simple and unsophisticated. Quite the contrary, in order to optimize the help of volunteers, careful attention must be paid to planning, targeting, and resource allocation. All of the basic principles of new-style campaigning apply to the grassroots operation. Because the "soldiers" in the grassroots effort are generally untrained, they need prudent supervision. Without order and direction, the work of well-intentioned volunteers can not only be unproductive, but detrimental.

This final chapter outlines some ways in which to optimize the aid of volunteers and other direct-contact activities, often termed fieldwork. Candidates like Stockman and Cooper can be successful with shear grit and determination. More likely, however, poorly planned and untargeted grassroots efforts can be disappointing. Cooper may have shocked the political community by knocking off a rising star in the Democratic primary, but his approach proved to be unsuccessful in the general election. The old-fashioned way of getting voters remains one of the best—that is, if it is combined with a new-style twist.

WHY DIRECT VOTER CONTACT WORKS

Elections are about getting information to voters in an effort to persuade at least 50 percent plus one to elect a candidate or not elect another. To persuade, the campaign must reach voters, and numerous voter contact methods are available. Because electorates are often large—in a congressional race there may be over 250,000 voters—and often geographically vast, campaign communication tends to be broad and indirect. In other words, most attempts to reach a large number of voters are simultaneous, such as through a mailing, a series of television spots, or radio ads. Individual voter effectiveness is sacrificed for efficiency—a broad reach.

Direct voter contact, while less efficient when it comes to reaching a large number of voters, is much more effective per voter. There is little debate that the best means to persuade a voter is through a direct appeal, and the foremost direct appeal comes from the candidate. Simply put, there is no better way of winning a vote than to have the candidate ask for it (Trent and Friedenberg 1991, 259, citing Robinson 1976). After the candidate's appeal come the direct requests of the candidate's spouse or other family members, friends, volunteers, party and interest group activists, and paid helpers, respectively. The closer the requestor is to the candidate, the more effective the appeal. This is especially true in low-level races that receive little media attention.

Direct voter contact is effective for a number of reasons. For one, it brings the voter to a different cognitive level than other campaign communications. There is a qualitative difference between a volunteer's talking with the voter on the front porch and a piece of campaign literature in a mail box. The voter becomes more engaged and is more attentive for a longer period of time.

Direct contact allows two-way communication. Voters are given information, and, at the same time, they are given an opportunity to provide information. When voters have the opportunity to give feedback, instead of simply viewing a television screen or reading a piece of paper, they become more invested. "Mass media messages cannot adapt and react to feedback, as can interpersonal communication" (Trent and Friedenberg 1991, 259).

Added benefits of direct contact are physical cues, not otherwise afforded by indirect means. For example, a voter may be persuaded by the physical appearance or kinetics (body language) of the candidate or volunteer. Facial expressions' hand movements, and voice intonations can mean a great deal in interpersonal communication. Some of this might be captured by radio or television spots, yet voters are not as engaged.

Grassroots campaigning also humanizes the candidate. Put a bit differently, campaigns conducted purely in the media, over the airways, or in the mail seem distant and impersonal. When a candidate or volunteer makes direct contact with the voter, a connection is made. Today, more than ever, voters need to be reminded that candidates are people, not products. Along similar lines, field-work gives the impression that there is a groundswell of support for the candidate. Voters, like most of us, like being on the winning side. A enthusiastic volunteer effort leads them to believe that others in the community are supporting the candidate. This can lead to more volunteers as well as support on election day. There are few better ways of getting the bandwagon rolling than with an outpouring of help by members of the community.

Fieldwork activities are not cost free, but they are much less expensive than indirect tactics. Campaigns with strapped budgets can make headway with a large volunteer pool, and most activities can be done quickly. If the campaign is out of funds and receives a last-minute endorsement, for instance, a massive volunteer literature operation could spread the message quickly.

Grassroots can be one of the most targeted voter contact activities. With careful planning it can bring the right message to the right voter. And there is generally little waste, as there is with most media activities.

Finally, fieldwork can lead to greater enthusiasm in the race, leading to more media attention and easier fund-raising. Campaigns engulfed by hordes of volunteers are conspicuous—they stand out and send a positive message. This leads potential contributors to take notice and catch the eye of news editors and reporters. Grassroots efforts can help move campaigns to the winning side of the all-important self-fulfilled prophecy.

The foremost downside to fieldwork is that it is less efficient; it takes much longer to reach voters. This is especially true in high-level races, such as statewide campaigns. Two points should be remembered. First, even the largest race can be brought to the grassroots with layers of organizations and networks of activists. All politics is local. Second, direct voter contact should never be the only mode of campaign communications, but rather a complement to indirect activities.

Where to Get Grassroots Help

The advantages of direct voter contact are numerous and great. But is it easier said than done? How does a campaign recruit personal assistance?

The first place to start is always the candidate. It is difficult to ask others to lend a hand if the candidate is unwilling to do so. More important, as noted above, the most persuasive message is the one delivered by the candidate. The candidate's family and network of friends is the next logical place. Often this takes a little prodding—those close to the candidate presume their efforts should be geared only to "strategy," as opposed to implementation. This notion should be revised early in the race.

Political parties are experiencing an organizational resurgence of late, as noted in the introduction. Many locals are as robust as at any time in the past thirty or forty years; this means a good pool of potential volunteers. On top of this, many party workers will have had experience. Grassroots campaigning is not difficult, but there are some "tricks of the trade."

Local organizations and interest groups can provide volunteers as well. Most Democrats benefit from in-kind assistance from labor unions; and many Republicans get a boost from business and manufacturing groups. If the candidate is a member of a group, certainly the other members can be approached. Yet another source might be student organizations at the local college or university.

A final suggestion is to approach senior groups in the community. Older Americans are politically active and often have more spare time. Many campaigns have benefited from the vigorous, unfailing aid of senior volunteers.

TYPES OF GRASSROOTS ACTIVITIES

The Importance of Targeting Grassroots Efforts

The difference between old- and new-style fieldwork is that the latter is systematically targeted. The limited reach necessarily accompanying direct voter contact can be minimized if it is done in the right places. There are two axioms of direct campaigning: it is the best means to win votes, and it is the slowest means to win votes. It is also true that time is a precious resource and the candidate's time is even more priceless. It makes sense, therefore, to optimize grassroots projects by conducting them in selected areas.

Numerous criteria can be used to target areas of the district for fieldwork. Demographic research, combined with polling findings, might indicate "target group" areas. Geography will certainly matter; it is much easier to conduct grassroots activities in urban and suburban areas than in rural ones. Possibly the race has remained stale in a section of the district, suggesting the need for a conspicuous show of strength. It is argued, nevertheless, that the best criteria to use when targeting direct voter contact efforts are prior election data (Chapter 5).

Grassroots activities are persuading, so it is logical to conduct them in areas of voters most susceptible to persuasion. "Swing" or "undecided" areas are defined through prior electoral research as those places in which voters have a history of moving from candidates of one party to the other, either in the same election or between election years. We might say that these areas are "fertile grounds."

Geographic considerations must be overlaid with the targeting data. An area may be a "swing" territory, but very difficult to canvas. In order to go door to door in most agricultural areas, for instance, the volunteer must drive between homes. Some areas of the district may simply be unsafe for direct contact activities, such as a few inner-city neighborhoods.

The Candidate Walk Plan

In congressional races and below, the candidate should be responsible for canvasing the prime swing areas—the most important marginal neighborhoods in the district. This does not mean simply sending him out to meet voters with a handful of literature. This activity should be meticulously planned, down to the finest detail. A good candidate walk plan consists of several elements:

Step 1: Walk Sheets. The first step is to acquire walk sheets. These registries contain the names (and in some states the party affiliations and a limited set of biographical data, such as date of birth and occupation) of voters at each house on each street in the area. They exclude those not registered to vote and list the households along each side of the street, rather than in numeric order. For example:

1. Alma Jones (R), Morris Jones (R); 1 Maple Street
2. Bert Smith (D), Carol Smith (R), April Smith (D); 3 Maple Street
3. Andrew Johnson (I); 7 Maple Street

4. Betty Hill (D), Stephen Fisher (D); 9 Maple Street.

This format allows the candidate to skip households with nonregistered voters, and to work each side of the street at a time. It can also be used to eliminate certain households based on targeting data, such as those with voters enrolled in the opposing party. Walk sheets can be purchased from the board of elections or the office of the secretary of state in most states and can be sorted by areas defined by the campaign. Another option is to purchase a list from one of the many list vendors (see Chapter 4).

Step 2: A Local Volunteer. The candidate should never go into the field unaccompanied. A volunteer, preferably one from the area where the candidate is assigned to walk, serves many roles. Volunteers can introduce the candidate to the resident, provide some background information on each voter ("Mrs. Smith is a retired teacher who loves to bird-watch"), or give a quick rundown of the neighborhood ("We used to have a zipper factory located in this area"). The volunteer can carry the walk sheet, allowing the candidate to shake hands with the voter. He or she can keep the candidate on task, provide directions, and most important serve as the "bad cop" if needed. If the voter is anxious to have the candidate in for coffee—or something that would take up a good deal of time—the candidate should always appear willing, but the volunteer should suggest that they need to moving along. Maybe the voter will be upset that they did not stay but will not blame the candidate.

Step 3: Pre-Walk Cards. Approximately two weeks prior to the candidate's walk in an area, pre-walk cards should be mailed to each household (if the campaign is strapped for funds, hand delivered). These cards contain a picture of the candidate and a small note, something like:

I'll be stopping by in the next few days to visit. I hope we get a chance to chat about your concerns and what I might do in the state legislature to help.

These cards serve several purposes. They get the candidate's name and message out, prime the voter for the visit, and provide a picture of the candidate so that when the visit takes place the voter knows who is at the door. Even if the voter is not home on the day of the visit, the cards suggest that the candidate is willing to "listen to average folks." A word of caution: Once the cards are sent, the candidate is obligated to walk in the area. Accordingly, pre-walk can also serve as a strong motivator and help keep the candidate on task.

Step 4: The Drop-off Pamphlet. After shaking hands with the voter at the door, the candidate should provide a pamphlet containing "feel good" information. The idea here is that after the candidate has departed, the voter will return to the couch with the material. He or she will settle back into the *Seinfeld* rerun but will glance at the literature occasionally—perhaps during commercials. This one-two punch of meeting the candidate at the door and then scanning the pamphlet provides powerful repetition—just what voter contact is all about.

Step 5: Careful Notes. Immediately after the candidate departs from each voter's doorstep, the volunteer should take notes about the content of the conversation: who was contacted, what were the voter's concerns, what did the vote say about the candidate, and so forth. This feedback information provides data for the "follow-up card."

Step 6: The Follow-up Card. If the voter is not at home at the time of the visit, the candidate should leave a *hand-written* note on the back of the literature:

Sorry I missed you. I stopped by to say hello and chat about your concerns, but you were out. Perhaps we can get a chance to talk another time. Please feel free to call.

These should be written in advance so that the candidate and the volunteer can move along on the night of the canvas.

To those voters who were home, a follow-up mailing should be sent about one week after the visit. It should thank the voter for his or her time and highlight the candidate's belief in voter input in government decision making. Additional content should, if at all possible, parallel the notes taken during the conversation (see Step 5). If, for instance, the voter was concerned about environmental issues, the follow-up should outline the candidate's environmental priorities.

Step 7: Additional Follow-ups. As a final step, any information or material requested by the voter during the visit should be mailed, delivered, or telephoned to the voter immediately. This can be done at the headquarters by a volunteer.

This multistep process is time and resource consuming. But if it is done in the prime swing area of the district, no cost would seem too high. The repetition and careful attention to the message distinguishes this walk plan from traditional canvases, in which the candidate simply knocks on doors. Many of the steps can be accomplished without the candidate, such as the follow-up operation.

The Canvas

In many ways the canvas mirrors the candidate walk plan. This time, however, other members of the campaign team walk from door to door. Instead of mailing a candidate pre-walk card, a note could be sent indicating that "a volunteer will be stopping by soon." The follow-up may say, "Thanks for chatting with one of my volunteers." At times, the canvas can serve as a "rapid-response" operation, also called a "door-to-door blitz." Here it may be impossible to follow the aforementioned steps. For example, if the opponent levels a powerful charge during the final days of the race, a canvas blitz might help limit its impact.

Door-to-door workers should have a clean-cut appearance and be somewhat familiar with the themes of the campaign. Training sessions and scripts are an excellent idea. The importance of careful records as to who was home and the interests of the contacted voters should be stressed.

Voter Registration Drives

Volunteers are a frequently used to find and register new voters. While it varies greatly from one district and community to another, as many as 50 percent of the voting-age residents may not be registered to vote. Enlisting these folks and getting them to the polls on election day is a good idea, and in a race where the candidate is behind it can help win the election.

The voter registration process is relatively uncomplicated. A walk sheet (see above) should be purchased. Nonregistered voters will be in houses on the street not listed on the registry. A campaign volunteer visits these homes and tries to convince the resident to fill out a voter registration card. The volunteer brings the completed cards back to the headquarters, where they are compiled into a list and then delivered to the local board of elections. (Check state laws as to the legality of this one-two step.)

Simply registering someone to vote does not guarantee his or her help on election day. Nevertheless, previously unregistered voters tend to be less partisan and, as such, less predisposed to particular candidates. The campaign should "work" this list repeatedly, including frequent mailers and perhaps a telephone call. Moreover, because they are new voters, it is likely that the opposition will not have them on their list. The only campaign material they will be receive during most of the race will come from your headquarters.

Voter registration drives are again time consuming and somewhat unpredictable. But they are a good way of keeping volunteers busy, and they can be a big help if the campaign faces an uphill battle. In some districts, such as those with a large college student population, registration drives make or break candidates. If nothing else, the goal of bringing more people into the political process is a good one.

Absentee Voters

Absentee voters can be of two types: those living in the district but unable to get to polls on election day because of a disability or illness, or those scheduled to be outside the district on election day, such as students, vacationers, and military personnel. Updates of the absentee list can be secured at the board of elections or the secretary of state's office throughout the campaign. Volunteers should carefully review these registries and compile a list of those who will not be in the district prior to the election (the latter of the two aforementioned groups). They are then mailed campaign literature throughout the race. Because they are not living in the district at the time, it is likely that these mailings will be the only information they receive.

Another approach is to encourage the use of absentee ballots among low-frequency voters. These people are registered to vote but have skipped a few recent elections. It may be, for instance, that the individual is finding it difficult to get to the polls because of a physical condition. Senior citizens often fall into this category. They should be mailed a packet containing an absentee application and, if allowed by state law, information on the candidate. If the latter is not possible, after this person has filed for an absentee ballot, he or she should be cultivated. This group can be especially fruitful, as they are generally less politically active and more open to candidate appeals.

Literature Drops

Literature drops are also targeted to swing areas. Unlike the canvas, drops do not entail meeting the voter but simply placing a piece of campaign literature on the porch or in the door jam. It can be done by anyone, including volunteers unfamiliar with the candidate or the issues of the race—and even kids. The idea is to cover an area quickly and provide material somewhere other than in the mailbox (to distinguish it from other junk mail). Drops are much less expensive than mailings (no postage is needed), but their overall effectiveness is speculative. They are perhaps most helpful in improving early name recognition (cognition) or during a last-minute push.

Telephone Banks

Telephone banks are an excellent means of reaching a large number of voters directly over a short period of time. They keep volunteers busy, particularly those who are not able to walk from door to door or to drop literature, and they are relatively cheap.

There are three possible goals in a telephone operation: pitching, identification, and activation. A pitch is simply providing targeted voters with a brief message. A script is devised and a volunteer conveys this information. Similar to an indirect voter contact activity, such as a television ad, the voter is not called upon to respond. The goal is to provide the voters with material believed to be in their interests.

More frequently, an identification process is undertaken. Here a pitch is provided, followed with a few short questions regarding the voter's preferences in the coming election—who they will be voting for, what their primary concerns are, and so on. This information is carefully recorded, and the voter is dubbed a "for," "against," or "undecided." Sometimes a numbering scheme is devised along the same lines.

Voters labeled "against" are removed from the phone list, and if they demonstrate a serious dislike for the candidate they may be removed from the mailing lists. Let sleeping dogs lie.

Voters noted as "undecided" are placed in a special file. They are given another call, mailed information on the candidate, and perhaps even visited by a volunteer. This group is cultivated extensively throughout the race so that, by the end, they see their choice as straightforward.

Activation occurs when favorable voters are called in order to get them to the polls on election day. At a minimum, this list is made up of those noted as "favorable" during the identification phase, but it can include other deemed likely to support the candidate. This can be done a few days early, or on election day. More will be said about the get-out-the-vote drive below.

One of the handy things about telephone banks is the control they afford. Callers are provided a precise list of voters and a carefully honed message. The number of contacts projected during a given time period can also be predicted with a good deal of accuracy. This is done by multiplying

- The length of the script, times
- The projected down-time between calls, times
- The number of volunteers, times
- The number of hours per evening called, times
- The number of days per week of telephoning.

Put a bit differently, a campaign can calculate about how long it will take to make X number of telephone contacts in a given period. This can be very helpful when it comes to overall strategy and timing.

There are some advantages to hiring a telemarketing firm to carry out this operation, namely the speed at which it can be done. At the end of the race, for instance, it may be necessary to complete 5,000 contacts over one weekend. This task would be difficult for most volunteer teams, but it could be accomplished easily by one of the large telemarketing firms now available. They generally charge a fixed rate for each completed call, such as $.50 or $.75, depending on the length of the script and the location of the district in relation to the telephone bank.

There are a number of benefits to keeping the operation local—and with volunteers. It is much easier to monitor the callers, leading to higher quality control. There is some flexibility as to when calls are made, and it yields greater security (Yeutter et al. 1992). If the telephone charges are donated, the operation is relatively cheap. Most important, voters often snub professional telemarketing pitches. If the call is coming from a volunteer, perhaps even a neighbor, the voter is much more likely to listen and be receptive.

In sum, telemarketing for votes is a powerful new-style tactic. In a way it bridges the gap between efficiency and effectiveness. It is quick, somewhat personal, and relatively inexpensive. Often a local law firm, real estate office or labor union will donate the use of their phones during the evening.

Coffees, Factory Gates, and Commuter Stations

There are many options when it comes to direct voter contact activities. A growing number of candidates are making hay out of coffees or cocktail parties. Here a supporter invites his or her friends and neighbors to a small gathering at his or her home, and the candidate drops by for a visit. Several gatherings held in the same areas of the district and on the same evening allows the candidate to touch base with a number of voters. This can also be a rather pleasurable form of campaigning.

Knowing when a factory shift changes can mean a lot of voter contact over a short period—several hundred workers might pass a point in fifteen minutes. Factory gate and commuter station activities can be especially effective if the candidate hands out coffee and donuts, for example, as well as a small piece of literature. Moreover, shift and commuter changes usually occur when little else is going on in the campaign, for example 7:00 a.m.

Why Not to Do Malls, Fairs, and Street Corners

One of the hardest things a consultant will confront is a candidate who is convinced that the best way to meet voters is to visit the local mall or fair or to stand on the street corner. "Thousands of folks go to the fair," they will exclaim. By now it should be apparent that this type of shotgun approach is antithetical to new-style campaigning. Not only do we not know where these voters live in the district, or what their partisan predisposition might be, but there is no evidence that they are registered to vote. They may not even live in the district! Such untargeted activities are generally a waste of time, a precious commodity in campaigns. They can even wake up sleeping dogs. Candidates must realize that productive campaigning is not simply meeting as many folks as possible, but rather meeting the right folks and providing the right message.

GET-OUT-THE-VOTE DRIVES

One excellent illustration of the importance of last-minute campaigning occurred when Rosemary Shea (this author's mother) ran her first bid for the Oneonta, New York, School Board. With one hour to go before the polls closed, the campaign team had exhausted their list of favorable voters. In fact, two or three calls had been made to each in order to get them out to vote. Determined to work until the last minute, the candidate herself scoured the list of those who had not voted. With fifteen minutes to go, she drove across town to pay a "visit" to a household of three would-be Democratic voters. She convinced them to jump into her car and be driven to the polls so that they could fulfill their "civic duty." With seconds to go, all three cast their votes. Out of the thousands of votes cast, Shea won that election by three votes.

Get-out-the-vote (GOTV) efforts can be the most important activity undertaken during a campaign. The record books are filled with elections won and lost by a handful of voters. In every election there are scores of congressional, state legislative, and even senatorial and gubernatorial races that are decided by less than 1 percent of the votes cast. Carefully orchestrated last-minute pushes can mean the difference between success and failure.

While it may be beneficial to our political system to have everyone vote on election day, the goal of GOTV drives should be to concentrate on those who are likely to vote for your own candidate. There are a number of ways to determine this, including telemarketing identification, demographic and survey research, and geography. Maybe everyone in the candidate's neighborhood should be encouraged to help their "gal" or "guy." Party enrollment is also often used. All things being equal, a person's party enrollment is the best single predictor of his or her vote choice. Conceivably the canvas records will produce a list of favorable voters. A good rule of thumb, suggests Cathy Allen, is to target roughly 10 percent of the votes needed to win (see Chapter 5). "If you are running a state legislative race and need 15,000 votes to win, you must have at least 1,500 identified supporters whom you will push to the polls" (Allen 1990c, 38). Whatever criteria are used, it is important to remember that last-minute pushes are designed to get *your* voters to the polls, not simply to kick up turnout.

Every consultant and party operative will advocate a slightly different GOTV approach. Some would rely upon canvasing, door-bell ringing, direct mail, and other tactics. Below is a technique that relies upon volunteer efforts and has proven to be quite effective.

Step 1: Early Planning. The team should begin planning the GOTV by about thirty days before election day. This means establishing a written plan of action and assigning a coordinator. The plan should lay out specific tasks, dates to accomplish these jobs, and who is responsible for completing them. Moreover, it lists the necessary resources needed (both money and people), supplies, and facilities.

Step 2: GOTV Mailer. Between three and five days before the election, a mailer should be sent to voters in all swing and favorable election precincts throughout the district. If it is determined that the swing group is not needed, they may be dropped (See Chapter 5). This mailing should stress the importance of the election and the difference every vote can make. It is a good idea to include an anecdote of an election won by just a few votes. If the campaign is strapped, a pamphlet can be dropped in target areas during the weekend prior to the election.

Step 3: Phoning Begins. On the eve of the election, the telephone operation should be in full gear. The target group for this phase is more refined than the mailer group. If at all possible, the entire 10 percent GOTV group should be contacted. The message should be similar to the message in the mailer.

Step 4: Poll Watching and Pickup. On the morning of the election, a "poll watcher" should go to each polling place and find a comfortable place to sit. The names of each person coming to vote are noted. These lists are picked up throughout the day, at about two-hour intervals, and brought to the headquarters. Here the names (the ones who have voted) are scratched off a master list of registered voters. This process indicates which registered voters have gone to the polls and which have not at various points of the day.

Step 5: Phoning and Assistance. It is really not necessary to begin calling until late in the afternoon on election day. Most people vote either early in the morning or just after work. Thus, by about 4:00 p.m. the telephone operation should be in action, focusing on those in the target group who have not yet voted. Very often people will need assistance to get to the polls: child care or a ride are quite common needs. The campaign should be prepared to provide these services. This process should continue throughout the evening, relying upon updated lists from the poll watchers in order to scratch off recent voters. There is no reason not to call prospective supporters who have not voted several times, right up until the close of the election.

Other GOTV Aids

The mailer-poll-watching-telephoning operation should form the core of the GOTV drive. Yet there are several other activities that might help. A rally might be held in a targeted area the weekend prior to the election. Massive literature drops can work, as can yard sign blitzes—again.

Unless the candidate is down in the polls and a large turnout is deemed the only chance, the campaign should steer clear of untargeted activities such as waving signs at intersections, handing out leaflets at shopping malls, and blanket canvasing. Remember, GOTV efforts are not about getting voters to the polls, but getting the right voters to the polls.

As for the candidate, this can be a difficult time. Months, if not years, of work are coming to an end. It is a good idea to give the candidate a specific task, perhaps calling his or her best supporters thanking them for their work. Another possibility is to have the candidate walk from door to door in the highest swing neighborhood in the district. More than anything else, he or she needs to be kept busy—for everyone's sake!

PARTING TIPS ON GRASSROOTS ACTIVITIES

On a crisp Saturday morning in October, a zealous campaign operative rounded up a team of volunteers to walk from door to door. Their race was located in the Long Beach area of New York's Nassau County. After two hours of work, the group became increasingly discouraged. Although cars were in the driveways, no one appeared to be home. Those who did answer the door, refused to open it more than a few inches. The canvas was soon canceled. Upon investigation, it was found that the area contained a large number of Orthodox Jews. Saturday, of course, was their Sabbath. Not only did these voters refrain from talking about politics on their day of reflection, they were insulted that the campaign workers did not understand this. Needless to say, it took considerable effort to offset the damage.

A core lesson to garner from this story is that volunteer efforts should always match the social, religious, and political norms of the area. In some places it is common to find door-to-door volunteers on Sunday; in others, this is taboo. The same can be said about the time of day voters should be disturbed. All campaigns should be wary of calling after 8:30 in the evening or before 9:00 in the morning. Yard signs are acceptable in some places but considered in bad taste in others.

Volunteers should always be supervised. Even well-intentioned workers can cause great damage. It is also imperative that there be things for them to do. As strange as it may seem, many campaigns languish without volunteers because there seems to be little for them to do. With that said, volunteers should always be made to feel appreciated. Workers are a rare commodity in politics these days. It is a good idea to bring the candidate to many of the volunteer functions so that the candidate can also express his or her gratitude. The volunteers should be made comfortable, and that means plenty of pizza, bagels, soda, and coffee. On election night there should always be an extravagant blowout.

Finally, it is important for candidates, consultants, and volunteers to bear in mind that elections should be fun. They need not be sober affairs, with stressed-out, sour faces and hot tempers. Campaigning can be one of the most rewarding jobs or activities anyone can undertake. The rush on election night is unmatched. You will always want to win, but it should never be forgotten that it is only an election. Win or lose, the world will continue.

NOTE

1. This information was compiled during a telephone interview conducted by Amy Sims in the spring of 1995. Ms. Sims, an honors student, was working on an independent study project under the supervision of this author.

Selected Bibliography

Adamany, David W., and George E. Agree. 1975. *Political Money: A Strategy for Campaign Financing in America*. Baltimore: John Hopkins University Press.

Adamany, David. 1969. *Financing Politics: Recent Wisconsin Elections*. Madison: University of Wisconsin Press.

Agranoff, Robert. 1972. *The New Style in Election Campaigns*. Boston: Holbrook Press.

Ahuja, Sunil, and Staci L. Beavers, Cynthia Berreau, Anthony Dodson, Patrick Hourigan, Steven Showalter, Jeff Walz, and John R. Hibbing. 1993. "Modern Congressional Theory Meets the 1992 House Elections." *Political Research Quarterly* 47:891-908.

Alexander, Kathy. 1994. "Television Is the Name of the Game." *Atlanta Constitution*. October 16, B1.

Alford, John, Holly Teeters, Daniel S. Ward, and Rick K. Willson. 1994. "Overdraft: The Political Cost of Congressional Malfeasance." *Journal of Politics* 56:788-801.

Allen, Cathy. 1995. "Women on the Run." *Campaigns and Elections* 16:28–29.

———. 1990a. "Peer-Pressure Politics." *Campaigns and Elections* 11:49.

———. 1990b. "Impressing the Press." *Campaigns and Elections* 11:62–64.

———. 1990c. "GOTV." *Campaigns and Elections* 10:38–44.

Ansolabehere, Steven, and Shanto Iyengar. 1995. "Winning through Advertising: It's All in the Context." In *Campaigns and Elections American Style*, edited by James A. Thurber and Candice J. Nelson. Boulder, Colo: Westview Press.

Atlas, Mark. 1989. "Gambling with Elections." In *Campaigns and Elections: A Reader in Modern American Politics*, edited by Larry J. Sabato. Glenview, Ill.: Scott, Foresman and Company.

Backstrom, Charles H., and Gerald Hursh-Cesar. 1981. *Survey Research*. New York: Macmillan.

Baer, Denise. 1995. "Contemporary Strategy and Agenda Setting." In *Campaigns and Elections American Style* edited by James A. Thurber and Candice J. Nelson. Boulder, Colo: Westview Press.

Bayer, Michael J., and Joseph Rodota. 1989. "Computerized Opposition Research." In *Campaigns and Elections: A Reader in Modern American Politics*, edited by Larry J. Sabato. Boulder, Colo.: Westview Press.

Beaudry, Ann, and Bob Schaeffer. 1986. *Winning Local and State Elections*. New York: Free Press.

Beck, Paul A., and Frank J. Sorauf. 1992. *Party Politics in America*. New York: Harper Collins.

Beiler, David. 1994a. "Abraham vs. Romney." *Campaigns and Elections* 15:30.

———. 1994b. "Day of the Iguana." *Campaigns and Elections* 15:48–51, 56.

———. 1994c. "The Harder They Fall." *Campaigns and Elections* 15:44–45, 61.

———. 1994d. "Return of the Plainsman." *Campaigns and Elections* 15:47–49.

———. 1990. "Precision Politics." *Campaigns and Elections* 10:33–38.

Benenson, Bob. 1995. "Jesse Jackson Jr. Wins House Seat." *Congressional Quarterly Weekly Report* 53:3836.

Bennett, John. 1987. "Plan to Strike Gold." *Campaigns and Elections* 8:51–59.

Berelson, Bernard R., Paul F. Lazarfeld, and William N. McPhee. 1954. *Voting*. Chicago: University of Chicago Press.

Blumenthal, Sidney. 1980. *The Permanent Campaign: Inside the World of Elite Political Operatives*. Boston: Beacon Press.

Bradshaw, Joel. 1995. "Who Will Vote for You and Why: Designing Strategy and Theme." In *Campaigns and Elections American Style*, edited by James A. Thurber and Candice J. Nelson. Boulder, Colo: Westview Press.

Broder, David S. 1971. *The Party's Over: The Failure of American Parties*. New York: Harper and Row.

Brown, James, and Philip M. Seib. 1976. *The Art of Politics: Electoral Strategies and Campaign Management*. Port Washington, N.Y.: Alfred Publishing.

Brown, Ron, and Nello Giorgetti. 1992. "Downballot Doldrums." *Campaigns and Elections*. 13:50–51.

Butler, David, and Austin Ranney. 1992. *Electioneering: A Comparative Study of Continuity and Change*. New York: Oxford University Press.

Cohen, Mary W., ed. 1992. *Congressional Campaign Finances: History, Facts, and Controversy*. Washington, D.C.: Congressional Quarterly Press.

"Colorado: Ben Nighthorse Campbell." 1993. *Congressional Quarterly* 51:20.

Conway, Margaret M., and Joanne Connor Green. 1995. "Political Action Committees and the Political Process in the 1990s." In *Interest Group Politics*, edited by Allan J. Cigler and Burdett A. Loomis. Washington D.C.: Congressional Quarterly Press.

Conway, Margaret, M. 1985. *Political Participation in the United States*. Washington, D.C.: Congressional Quarterly Press.

Cotter, Cornelius P., James Gibson, John F. Bibby, and Robert J. Huckshorn. 1984. *Party Organizations in American Politics*. New York: Praeger.

Cover, Albert D. 1977. "One Good Term Deserves Another: The Advantage of Incumbency in Congressional Elections." *American Journal of Political Science* 21:523–41.

Craney, Glen. 1990. "Kentucky." *Congressional Quarterly* 48:3311.

Crespi, Irving. 1988. *Pre-Election Polling*. New York: Russell Sage Foundation.

Cross, Al. 1994. "Kentucky Derby." *Campaigns and Elections* 15:44.

Dahl, Robert A. 1961. *Who Governs?* New Haven, Conn.: Yale University Press.

Daley, Steve. 1995. "Lawmaker Who Got Fax Had Warned Reno." *Chicago Tribune*, April 25, 1.

Dawidziak, Mike. 1991. "Use Ethnic Targeting to Focus Mailings." *Campaigns and Elections* 12:52–53.

Diamond, Edwin, and Stephen Bates. 1992. *The Spot: The Rise of Political Advertising on Television*. Cambridge, Mass.: MIT Press.

Dimock, Michael A., and Gary C. Jacobson. 1995. "Checks and Choices: The House Bank Scandal's Impact on Voters in 1992." *Journal of Politics* 57:1143–59.

Dinkin, Robert J. 1989. *Campaigning in America: The History of Election Practices*. New York: Greenwood Press.

Dowd, Matthew. 1992. "Botton of the Ninth: If You Target Them, They Will Vote." *Campaigns and Elections* 13:39–40.

Dunn, Anita. 1995. "The Best Campaign Wins: Local Press Coverage of Nonpresidential Races." In *Campaigns and Elections American Style*, edited by James A. Thurber and Candice J. Nelson. Boulder, Colo: Westview Press.

Edmondson, Brad. 1994. "Crime Crazy." *American Demographics*. 16:2.

Ehrenhalt, Alan. 1991. *The United States of Ambition*. New York: Random House.

Fairbank, John. 1993. "Proving Conventional." *Campaigns and Elections* 10: 44–45.

Fairbank, John, and Paul Goodwin. 1993. "When Two's a Race and Three's a Crowd." *Campaigns and Elections* 13:51–52.

Farinella, Marc. 1992. "Research Resources." *Campaigns and Elections* 12:43–48.

Faucheux, Ron. 1994. "Don Beyer, Mike Farris, and the Wizard of Oz." *Campaigns and Elections* 15:62–63.

Fiorina, Morris. P. 1981. *Retrospective Voting in American National Elections*. New Haven. Conn.: Yale University Press.

Fenno, Richard, F. 1989. *The Making of a Senator: Dan Quayle*. Washington, D.C.: Congressional Quarterly Press.

———. 1973. *Congressmen in Committees*. Boston: Little, Brown.

Ferejohn, John A. 1977. "On the Decline in Competition in Congressional Elections." *American Political Science Review* 71:166–76.

Fowler, Floyd J., Jr. 1993. "Survey Research Methods." *Applied Social Research Methods Series*. Newbury Park, Calif.: Sage.

Fowler, Linda L. 1995. "Campaign Ethics and Political Trust." In *Campaigns and Elections American Style*, edited by James A. Thurber and Candice J. Nelson. Boulder, Colo: Westview Press.

———. 1993. *Candidates, Congress, and the American Democracy*. Ann Arbor: University of Michigan Press.

Graber, Doris A. 1993. *Mass Media and American Politics*, 4th ed. Washington, D.C.: Congressional Quarterly Press.

———. 1987. *Mass Media and American Politics*, 3rd ed. Washington, D.C.: Congressional Quarterly Press.

Greenblatt, Alan. 1995. "Republican Wins Minnesota Seat." *Congressional Quarterly Weekly Report* 53:3835.

Gruenwald, Juliana. 1995. "Wayden, Smith Vie for Center in Race for Packwood Seat." *Congressional Quarterly Weekly Report* 53:3755.

Guzzetta, S. J. 1987. *The Campaign Manual: A Definitive Study of the Modern Political Campaign Process*. Anaheim, Calif.: Political Publishing Company.

Hart, Nessa. 1992. "Buddy, Can You Spare a Grand?" *Campaigns and Elections* 13:47–50.

Hart, Roderick P. 1994. *Seducing America: How Television Charms the Modern Voter*. New York: Oxford University Press.

Henry, Gary T. 1990. "Practical Sampling." *Applied Social Research Methods Series*. Newbury Park, Calif.: Sage.

Herrnson, Paul S. 1995. *Congressional Elections: Campaigning at Home and In Washington*. Washington, D.C.: Congressional Quarterly Press.

———. 1994. "Party Strategy and Campaign Activities in the 1992 Congressional

Elections." In *The State of the Parties,* edited by Daniel M. Shea and John C. Green. Lanham, Md.: Rowman and Littlefield.

―――. 1988. *Party Campaigning in the 1980s.* Cambridge, Mass.: Harvard University Press.

Hershey, Marjorie R. 1984. *Running for Office: The Political Education of Campaigners.* Chatham, N.J.: Chatham House.

Hesla, Maren. 1992. "Credibility Crusade." *Campaigns and Elections* 12:53–57.

Himes, David. 1995. "Strategy and Tactics for Candidate Fund-Raising." In *Campaigns and Elections American Style,* edited by James A. Thurber and Candice J. Nelson. Boulder, Colo.: Westview Press.

Hood, John. 1993. "The Third Way." *Reason.* 24:40–43.

Hyman, H. H., and P. B. Sheatsley. 1950. "The Current Status of American Public Opinion." In *The Teaching of Contemporary Affairs,* edited by J. C. Payne. Twenty-first Yearbook of the National Council of Social Studies, 1950, 11–34.

Jones, Ruth. 1984. "Financing State Elections." In *Money and Politics in the United States: Financing Elections in the 1980,* edited by Michael Malbin. Chatham, N.J.: Chatham House.

Idelson, Holly. 1990. "Michigan." *Congressional Quarterly* 48:3318.

Ifill, Gwen. 1992. "Democrats Exercising Their Legs and Lips." *New York Times,* July 20, A22.

"Illinois: Carol Moseley-Braun." 1993. *Congressional Quarterly* 51:32.

Ireland, Doug. 1995. "The Rich Rise of Lamar Alexander." *The Nation.* 260:517–522.

Jacobson, Gary C. 1987. *The Politics of Congressional Elections.* Boston, MA: Scott, Foresman & Company.

Jamieson, Kathleen Hall. 1992. *Dirty Politics.* New York: Oxford University Press.

―――. 1984. *Packaging the Presidency.* New York: Oxford University Press.

Johnson, Clarence. 1992. "Marks Absent from New Ad." *San Francisco Chronicle,* April 20.

Johnson, Dick. 1995. "Victory His, Jesse Jackson Jr. Heads to Congress." *New York Times,* December 14.

Johnson, Wayne C. 1992. "First Do No Harm." *Campaigns and Elections* 13:51–52.

Johnson-Carter, Karen S., and Gary A. Copland. 1991. *Negative Political Advertising: Coming of Age.* Hillsdale, N.J.: Lawrence Erlbaum Associates.

Jones, Ruth S. 1993. "Campaign and Party Finance in the American States." In *Campaign and Party Finance in North America and Western Europe,* edited by Arthur B. Gunlicks. Boulder, Colo.: Westview Press.

Joyella, Mark. 1994. "Beating the Son King." *Campaigns and Elections* 15:44–45.

Kanfer, Ron. 1991. "Direct to the Bank." *Campaigns and Elections* 12:22–27.

Kaplan, Robert L. 1991. "Psychology of Silence: Raising More Money by Psyching out Donors." *Campaigns and Elections* 12:54–55.

Kayden, Xandra, and Eddie Mahe, Jr., eds. 1985. *The Party Goes On.* New York: Basic Books.

Koelemay, Douglas. 1994. "Clay vs. Corbett: How a State Senate Incumbent in Alabama Was Out-Campaigned in an Upset Primary." *Campaigns and Elections* 15:48–49.

Krasno, Jonathan, S. 1994. *Challengers, Competition, and Reelection.* New Haven, Conn.: Yale University Press.

Krehbiel, Keith, and John R. Wright. 1983. "The Incumbency Effect in Congressional Elections: A Test of Two Explanations." *American Journal of Political Science* 27:140–57.

Krueger, Richard A. 1994. *Focus Groups: A Practical Guide for Applied Research.* Thousand Oaks, Calif.: Sage.

Lane, Mary Beth. 1994a. "Voinovich Plans $57-per-Head Party." *Cleveland Plain Dealer,* June 25.

―――. 1994b. "Voinovich Campaign Has $1.9 Million on Hand." *The Cleveland Plain Dealer,* July 1.

Lau, Richard. 1994. "An Analysis of the Accuracy of 'Trial Heat' Polls during the 1992 Presidential Election." *Public Opinion Quarterly* 58(1):2–20.

Lavrakas, Paul J. 1993. "Telephone Survey Methods: Sampling, Selection, and Supervision." *Applied Social Research Methods Series.* Newbury Park, Calif.: Sage.

Longley, Lawrence D. 1992. "The Institutionalization of the National Democratic Party: A Process Stymied, Then Revitalized." *Wisconsin Political Scientist.* 7:9–15.

"Louisiana - Fourth District." 1993. *Congressional Quarterly* 51:90.

"Louisiana 14th District - Cleo Fields." 1993. *Congressional Quarterly* 51:90.

Luntz, Frank I. 1988. *Candidates, Consultants, and Campaigns: The Style and Substance of American Electioneering.* Oxford, England: Basil Blackwood.

McGinniss, Joe. 1969. *The Selling of the President 1968.* New York: Trident Press.

Maisel, L. Sandy. 1990. "The Incumbency Advantage." In *Money, Elections, and Democracy: Reforming Congressional Campaign Finance,* edited by Margaret Latus Nugent and John R. Johannes. Boulder, Colo.: Westview Press.

Malbin, Michael, J. 1995. "1994 Vote: The Money Story." In *America at the Polls: 1994,* edited by Everett Carl Ladd. New Brunswick, N.J.: Roper Center for Public Opinion Research.

Manes, Susan. 1990. "Up for Bid: A Common Cause View." In *Money, Elections, and Democracy: Reforming Congressional Campaign Finance,* edited by Latus Nugent and John R. Johannes. Boulder, Colo: Westview Press.

Marquette, Jesse F. 1991. *Response Form Effects in Election Polling Process.* Phoenix: American Association for Public Opinion Research.

Marrison, Benjamin. 1994. "Campaign Donors Seeking Stake in Ohio Politics." *Cleveland Plain Dealer,* November 4, 1.

Martindale, Rob. 1994. "Ex-Teacher Tops Veteran Lawmaker." *The Tulsa World,* September 21, 1–3.

Mayhew, David, R. 1974a. "Congressional Elections: The Case of the Vanishing Marginals." *Polity* 6:295–317.

―――. 1974b. *Congress: The Electoral Connection.* New Haven, Conn.: Yale University Press.

Melder, Keith, E. 1992. *Hail to the Candidate: Presidential Campaigns from Banners to Broadcasts.* Washington, D.C.: Smithsonian Institution Press.

"Missouri: Second District." 1990. *Congressional Quarterly* 47:3326.

Morris, Dwight, and Murielle E. Gamache. 1994. *Gold-Plated Politics: The 1992 Congressional Races.* Washington, D.C.: Congressional Quarterly.

Napolitan, Joseph. 1986. "Some Thoughts on the Importance of Strategy in a Political Campaign." In *The National Republican Congressional Committee Campaign Starter Manual.* Washington DC: The Republican Congressional Campaign Committee.

―――. 1972. *The Election Game and How to Win It.* Garden City, N.J.: Doubleday.

Nelson, Michael. 1995. "Evaluating the Presidency." In *The Presidency and the Political System,* edited by Michael Nelson. Washington, DC: Congressional Quarterly Press.

"New York: Peter King." 1993. *Congressional Quarterly* 51:110.

Nie, Norman H., Sidney Verba, and John R. Petrocik. 1976. *The Changing American Voter*. Cambridge, Mass.: Harvard University Press.

Nieves, Evelyn. 1992. "Spelling by Quayle (That's with an E)." New York Times, June 17, A17.

Nimmo, Daniel. 1970. *The Political Persuaders*. Englewood Cliffs, N.J.: Prentice-Hall.

"Pennsylvania-13th District." 1993. *Congressional Quarterly* 51:132.

Persinos, John F. 1994. "Gotcha!" *Campaigns and Elections* 15:20–23, 56–57.

Phillips, Gerald M. 1984. *How to Support Your Cause and Win*. Columbia: University of South Carolina Press.

Pomper, Gerald M. 1974. *Elections in America*. New York: Dodd, Mead.

Power, John. 1992. "Learn to Habla Espanol." *Campaigns and Elections* 9:63.

Pressley, Sue Anne. 1994. "The Comeuppance of Texas Icon Mirrors Nation's Political Revolt." Washington Post, December 7, 1.

Randolph, Sallie G. 1989. "The Effective Press Release: Key to Free Media." In *Campaigns and Elections: A Reader in Modern American Politics*, edited by Larry Sabato. Glenview, Ill.: Scott, Foresman and Company.

Reeves, Richard. 1994. "Synar's Defeat Gives Politicians the Jitters." *The Tulsa World*, September 28, 27.

Ridder, Rick. 1984. "Do's and Don'ts of Opposition Research." *Campaigns and Elections* 15:58.

Rieter, Howard L. 1993. *Parties and Elections in Corporate America*. New York: Longman.

Riordon, William L. 1948. *Plunkitt of Tammany Hall*. New York: Alfred A. Knopf.

Robbin, Jonathan. 1989. "Geodemographics: The New Magic." In *Campaigns and Elections: A Reader in Modern American Politics*, edited by Larry Sabato. Glenview, Ill.: Scott, Foresman and Company.

Roberts, Steven V. 1987. "Preserving Reagan's Legacy." *New York Times*, May 7, A27.

Sabato, Larry J. 1991. *Feeding Frenzy: How Attack Journalism Has Transformed American Journalism*. New York: Free Press.

———. 1989. "How Direct Mail Works." In *Campaigns and Elections: A Reader in Modern American Politics*, edited by Larry J. Sabato. Glenview, Ill.: Scott, Foresman and Company.

———. 1981. *The Rise of Political Consultants: New Way of Winning Elections*. New York: Basic Books.

Salmore, Barbara G., and Stephen A. Salmore. 1989. *Candidates, Parties, and Campaigns*. Washington, D.C.: Congressional Quarterly Press.

Schlesinger, Joseph A. 1991. *Political Parties and the Winning of Office*. Ann Arbor: University of Michigan Press.

Schuman, Howard, and Stanley Presser. 1981. *Questions and Answers in Attitude Surveys*. San Diego, Calif.: Academic Press.

Selnow, Gary W. 1994. *High Tech Campaigns*. Westport, Conn.: Praeger.

Semiatin, Richard J., and Tari Renner. 1994. "Much Ado about Nothing? The Impact of Check Bouncing on Members Returning to Congress." Paper presented at the 1994 Annual Meeting of The Midwest Political Science Association, Chicago, April 14–16.

Shapiro, Beth S. 1992. "It's A Man's World: Unless You Know the Right Questions to Ask." *Campaigns and Elections* 13:52-54.

Shea, Daniel M. 1995a. *Transforming Democracy: State Legislative Campaigns and*

Political Parties. Albany: State University of New York Press.
————. 1995b. "Lessons from a Challenger Upset: The Voters Have the Floor." Unpublished Manuscript.
Shea, Daniel M. and Stephen C. Brooks. 1995. "How to Topple an Incumbent." *Campaigns and Elections* 16:20–29.
Shea, Daniel M. and John C. Green, eds. *The State of the Parties*. 1994. Lanham, Md.: Rowman and Littlefield.
Sheingold, Larry. 1993. "One More Hurrah: How Milton Marks Beat the Odds." *Campaigns and Elections* 14:40–41
Smith, Averell "Ace." 1992. "Fighting Fire with Electronic Fire." *Campaigns and Elections* 10:51.
Snider, Steve. 1990. "What Makes a Press Release Sing." *Campaigns and Elections* 7:51–52.
Sorauf, Frank J. 1995. "Competition, Contributions, and Money in 1992." In *Campaigns and Elections American Style*, edited by James A. Thurber and Candice J. Nelson. Boulder, Colo: Westview Press.
————. 1988. *Money in American Politics*. Boston, Mass: Scott, Foresman and Company.
Sutherlin, Allan. 1992. "Political Processing." *Campaigns and Elections* 9:43.
Sweeney, William R. 1995. "The Principles of Planning." In *Campaigns and Elections American Style*, edited by James A. Thurber and Candice J. Nelson. Boulder, Colo: Westview Press.
Thurber, James A., and Candice J. Nelson. 1995. *Campaigns and Elections American Style*. Boulder, Co.: Westview Press.
Tourangeau, Roger, and Kenneth A. Rasinski. 1988. "Cognitive Processes Underlying Context Effects in Attitude Measurement." *Psychological Bulletin* 103(3):299–314.
Trent, Judith S., and Robert V. Friedenberg. 1991. *Political Campaign Communication: Principles and Practices*. New York: Praeger.
Troy, Gil. 1991. *See How They Ran: The Changing Role of the Presidential Candidate*. New York: Free Press.
Tufte, Edward R. 1975. "Determinants of the Outcomes of Midterm Congressional Elections." *American Political Science Review*. 69:812–26.
Uslaner, Eric M. 1981. "The Case of the Vanishing Liberal Senators: The House Did It." *British Journal of Political Science* 11, pt. 1:105–113.
Varoga, Craig. 1995. "The Lone Star Upset." *Campaigns and Elections*. 16:34–35, 58.
Wachob, Bill. 1991. "Tapping the Local Till." *Campaigns and Elections* 12:51–52.
"Washington: Patty Murray." 1993. *Congressional Quarterly* 51:33.
Wattenberg, Martin P. 1990. *The Decline of American Political Parties 1952–1988*. Cambridge, Mass.: Harvard University Press.
Wayne, Stephen. 1982. "Great Expectations: What People Want From the Presidency." In *Rethinking the Presidency*, edited by Thomas E. Cronin. Boston, Mass.: Little, Brown.
Whillock, Rita Kirk. 1991. *Political Empiricism: Communication Strategies in State and Regional Elections*. New York: Praeger.
Yeutter, Clayton, Jeanie Austin, James S. Nathanson, and Jane Hershey Abraham. 1992. *The NRC Campaign Encyclopedia*. Washington, D.C.: The Republican National Committee.

Index

About the Author

DANIEL M. SHEA is assistant professor of Political Science and Research Fellow at the Ray C. Bliss Institute of Applied Politics at the University of Akron in Ohio. Prior to teaching and conducting research, Dr. Shea was Regional Coordinator of the New York State Democratic Assembly Campaign Committee. He is the author of *Transforming Democracy* (1995), and co-editor of *The State of the Parties, 1st and 2nd Editions* (1994, 1996). He has also published extensively in leading political science and campaign management journals.

ISBN 0-275-95458-7

EAN

9 780275 954581

HARDCOVER BAR CODE

90000>